Child of A Mountainous Land

Odyssey of a Haitian Refugee

By

Marie-Solange Benedict

Copyright © 2007 by Marie-Solange Benedict

Child of A Mountainous Land
by Marie-Solange Benedict

Printed in the United States of America

ISBN 978-1-60477-127-5

Library of Congress Cataloguing-in-Publication Data
Benedict, Marie-Solange.
Child of A Mountainous Land: odyssey of a Haitian refugee/
Marie-Solange Benedict
1st ed.

All rights reserved solely by the author. The author guarantees all contents are original and do not infringe upon the legal rights of any other person or work. No part of this book may be reproduced or transmitted in any form, or by any means, electronic or mechanical, including photocopying and recording, or by any information storage and retrieval system, without permission in writing from the author. The views expressed in this book are not necessarily those of the publisher.

All scripture quotations, unless otherwise indicated are taken from the HOLY BIBLE, NEW INTERNATIONAL VERSION. Copyright © 1973, 1978, 1984 by International Bible Society. Used by permission of Zondervan Publishing House.

Scripture quotations marked (KJV) are taken from the King James Version.

The names of people, except for immediate family members and public figures have been altered to protect their privacy. This is a work of non-fiction. Unless otherwise noted, the author and publisher make no explicit guarantees as to the accuracy of the information contained in this book.

www.xulonpress.com

To: Marie-Yolette Marcellus

In appreciation of your caring and gentleness as one of the best Dental Assistants I have ever met.

God Bless You and Your Family,

David L. Pany Benedict

Dec. 2007

Contents

I.	Child of a mountainous land	13
	Chapter 1	15
	Chapter 2	37
II.	Child of the Catholics and of the Protestants	57
	Chapter 3	59
	Chapter 4	77
	Chapter 5	95
III.	The making of a refugee	103
	Chapter 6	105
	Chapter 7	129
IV.	Refugee	139
	Chapter 8	141
	Chapter 9	155
V.	A single blue suitcase, well traveled	173
	Chapter 10	175
	Chapter 11	193
	Chapter 12	205
VI.	Liberated daughter of a troubled people	217
	Chapter 13	219
	Chapter 14	237
	Chapter 15	259
	Chapter 16	269

VII.	A branch connected to the True Vine	279
	Chapter 17	281
	Chapter 18	301

Introduction

The Pastor of the church I was attending at the time walked down from the pulpit towards me midway through his sermon and handed me a pen.

" The Lord told me to give this to you." He said. "I do not know why. It is my good pen too!"

I knew immediately why God was sending me this illustrated message via the pastor's reluctant gift. God knew that He had created me to be a writer and that I had chosen to be a procrastinator. There was a story that I had avoided, that needed to be told. It was my own story as a ten years old refugee from the Haitian Duvalierist Dictatorship in 1962. The story is also that of a people, destroyed one family at a time and of a country in ruins.

In recent years, I have had the opportunity to interview my parents, now retired, about the events in Haiti that had forced us to leave the country. My father had escaped a plot to assassinate him: a Duvalierist had wanted to remove him from the job he had held for twenty years as a Dentist at the government owned hospital. The man simply wanted the position for one of his cronies. So many people had lost their lives, and many families had been destroyed in much the same way. After a sixteen years exile, my parents returned to work in Haiti but found it impossible again to remain there. This time they left Haiti forever.

For years, as I traveled and lived in Liberia, West Africa, England and after immigrating to the United States in 1968, I recalled vignettes of our family's escape for new acquaintances, explaining my presence on foreign land even as I tried to understand why I had lost my home and country. I was also in search of a homeland. What I did find twenty-seven years ago, was salvation in the lord Jesus Christ and an extraordinary perspective of my challenges.

My purpose in telling my story then is two fold. First, I want to recall the events that forced me into becoming a refugee, dismantled a country and the corrosive residue that continue to displace people from their native land. Violence against children, the poor, the women, and the disadvantaged is endemic in Haitian culture as is idolatry and rejection of God. As I watch each new wave of Haitians seeking refuge primarily on the shores of South Florida, where I live, and from observations, on visits back to Haiti and in reading news accounts of the latest political upheaval, I want to denounce this flaw as the root cause of recurring dictatorships and political turmoil.

Secondly, I want to testify to how my walk with the Lord over the past twenty-seven years had rescued me from anger and bitterness, allowed me to overcome the negative experiences of my childhood and youth. My faith in God continues to sustain me through the many frustrations of life as a Black woman in the United States. I hope that the story of my walk with God will inspire others to Trust Him. The transforming power of the Gospel can rescue anyone, even an entire nation.

Dedication

To my parents:

Marguerite Marie Toulmé Benedict and Duplessis Charles Solanges Benedict, for modeling integrity, generosity, and a sense of duty towards family, and our fellow man.

Acknowledgments

I would like to thank my sisters Florence Benedict Holly and Maryse Benedict Cartright for their encouragement, my daughter Marlo Johnson and her fiancé, my son in training Vernon Lawrence for their help and technical assistance.

I. Child of a mountainous land

" For I know the thoughts that I think toward you, saith the Lord, thoughts of peace, and not of evil, to give you an expected end." Jeremiah 29:11(KJV)

1

The secret had been so well guarded that I never knew it. Yet, because of it, I was about to lose some of my life before even half of the year had passed in April 1962. I was ten years old. People, mostly strangers with an occasional acquaintance, had been disappearing for some time now from my hometown. This was no secret in our town of Les Cayes, a sun drenched port on the Southern coast of Haiti, my native land. I, and the townspeople, accepted that the cycle of bloody revolutions and political repressions, never too far from our lives, had birthed something new. It was inevitable, something having to do with our cursed heritage. So the adults said. This new thing, however, fed a greater fear than even Satan worshipers or *vodooisants* could when they snatched one or two dead bodies from a freshly dug grave. As news filtered in from the capital city of Port-au-Prince and the other outlying provinces, we knew that these disappearances were spreading throughout the land. It was the work of *Tontons Macoutes*, someone whispered. There was a collective knowing look in the eyes of the people of Haiti. In our native Kreyol, *Tontons Macoutes* were surreal, malevolent beings that ambushed children and carried them off in the night. They were the mainstay of our folk Tales and the suspects in many more acts of evil in our society. *Tontons Macoutes* were now causing all sorts of people, young, and old, in the night and in the light of day, to vanish from our midst. That very discovery haunted our sleep and dogged our every thought. I already knew too much, as a precocious child, about the cares of my world. The vanished: I knew, were dead.

Some time before, when I was still an untaught child, my parents had driven to a distant place in the countryside, with me in the back of their car, to a certain field where people were killed and buried. From my seat, I could see most of the land around us. There were no trees in the stretch of bleak dusty miles we traveled on. No man or beast dared to be seen. The earth looked turned over; just like the patches of ground, I had seen farmers till in preparation for planting their crops. The open windows of the car let in the raw smell of rain hitting the parched soil, as a brief shower scurried past the hardened, unrelenting, furrows. In this field, only death had been sowed. Snatches of my parents' low-voiced conversation revealed that a man they knew in our town had been here to face a firing squad. His body drenched in blood, wrapped in a military blanket, was buried with many others underneath the earth below us. No stone, wreath, or even a cross, made with twigs marked the spot where the dead man laid. Myth and reality had collided for me on that day. I learned then what the *Tonton Macoutes* did.

Those to whom we in our town, our country, and the outside world later gave the name of *Tontons Macoutes* were human. They were our neighbors. We whispered about them and what they did, inside our bedrooms, in the schoolyard corner and in a furtive huddle with the two or three families who came to visit us in our home on the outskirt of town.

As a Haitian child I knew that our country became an independent nation because our heroes subscribed to the motto that our enslaved ancestors should *"koupe tèt, boule kaye"* that is cut off the heads and burn the houses of their French oppressors. For the first and last time in their history the Black and Mulatto inhabitants of the French colony of Saint

Domingue, Haiti's former name, were united. They freed themselves from slavery on the western side of the island: a territory the size of the American State of Maryland. The French, slave owners and settlers alike, were driven out to sea at the end of a twelve years war and in 1804; the Republic of Haiti was born. The dead numbered over three hundred thousand. Scores of the sons and daughters of the Revolution eventually perished as some of our revered heroes turned on each other. That was over two hundred years before. *"Their blood swirled in our hills" w*as a patriotic song I was taught in school. My child's mind did not ponder the fact that even though " they" no longer threatened us, blood still flowed down the rocky mountain paths of Haiti. I knew without ever saying it that I lived in a blood-soaked land.

Our hometown sat on a plain surrounded by the mountains that gave Haiti its name. *Hayiti,* The older version of the word, according to history, means mountainous land, in the language of the native Arawak who peopled the entire island of Hispaniola when Christopher Columbus discovered it in 1492. The lush green of the tropical slopes as well as the denuded earth of jagged cliffs and cave lined crevices, invite speculation. It is easy to wonder about the secrets hidden within the troubled ground. Historians have tried to make an inventory of the different African tribes living in the French colony of Saint Domingue in the late 1700's and agree for the most part that they originated from the West part of the old continent. Once in the New World and stripped of their native customs and mores these Africans had to adopt a new identity. This was crucial for those who would reclaim their God given rights of freedom. Another ancient people had been enslaved for four hundred years, and had been freed after a series of spectacular events. Whereas the former started on this quest with many names from the number of tribes to which they and their ancestors belonged in Africa, the latter could trace their ancestry to one common family.

They took the name of their father Israel whose father and father's father were given a name, an identity. The children of Israel were known as the "children of God". Even though scattered from the land of their father, this people retained their identity. They had a special mission. It was the particular destiny of these children of God to lay the foundation for other peoples of the world to also become "children of God". Many believers in the God of the children of Israel did become children of God. These adopted children became known as Christians. Tragically too many of the people of the world who called the God of Israel, their father, lied. These false children did the very thing that proved their true parentage: they persecuted the children of Israel, the Hebrews, known to the world as Jews. Western civilization built on the Judeo-Christian faith set about denying its fundamental tenets by committing fratricide. From there, it was easy for the so-called Christians to slide into wholesale slaughter and exploitation of other people who did not call themselves children of God. The children of Africa and those of a mixed race saw in their murderers and exploiters a grotesque misrepresentation of Christianity and God. Slave owner and slave both created in the image of His maker, both ignorant of the one who yearned to be called "Father" by humankind, His creation. Both unable to see the promise in the words: "*If my people which are called by my name...* "Second Chronicles 7:14 (KJV).

Legend has it that the freed slaves sold their infant country to the Devil in a pact to defeat the French. In their quest for a national identity, the Revolutionaries of Saint Domingue for want of their own, borrowed many emblems from their enemies; singing *La Marseillaise,* France's National Anthem that had its birth from that country's own Revolution. On the North American continent, that same irony was played out in the situation of the Black soldiers who fought the British for the freedom of a Nation whose Constitution extolled the *inalienable rights of man*, that many soon realized excluded those of African descent. In a further twist of fate, the Revolutionary army of Saint Domingue counted as one of its leaders, General Henri Christophe who as a youth fought for the American Revolution in a French battalion commanded by the Marquis de La Fayette at the battle of Savannah in the then colonial territory of Georgia.

In seeking freedom from slavery, the enslaved Africans had to integrate their separate tribal identities into one fighting unit against a common enemy. *"L'Union Fait La Force" Unity creates might* is the slogan inscribed on the Haitian flag. The struggle for freedom gave birth to a Nation. The French name of Saint Domingue was discarded and replaced by its pre-Columbian name of *Ayiti* or Haiti the Arawak word for *mountainous*. Its citizens now had a new identity along with their new status of Citizen: *Haitien* (Haitian in English). Those who had been born in the land with no more identity than that of *negre* or Negro as well as those who were brought in directly from Africa, relinquished their separate tribal identities to become a citizen of the Republic of Haiti. It is easy to speculate what the word "Haitian" meant in those days depending on whose lips framed that word. For obvious reasons, some denied its existence while others reviled it. Contemporary European Historians took the French lead to describe the twelve years war of Haitian Independence as an "uprising". It certainly inspired a number of "uprisings" among the enslaved throughout the Caribbean.

The identity of the citizen of Haiti had been bought at a high costs; those first Haitians made certain that each subsequent generation never forgot it. Surrounded by a hostile slaveholding world they had no choice but to extol their own virtues and proclaim their own worth, endlessly. Small wonder then that lessons in pride took such preeminence in a child's education. The word Haitian soon grew to mean pride. Yet, the ancient promise in the book of second

Chronicles states that "if my people which are called by my name, would humble themselves". Surely, this did not apply to a Haitian? That name also spoke of trouble. Year after year and decade after decade, one century after the next of the declaration in 1804 of the birth of an independent nation there has been trouble in the land. Some will say that country has "bad luck". Haitians are even reluctant to acknowledge any "good luck". One common reply in response to 'how are you? In the country is *"moin pa pli mal!"* which literally means: "I am not too bad". Haitians remained proud of themselves and of their offspring.

At my parents' wedding reception in 1950, my maternal grandfather raised his champagne cup in front of the assembled guests, hand, and voice shaking, to toast the newlyweds:

"You are getting a soldier's wife!" He sputtered, eying the groom.

My grandfather was sobbing. He had been so accustomed to the way his daughter kept his house in Port-au-Prince that even after giving his consent to the wedding he tried to convince her to stay home instead. She was an accomplished homemaker. Grandfather Toulmé was proven right in his assessment of his industrious daughter. Whatever happened around her, *Marguerite Marie Toulmé Benedict,* who became my *Manman*, could always be counted on to stand, her sturdy five- foot frame erect, head held high, and to pick up the pieces after whatever set back and move on.

When my parents had saved up enough money to build the house on the outskirts of town it was my mother who went early in the morning, wearing a large straw hat, to count the cement sacks and lumber and keep an eye on the workers until the day's work was done. Haitian workers are notorious for absconding with construction material right under the nose of their foreman. At the end of the day, *Manman* supervised the loading of a borrowed flat bed truck and the delivery of the supplies into another friend's warehouse for safekeeping through the night.

Part of my mother's formal education, while she was a young woman awaiting a suitable husband, included sewing lessons, so she was skilled in making her own patterns for everything from brassieres to men's boxer shorts and collared shirts. Manman sewed everything in our home; except my father's dress shirts, pant suits and our socks. She embroidered all of our linen including an intricate white runner that she spread on top of the large mahogany dining table. On more than one occasion, she made uniforms for an entire soccer team in record time. Having a ferocious contempt for idleness: she had my sisters and I clean the bales of raw cotton she used to stuff the mattresses she made. As the oldest child, I helped with the simpler stitching on her foot-operated sewing machine. The sewing for our household, friends and acquaintances, was endless.

Manman's cooking style leaned towards the adventurous. She coached our cook for the ordinary meals that were prepared in the main kitchen, a structure separated from the house by a rocked paved yard. Just about every part of a cow, goat, pig, seafood, and poultry except for the hide and feathers was made edible in that room. Once, Manman tried her hand at drying meat by having it spread out in the sun on the kitchen's tin roof. That particular experiment ended when everyone complained of the stench. The smaller kitchen inside our house, adjoining the dining room, sported a kerosene refrigerator, stove, and oven, and was for my mother's exclusive use. There, she taught me to bake the special dishes we reserved for festive days. "One day" my mother told me as I watched her dissect all the bones out of a turkey she was about to stuff, " I will teach you how to prepare this *dinde farçie"*

Manman never passed up an opportunity to remind me that it was my duty to *"ran sèviss"* or give help to anyone who asked. She and my father modeled more than anyone that I would ever know that sense of responsibility for other fellow humans. It was part of our own family heritage. Numerous times as I helped set the diner table Manman would point to the thinly plated silver ladle that had been passed on to our family from Papa's mother. It always reminded Manman of her mother-in-law seated at one end of the meal table patiently dipping from a large bowl of pureed red beans unto the plates of white rice being passed around to any number of children, older relatives, and other people who happened to stop by. Both Georges and Christine Ledan Benedict, Papa's parents had died before I could know them but their memory lived on in the stories I would hear of their generosity and work habits. A network of family and friends lived by that code of ethics.

One day in 1955, the large round ball that my mother had become yielded the promised, not one but two babies: one light skin and the other brown. I was three years old when my twin sisters were born and became an instant celebrity at the *Ecole Maternelle* I attended in Les Cayes. While my classmates had one new brother or sister, I had two babies to call my own. I took charge immediately, insisting that both infants be placed in my lap so I could lull them to sleep in a rocking chair with the tips of my toes stretched to tap a nearby stool since my feet did not reach the floor.

"No, I am not tired"

I would insist as sweat trickled down the side of my cheeks and both my arms grew numb under the babies' weight. The town people of les Cayes streamed in to visit our family on the chance that they would be allowed a glimpse of the "*petites Jumelles*"; my twins. Caridad Elizabeth Florence was the larger of the twins and of the same light complexion as Manman, our mother, and I. The smaller twin was given the names Carmelle Elizabeth Maryse. Her skin was darker brown like our Papa's. A family friend nicknamed the twins "*bonbon sucre*" and "*bonbon sirop*" for sugar and molasses cookie because of the difference in their complexions. As they grew, "*Bonbon sirop*" was re-nick-named. So was her sister.

Bonbon Sucre, was a head taller and larger than her twin and became known as "*gros Pepe*" because her habit of sucking one thumb while twirling a strand of her soft curly hair around the fingers of her other hand, eyes drifting into space made her appear "slow". Pepe sat silently close to anyone who stood still, tucking her small round legs under her thin cotton dress, leaning unto anyone or anything, falling asleep at times seemingly unaware of the adults whispering about the events of the day. She was not a talker. Then, unexpectedly, with an imperceptible thud as she pulled out her wet thumb to unstop her mouth Pepe would throw our household into a panic with a lisped but precise version of something she had overheard someone say. Most unnerving was when she would call out *"Vive Deja!"* in honor of a political candidate whose name she could not pronounce. Louis Dejoie had lost the presidential elections and in the Haitian tradition had to flee the country to escape his victorious opponent's murderous wrath. Anyone breathing Dejoie's name would be instantly condemned for anti-government sympathies.

Pepe's twin was smaller, a head shorter, and a whirlwind of activity. The first thing one noticed about my smaller sister was her dark, shining eyes. They lit up her small brown face with their intensity. Someone watching her small body, her slim arms and legs and their seemingly boundless energy thought that she looked like a hummingbird poised in flight dipping its diminutive beak into a flower. In Haitian Kreyol small things are frequently called a "Ti -kikite" so the name stuck to the very small species of hummingbird that lives in the country and to our sister. From "Ti -kikite", her nickname was shortened to Tikite. She was fearless. Whether in defense of her twin or in response to a challenge Tikite was quick on the draw with her tongue. Pepe on the other hand, needed to be rescued frequently especially when both girls started school. One particular teacher, at the time the twins were about five or six years old, struck terror in Pepe's little heart whenever the swish of petticoats announced the woman's approach. Pepe would crouch nervously over her desk and the eraser end of the pencil she worked with her small clenched fist would erase and erase and erase until a glaring hole appeared on the page of her copybook.

Our Manman's mother Amelie Pilet Toulme a first generation Haitian had caramel colored skin. Manman's father Victor Auguste Toulmé, who had a French father and mulatto mother, looked White. The members of both my parents' families were of varying shades of light to dark brown. Anyone trying to group us by skin tone would match Papa with Manman's dark skinned brother and sister whereas several acquaintances have thought that I was the daughter of uncle Miyou, Papa's older brother whose other nickname was Blanco because of his very light complexion. My sisters and I simply referred to our parents as " Manman" and "Papa".

African, French and the very distinctive features of Lecilina Lebrun Ledan the half Arawak, a now extinct native Caribbean people, and half French matriarch of the Ledan clan make up the racial mix on my father's side of the family. Great grandmother Lecilina's husband, Louis Duplessis Ledan, a diminutive black man who was fond of wearing knee high riding boots, was an associate pastor to the more robust African looking Charles Emmanuel Benedict, Papa's other grandfather. According to family history, *Pasteur* Ledan was reputed to have ridden on a horse from Les Cayes, stopping only to change his mount, all the way to the capital city of Port-au-Prince, galloped past a sentry straight into the National Presidential Palace into the President's office to demand the release of his son David. Papa's uncle David had been a medical student in Port-au-Prince. David Ledan apparently had been so engrossed in a textbook he was reading while seated on an open porch that he did not stand up to show respect to the president of Haiti as the latter's carriage drove by in the street. The presidential escort had promptly clapped young David Ledan in the city jail. In the most notorious arbitrary mass execution at that same Port-au-Prince, city jail three hundred men had been executed one July morning in 1914. His father's timely horse ride caught the authorities off guard and David Ledan lived to return to his native Les Cayes as one of its hardworking physicians. Papa moved into his house when he returned to Les Cayes in 1940. This was expected. A young single man moving to a town would live with whichever older relative had room. Papa had left Les Cayes at 10 years old when his father had been transferred to *Sainte Trinite* the Episcopalian Cathedral in Port-au-Prince and moved the family there. Grandfather Benedict also taught at the Episcopalian Seminary there. Relatives from the provinces, mainly les Cayes squeezed into the family home in Port-au-Prince as the need arose.

The townsfolk of Les Cayes kept a watchful eye, because he had a profession and a paying job, on Dr David Ledan's very eligible dentist nephew. Everyone knew that the young Dr Benedict was spoken for and had a fiancée in Port-au-Prince. Yet, mothers with daughters of marriageable age set their wishing cap in his direction. When Papa, at five feet five a whole five inches taller than Manman, brought his bride to the town on the afternoon of their wedding day word quickly spread that they both looked like a couple of turtle doves. So for quite a while the newly weds were both referred to as " *Les deux poulies*": a Haitian version of the French idea of lovebirds. Manman was from the much larger city of Port-au-Prince. She immediately labeled the town's people as "*Tripotes*" or "nosey" and fiercely guarded her privacy. Living in a province instead of the Capital city was a disappointment to Manman. For years she would cite the twelve years she spent in Les Cayes as evidence that she was a dutiful wife and virtuous woman.

"Your Papa's umbilical cord is buried in that place!" she would exclaim on occasion. His love for his hometown was a source of irritation to her. Papa nurtured the hope that he would spend the rest of his life there and never understood why Manman should miss the crowded social clubs, theatres, and the frenetic bustle of Port-au-Prince. Manman voiced her opinion often enough that no Costume ball or New Year's Eve dances in Les Cayes came close to her standards. Characteristically, my mother did not idle away her time mulling over her disappointments. There was always a shirt to sew, the layette for a newborn or a *paillase* (straw filled mattress) to make for one of our large circle of acquaintances. Had she charged money for her talents or even her supplies, my mother would have accumulated a tidy sum in those days. Papa, although a recognized professional, did not collect fees either for a substantial number of his private patients. It was his duty to care for anyone remotely related by blood or association to his ancestors in addition to the needy.

The Benedict family in Haiti originated with, a stocky African-looking man of unknown origins and the English surname of Benedict, who arrived in Les Cayes in the mid eighteen hundreds with a light-skinned Haitian wife. He was an associate of James Theodore Holly, a Black American who in response to racism in the United States, left there with a group of pioneers to settle in the new republic of Haiti. Bishop Holly founded the Episcopalian Church in Haiti and sent the young Charles Benedict to an American Seminary in Philadelphia, U.S.A. before appointing him to start an Episcopalian congregation in Les Cayes. Whatever his earlier background, great-grandfather Benedict had left the legacy of a good name to his nine children and their descendents and a firm place in the Haitian middle class. The town's people of Les Cayes paid homage to this legacy. My father was respected because of his inheritance of the Benedict and Ledan (his mother's family) reputations even before he made his mark in the town as a trusted dentist. At ten years old, I was poised to reap the rewards of my ancestry.

Brave ancestry and family honor count in Haitian circles. Survival in this troubled country was in itself a badge of honor. Before Manman had even been born her own father had had two death sentences passed on him: one by the Haitian government, and the other by the French. It seems that Victor Auguste Toulmé, quite wild in his day, was frequently embroiled in some political dispute. One day, the government against which he and a group of friends had been demonstrating rounded up and summarily sentenced the young men to die by firing squad. The condemned men were all in a jail cell when one of them called out to the prison guard.

"Hey! You cannot execute a Frenchman... There he is right there, the fellow with the blue eyes and blond hair: Auguste Toulmé! Do you people want trouble with the French?"

Auguste Toulmé had refused to save himself insisting that his companions and he had gotten into trouble together and therefore should face the consequences as one. It was a matter of honor. His friends shook their heads as they bade him adieu. In their situation, French Citizenship was the only card left to play.

Auguste Toulmé later known as *Pe Toulmé* to acquaintances, having survived the time when proud mustachioed males died for the sake of honor was known as Papa Gus to my generation. He was born in the Haitian city of Cap-Haitien but his parents both French citizens, his father was reportedly born in France and his mother came from Martinique a Caribbean colony of France, had registered him with that country's consulate as a Frenchman; a fact that never prevented the younger Toulme from being the most patriotic of Haitians. The French government however, had not forgotten about him. When the First World War broke out in 1914 Papa Gus, by then married with young children, received a draft notice from Paris, France. He had never set foot in Europe. The French insisted that he fulfill his duty to *"La Patrie"*. When he refused to go to France, the French government declared him a deserter, tried him in one of their Tribunals in absentia, and pronounced a death sentence on him. Papa Gus quickly applied for Haitian citizenship and stopped traveling in the Caribbean for fear of falling into the hands of a French naval vessel and being deported to France to face yet another firing squad.

My grandfather's penchant for meddling with Haitian politics earned him other brushes with death. Manman remembers her father hobbling home one night with a bullet in one leg and of having a group of *Cacos*, the redoubtable revolutionary men from the North of Haiti, turn her family home, late one other evening, into an impromptu overnight safe house. She and her two sisters became experts at hiding their father's activities from prying neighbors. Then the Duvalierists came into power in Haiti. Papa Gus realizing that the days of riding on horseback, shooting pistols off in the air and rum fueled heated political debates were gone, retired from politics, and watched from the sidelines.

Against all odds, Papa Gus held on to his job at the country's Ministry of Finance as an accountant until a broken hip forced him into retirement at the age of ninety. One of his techniques for staying employed as a political appointee was to never train any newcomer who might one day replace him. He carefully guarded the secrets of his neatly inscribed accounting ledgers. Tall, by then silver haired with an antiquated thick mustache, he cut an elegant figure in his crisp white linen suits, impeccably charming to the ladies but the bane of the life of would be suitors of his daughters.

I was both fascinated by and afraid of my grandfather's stern face. There was a barely perceptible twitch of his moustache when he spoke. Occasionally I would catch a glimpse, from under this gray bush that hid his upper lip, of sturdy teeth, stained orange yellow, as were his fingertips with years of cigarette smoking. My sister Pepe, when she was a baby, would burst out in loud sobs if he looked at her. On the other hand Tikite's unblinking gaze studied his face intently as he held her in his arms crooning, his voice raspy and droll, with his own version of a lullaby. My aunt Christine shared the same house with Papa Gus with her children and our unmarried aunt Andree. They were puzzled by his tenderness towards the twins. *Papa Gus* was the undisputed head of the household that felt the weight of his iron rule. Everyone knew that he was displeased by the pronouncement, resonating throughout the large house, of his own inimitable thundering of *"Tonnèrres!"* which is the French word for thunder. Family, friends, and foe spoke of Auguste Toulmé as a man of indisputable integrity.

Although in Les Cayes, we lived eight hours away from our parents' immediate family in the capital city of Port-au-Prince, our ancestors, or as we said in Kreyol " *granmoun lontan*" held an integral place in our daily lives. Some of the older generation, like Manman's maternal grandfather Paul Pilet who had been born in Guadeloupe, left a less distinct record. The latter had been made to relinquish his French merchant marine commission at the insistence of the family of the Haitian beauty, great grandmother Aldéda Aclocque whom he married. Paul Pilet never returned to his native Caribbean island even after the premature death, from a fall off a balcony, of his beloved. His wife's family took charge of their fifteen children placing them in the care of various relatives. Amélie the thirteenth child, who became my grandmother Man Lillie, was three years old at the time of her mother's death, remembered only brief chance encounters with her grief-stricken father.

Adults used stories of the deeds of the elders, alive or dead, with minute details of their way of thinking, as the unwritten instructional manuals for the new generation. I grew up with the knowledge that those who had preceded me were decisive, hard working and strong-minded men and women who did not hesitate to take action even to the point of risking death in defense of family honor and National freedom.

Why Haitian parents take the trouble to name their children is a mystery. They invariably allow friends, relatives, and their very own fancies to saddle a small child with the most cumbersome of sobriquets. A family friend thought that I, upon my entry into the world with a large round hairless head and plump cheeks, looked like a tomcat. So family, friends and any number of acquaintances all somehow agreed that I looked like a *Matou Chatte,* and since I was an infant someone stretched out the first part of the Kreyol appellation into *Matoutou* to make it sound endearing and dropped the *chatte* or "cat" part. I became *"Matoutou".* There was no connection, even remotely, to the names inscribed on my birth certificate of Claire Marie-Solange Bénédict. In Haiti, the introductory name such as in my case is not used. My first name is Marie-Solange.

By the time I was ten years old I answered to *Matoutoucha, Matoutou, Titoutou, Toutsi* and briefly, when my frequent visits to a street vendor who parked her fried *"griot"* and *"banan pese"* pots on the other side of our fence caused my weight to soar: *"Tibouloune!"* All of my nicknames pointed to my chubby appearance: a fact that encouraged some unfortunate errand boys in Les Cayes to risk a vicious tongue-lashing. I took no prisoners when it came to ego bruising contests. My hair, when it finally came in, leaned towards a reddish tint in addition to being plentiful and very coarse.

This meant that, according to local custom, I would be called a "*grimelle*". I, however, was not inclined to acquiesce to anything that held me up to ridicule, so the cautionary word circulated about town:

"Don't tell Matoutou Bénédict that she is a *grimelle!*"

Our official first names although rarely used audibly were not light stuff either because of the inherited French predilection for double-barreled first names that, by my own unofficial tally, affects a good third of the Haitian population. The deluge of Marie-Louise, Marie-Jeanne, Marie-Carmelle for girls and Jean-Pierre, Jean-Robert, Jean-Marie, Jean-Jacques for boys even led to the custom in school of abbreviating the "Marie" with a "Mie" and using "Jn" for "Jean" at least on copy books. Other hyphenated appellations taxed the patience even of their owners who in turn gratefully responded to anything monosyllabic. For my parents' generation there was a purpose for the name changes. Someone had noticed that voodoo malefactors who turned people into zombies needed the real name of the victim to exert their power over them. Children were deemed to be especially at risk of being snatched. That is why birth certificates are carefully crafted to list several names and relatives use a secret list of others to call each other by. Real birth dates were also frequently hidden for the same reason. For years, I was confused as to when I should wish my father "Happy Birthday".

My parents, in their attempt to help those who asked, hired more people than we needed to work in our house. Besides room and board, their employees had a monthly supply of toiletries and any medical care they or their close family members needed. "*Poulie*". Manman would say. "You can't allow so and so to walk around with a big gap in the front of her teeth!" In turn Papa would recommend that someone should "go see *madanm doktè*" for some clothes. Married women in our town were frequently referred to as the wife (*Madanm*) of the doctor (*doktè*), engineer (*ingeniè*), inspector (*inspektè*), or captain (*kapitènn*). In Les Cayes there was an informal system of trading: Papa could send one of his protégés to a colleague for free medical care just as he would attend to someone showing up to his private clinic with a plea for help. My father, vulnerable to sad stories, was slow to detect the inevitable con artists. Maman was a better judge of character and early on instructed me to be suspicious of anyone she disapproved of which included everyone not related to her side of the family. Several members of Papa's family had offended my mother and she would never forgive them. Once someone was on Manman's black list, they remained there for life. Yet, she was fiercely loyal to the few who earned her trust.

I forget when my mother taught me a certain expression in Haitian Kreyol that became a stock phrase in her vocabulary, whenever she wanted to drive home her point that she chose to accept certain situations in life. Her personal priorities were her husband, her children, and her reputation as a virtuous wife, mother, and housekeeper. She told me that she trusted in God, but she also relied heavily on the folk remedies she had learned from her childhood and youth. Now as a woman in her own house, Manman adhered to the prescriptions for life in a Haitian community that generally held an innumerable list of negatives.

"*Ça pa bon!*"

Curiously, I do not remember children using that phrase. Literally, it means; *this is no good!* No child dared question an adult of a certain standing in our society as to why any activity was labeled thus. I had the vague impression that doing something that I was told was "no good" invited retributions from a higher power. It was generally understood around me that God would strike one dead if he wished at any time for some infractions. Most likely, however, doing something that our religious leaders had neglected to warn us against might fall under the vigilant doctrine of "*Ça pa bon"*. As a result, my parents do not have any pictures of their wedding ceremony or even of themselves on that day because someone in authority in their families had declared this activity as one; "*Ça pa bon*".

I had determined very early on that my mother, although she did not receive a University education, was a very intelligent woman who understood life better than her educated contemporaries. She prided herself on having the strength of character to choose her own fetters. Manman's personal mantra, another kreyol saying, was:

"*Bouche nin bwè dlo santi!*"
Pinch your nose and swallow the stinking water!

I had become very well acquainted with that phrase. My mother was one of the rare adults in Haiti who took the time to explain our sayings. She taught me the meaning of this particular phrase, and it was important to her that I understood, that she had a nose or "*nin*" on her face. Another Kreyol saying judged an individual who did not exact revenge for an insult as someone "*without a nose in his face*". One way of dealing with an insult was to avoid its stench by pinching one's nose. Manman pinched her nose many times throughout her life for the sake of others: her father, brothers and sisters, her husband, her children and her home. She kept a meticulous count of these events, admonishing me to do the same.

"*Songé!*" or "Remember!"

In our home, I had my share of challenges. I do not remember how and when *Clothilde* joined our household in Les Cayes when I was a child, or why she remained there. At some point, Maman must have pointed out her shortcomings to me. I do recall that what I most disliked about this particular woman was her hypocrisy. When *Clothilde* realized that I had seen through her toothy minutely crafted theatrical smile, she grasped at every opportunity to discredit me through lies and the most elaborate schemes. She was a servant, resented her position in life, and sought to use her association with our family to elevate her status within Haitian society. Carefully styling her hair, and appearance to blend in with our family circle, she set herself above the rest of the staff. Manman disliked her and the woman was fired at least twice yet always managed to worm her way back into our home. My gullible father punished me time after time, because of this woman's deception. One evening, *Clothilde* decided to entertain a male visitor in my parent's sitting room in their absence, without their permission, and tried to coerce my curious sisters into going to sleep earlier than their usual bedtime. My bedroom adjoined that of the twins and I could hear *Clothilde*'s rising voice. I had been bred to protect my younger sisters and everyone acquainted with us knew this. In our home, the servants were allowed to give the twins a mild swat to correct them. This woman had crossed the line. The sound of my sisters' screams as she physically disciplined them, stirred me into action. I dropped whatever I was engaged in to charge across the distance between our rooms and pounced on the woman, pinning her skinny arms to her sides squeezing her body with all the strength of an oversized nine years old and lifted her off her feet. As *Clothilde* and I panted, her head and feet swinging wildly, I dragged her out of my sisters' room and tried to throw her off the back porch of the house.

Some other adult must have rescued my enemy and advised her to stay away from me, since I remember nothing else of the incident except my fear of reprisals. Predictably, the next day, *Clothilde* walked from our home into town to complain to my father at his office. Papa reacted immediately; jumped into his car, drove home in a rage, unbuckling, and pulling off the belt holding up his pants as he stormed into the house, bellowing out my name. The whirr of Manman's sewing machine slowed to a halt as she lifted up her feet from the cast iron pedal.

"Who is the mistress of this house?"

Manman demanded, without raising her voice. My mother remained seated in front of her sewing machine barely turning her head, but there was that certain characteristic tilt in her jaw. She was already resuming her interrupted task, but the weight of each of her words had the intended effect:
" I did not give *Clothilde* permission to leave her work in my house to go into town. Why did she go to you instead of coming to me?"
I knew not to openly gloat and slipped off discretely to savor my reprieve. From then on *Clothilde* and I contented ourselves with glaring at each other as our mutual hatred intensified. Meanwhile, I maneuvered through the traditions of my elders tending to my duties quite well, or so I thought. One of my duties as the oldest child in our family was to listen for anything my younger sisters would say that might endanger our home if heard by the wrong ears. The role of official sensor and guardian of the deeds of ones' siblings was an arduous and thankless job. Adult Haitians invariably questioned the oldest in any group of children who would then suffer the consequences for whatever trouble took place. The lines of authority, was established as soon as a baby ventured out of his or her crib. Out of a sense of self-preservation the older child in our society kept the younger set on a short leash. For my generation the burden of the first born, keeper of family secrets had been saddled with a more vital responsibility. At least I shouldered the unwelcome burden of guarding my tongue so as not to divulge any information about us to the outside world. Towards the start of the nineteen sixties, however, something had occurred that added to my load. I do not remember when I first became aware of it. Imperceptibly, the stack of secrets to keep safe grew daily and eventually weighed upon my most ordinary thoughts.

2

On that April morning of 1962, one more secret was being carefully guarded about our household and I did not know it. I walked, on that day, into our bathroom as Manman took a shower. She wore the familiar plastic bonnet on her head I remember noticing, as she leaned out from behind the shower curtain. We had talked about many things in just that way. Often, she recited in detail the plot of a movie she had seen with Papa at the town's theatre the previous night. Her keen memory painted such vivid pictures that decades later, I would instantly recognize the story of a movie from that period after watching the opening scenes. Manman splashed water on her body and the plastic drape as I nestled on top of the toilet seat cover, shouting out my questions above the noise of the shower alcove. It was our routine. What my mother said to me on that particular day, however, hit me with the force of a sudden billowing storm. It was more frightening than the story of Godzilla, or the scene of one of Alfred Hitchcock's characters dangling from the side of a cliff. Our family, Manman said, was leaving our home, our town, family members, friends and country right away to go to a far away land. The house we lived in, our home, was already sold with the furniture in it. We were to travel within two days to Port-au-Prince, the country's capital city to stay with my mother's family so my father could escape ahead of us out of Haiti.

I have forgotten how I reacted then. At ten years old, I most certainly did not voice any fear, anger, or anxiety: that was not allowed in my world. If I shed any tears, I must have done so in secret. Increasingly I disliked leaving my home to go anywhere. In years, since that day in our small bathroom, I have felt an indescribable sense of loss, which would cling to me and often usher in thoughts of foreboding. When I force myself to travel to any new place, even today, it weighs on my mind, this mostly irrational malaise. I had, as the average child in Haiti living in a town who also attended school, been nurtured on a steady diet of patriotic propaganda. Every morning our country's flag was raised up the schoolyard pole as the entire student body stood in formation singing *La Dessaliniènne* our national anthem, which extolled the virtues of dying for country and ancestors. My companions and I marched daily in a sort of physical education exercise to the tunes of revolutionary songs. Lyrics that told of French blood sloshing around Haiti's mountains sprang out of the mouths of small schoolgirls and older ones alike as the French nuns who were in the higher echelon of our religious school system stood by.

If French historians have by and large ignored the story of their country's defeat in 1804 at the hand of the largely Africans Revolutionaries of Saint Domingue, the transformation of their old colony into the Republic of Haiti is a much retold tale in that island nation. Generations, named heir sons, Toussaint, Dessalines, Pétion Christophe, Boirond, Capois, Boyer, and so on to keep alive the memory of the heroes of *"La Guerre de L'indépendence"*, The war for independence. Haitians who can trace their ancestry back to the days of the Revolution are very proud of being what is known as an *authentic* Haitian. Children my age, even most who had never set foot in a school, *knew* that Toussaint L'Ouverture, the chief architect of the abolition of slavery in Saint Domingue and the establishment of a free state on the French colony was a brilliant man. He had given his life for this cause. The French captured him, deported him to France, and threw him in a dungeon in their Jurat Mountains where he died. We knew that Jean-Jacques Dessalines who united the Revolutionary armies for the final push against the French military expedition, gave no quarters to the enemy, neither did other generals like Henri Christophe. My grandfather, with all the French blood coursing through his veins, was proudest of his African heritage. He admired men like Capois La Mort, the Cavalry officer, who at the battle of Vertièrres, when his horse was shot down from under him rose up to continue the charge he was leading on foot. I loved to hear how the French commander opposing Capois stopped the battle to salute the bravery of the man who from then on had the words " *La Mort*" or *death,* added to his name. The enslaved Africans of the former Saint Domingue had wrested their freedom from the seasoned troops of the great Napoléon Bonaparte himself. Close to 300,000 of them perished along with approximately, 50,000 French soldiers and a great number of civilians in a vicious twelve year long struggle, which also irreparably scarred the land. The French commander in chief of the Saint Domingue campaign, Donatien-Marie de Rochambeau, and his chief, Napoléon Bonaparte are revered in France just as Toussaint, Dessalines, and Christophe are in Haiti. There are no victims' memorials that I know. The Haitian revolution's rallying cry was "V*ivre libre ou mourir"*: "Live free or die". Those very words had been the slogan of the French Revolution, a continent away. What had been drummed into my and my contemporaries' minds was that no one could enslave a Haitian. We should all be willing to die first.

    An independent Republic of former slaves in the Western Hemisphere in 1804 was a threat to a slave holding world. Slaves had never before succeeded in setting up an independent State. On the world stage westerners, set themselves up as superior to people of color, had the military power to dominate, and could point to Rome's one thousand year reign. At that point, I knew nothing of the kingdom of Dahomey and other African territorial powers without which the Slave Trade could never have existed. Europeans in Europe and their descendants in the newly formed United States of America needed to feel superior to the Africans. How else could they justify the kidnapping, maiming, torture, and murder of over 22 million Africans and the brutality of the Slave Trade and Slavery? Rome was still revered for its might, no one appearing to question the centuries of brutality perpetrated in its Coliseum alone. The moral fortitude of men and women like William Wilberforce in England and others fought an uphill battle against the perverse greed and depravity of humanity. Saint Domingue was a considerable source of income to France for a reason. It killed people at such a rate that the French planters had to import more and more Africans to replace the dead. During the Revolutionary war, the French attempted to restore Slavery through genocide of the Colony's Blacks with the idea that they would replace them with slaves that had not been infected with the freedom bug. *"You are just cutting the tree"* Toussaint L'Ouverture was reported to have told his French captors. He prophesized that the roots of that tree; freedom would continue to sprout and grow and become unstoppable. For these surviving sons and daughters of Africa, however, isolation from the world was yet another price paid for freedom.

There was a pervasive national paranoia in Haiti against foreign domination, which peaked during a nineteen-years occupation by the United States at the beginning of the twentieth century. Individually, men and women sought refuge in Haiti, especially before the abolition of slavery in the remainder of the Caribbean islands. They were welcomed and as for so many in my own family, integrated themselves as citizens of the *République*. White soldiers on Haitian soil, however, immediately trampled on national pride. People who recalled that period were convinced that the United States Marines were all racists who harbored evil intentions toward Blacks. Haitian men died in countless incidents, I was told, of sometime merely symbolic gestures of patriotism. Others like Charlemagne Peralte, the commander of the Leogane *Arrondissment* who refused to surrender to the Americans, mounted a guerrilla resistance until a Haitian sold him out to a Marine patrol. There were also the suicidal campaigns of the *Cacos* the *paysans* fighters of the North. I knew that the memory of American Marines, in the cherished land, was still a topic of bitter debate for the older folk. Therefore, in my generation, a copious amount of pride was fed to every Haitian child from birth. In addition, this was nourished by regular reminders of the bravery of the heroes of the Republic whether from the *Révolution* or the *Occupation*. Local poems extolled the bravery of these *Grands Patriotes*! The fact that they murdered their competitors and abused their own people was left out. My classmates and I bought into the notion that no land on earth compared to our darling Haiti. Haitians who went to foreign lands to study or visit in my recollection always came home because of their intense grief at being separated from the motherland.

Another reason for the collective homesickness of the exiled was that family ties were tightly woven with several generations living under one roof. Our relatives were no exception. Extended families included godparents, in-laws, and honorary relatives, binding groups of people with ties of reciprocal relationships. People endured poverty, sickness, aggression, and death but remained loyal to family and country. On that morning in 1962, it must have shocked me beyond description to hear my mother, as she wrapped her wet body in a towel and casually stepped out of the puddle of water she had made on the bathroom floor, announce that we were about to abandon our native land, our Haiti.

My sisters and I loved to sit around the small table our father used as a makeshift dental lab bench. He and the other four or five dentists in our town did much of their own prosthetic work. Therefore, at the end of the day Papa brought a small alcohol lamp and a mounted plaster cast of a client's mouth to our home. I was fascinated by the dexterity of Papa's thick brown fingers as they scooped up little globs of softened wax on the tip of an instrument that looked like a miniature Roman soldier's lance. His baldhead with its small tuft of black hair adrift in the middle of a glistening brown scalp leaned over his work, tensing at times into faint ripples of skin in harmony with the ebb and flow of his thoughts. The twins and I found it highly entertaining to watch the fake teeth of someone, very often someone we knew, being placed one by one on their dentures. Our shoulders propped against each other, shielding the blue flame of the work lamp from the gusts of the large fan set up to sweep away the mosquitoes.

In those times, we heard the tall tales our Papa concocted for us. We waited also hoping that he had mixed just a little too much of the fragrant pink or brown material that would harden and eventually hold the imbedded teeth in a row and form the dental plate. I suspect that he often deliberately allowed for the soft little ball of surplus denture material so he could fashion the tiny figures that my sisters and I loved to play with.

Papa's main hobby was photography. His income, however, did not allow him access to expensive equipment so he made his own to develop and process the rolls of black and white shots he took. His enlarger, I remember was fashioned out of an empty lard tin can with its label and both ends cut out. My sisters and I, and members of our household were his main subjects out of necessity, since the two small antique cameras Papa possessed were ill suited for scenery shots. He printed some of the photographs of the family on postcards that we mailed to relatives. The one inconvenience caused by Papa's activities was that our sole indoor bathroom (the children were not allowed to use the outhouse in the backyard) served as his dark room.

Another hobby was to surprise us with a small brown paper bag filled with sweets from a local candy maker or with an impromptu trip to one of the rivers bordering our town or the beach. The twins and I would squeal with delight upon discovering his elaborate secret plans. Generally, he coaxed good behavior from us in so many ways. We knew that our parents as good Haitians did not tolerate *"Ti-Moun mal eleve"* or spoiled brats but knew that the three of us were at the center of their plans. Both were involved in our education from the start of our lives. In our home, the belt was used only on rare occasions. Lectures and "the look" a silent communication tool mastered by my mother served to correct our behavior. In our home Papa was king. Our household made sure that everything was done to please him. That was the Haitian way. In comparison to other Haitian fathers, he was a benevolent king; except when he indulged in a fit of anger. When this happened the servants, the twins, the dog, and I would scatter to various parts of the house. Manman would continue with whatever activity she was engaged in, seemingly unconcerned. Haitian men were entitled to throw tamper tantrums so I never heard my mother try to calm my father down or suggest to him that he should control his outbursts. Instead, she meticulously instructed everyone in our home on how to avoid upsetting our father. Her reason was that she did not like the noise that angry men make. She had done everything to avoid her own father's tirades when she lived in his house. As she told me several times, she was afraid that she would not be able to control her own reaction.

"The day your Papa gets on my nerves I might get a large stick, hit him on the head, crack his skull and kill him!"

I never doubted that she would. There was something about Manman's compact frame and square jaw that made her silence more menacing. Papa must have noticed it too since he seemed to respond to the glint that would suddenly appear in her eye, by shutting down his own eruption. Naturally, my sisters and I preferred the good side of our father. Manman made sure he always had a crisp clean white handkerchief in his pants' back pocket. He could always be depended upon to sacrifice its pristine folds to soothe a feverish brow, comfort a scraped knee, wipe a smudge, or my sisters' tears. He would lean forward to inspect it when one of the twins would try to return the damp cloth after blowing a nose in it.

" Go give this to Lorsa, or Marianne, or your mother." He would say.

As the oldest, I benefited the most from Papa's good graces. I traipsed after him on fishing trips with his friends strictly as a spectator since I never handled the fish and tried to keep my toes from touching the scales of the catch writhing at the bottom of the boat. Once when one of his companions, underestimating my weight, insisted that I jump down into the man's arms as we dropped anchor on a beach, Papa gallantly gave me his undershirt to wear until my clothes dried. He did not take me hunting, another of his weekend pastimes, until the *Tonton Macoutes* banned firearms use by civilians. Instead, we became inseparable during soccer season. Papa was the president of a soccer team for as long as I could remember. Our latest team wore black shorts with a yellow jersey. My favorite player was a cinnamon skinned lithe young Center Forward that our local fans idolized. His nickname was *Cacao*.

"*Cacao!*" The crowd would shout as the young man dribbled the ball past one, two defense players.

"*Cacao! Cacao*! : Screeched, the young women as our hero neared the penalty box.

"*Baye-Li gol*!" In other words: "Score!"

As with each time a player on our team got the ball, Papa would walk up and down the field, following the action. No one was supposed to walk on the edge of the field, but he was *Docteur* Benedict as well as the president of the soccer club. Both titles entitled him to certain privileges. Wearing his white handkerchief, with four knots at each corner, to protect his scalp from the blistering mid afternoon sun, he was easy to spot. Manman would instruct me before we left the house.

"Keep your eye on your father and don't let him scream and hurt his voice".

Cacao, however, had scored a goal!

"W-o-o-o-h!

Our fans erupted in a deafening roar and the crowd standing around the field swayed from side to side.

"*Cacao! Cacao! Cacao!*"

I had been caught up in the frenzy and chanted as loud as anyone next to me: "*Cacao! Cacao! Cacao! Cacao-o-o-o!*"

Our town's soccer field was shielded from those who could not pay the admittance fee by a wall made of coconut fronds weaved onto a frame of wooden poles. Manman, a passionate soccer fan in her youth, was used to the sophistication of Port-au-Prince's stadium and never attended our games. She thought that standing around a field, with sweating, screaming people, was not worth her time. The gendarmes who patrolled, *Rigoaz* in hand would pretend not to see the young boys who stood outside, tearing up the coconut fronds to push their faces in some small opening to look in. Invariably I would have to search for the yellow jersey of one of our team players in the crowd after the game.

"Matoutou, you are looking for your Papa?"

The player would hoist me atop his shoulders so that I could scan around the sea of bodies for that white kerchief coif. Papa would have found a *Machann Fritailles* and bought us both a generous portion of fried pork or plantain. *Griots* and *banan pésé* were part of the attraction to soccer games as well as the ice cream. I have never tasted ice cream like the *crème corosol* or *crème cayimite* of Les Cayes' street vendors. One or two of Papa's friends would also offer me some *kola* to wash it all down. When a fight erupted among rival fans, Papa would quickly drive me home and then go to the hospital. Doctors, dentists, pharmacists, nurses would volunteer to help the hospital staff treat the wounded. Papa would spend hours suturing lacerated scalps. It was a predictable post game ritual. If our team won, there would be a parade. The players, fans and I would squeeze into several cars for the impromptu single filed drive, horns blasting, chanting and singing our victory songs at the top of our voices, for a spin around the streets of the town, slowing down on the last leg of our victory march the whole length of the *Grande Rue*. Manman would greet our return with a knowing look:

"You have lost your voice, haven't you?"

Haitian tradition demanded respect for all elders. The education of children whether in or outside of the home is very important to Haitians. Small farmers in the countryside, especially the women toil endlessly to pay for the schooling of their offspring; the male children, that is. Girls were taught, in various private academies, to care for the family home unless they were hired out as servants and cooks to more prosperous families. Our schoolteachers rapped us across the knuckles with rulers as they did their other pupils but were restrained from using the *rigoazz,* a horsewhip made out of braided rawhide, to discipline the Benedict girls. Manman had made her views about the use of the *rigoazz* known. She was an outsider from Port-au-Prince and townspeople were unsure as to what the straight-backed *Madame Docteur Bénédict* was capable of if anyone harmed her girls. Most other students were no so protected.

Pepe, Tikite, and I were the family representatives for our town's *Premier Janvier* ritual. Manman prepared for it weeks in advance sewing and embroidering three matching dresses, purchasing the matching hair ribbons and socks that my sisters and I would wear with the new shoes our local shoemaker made in time for the new-year deadline. January first was the anniversary of the Haitian declaration of independence as well as the day everyone in town was expected to wish each other a good year. In addition to saying *"Bonne Année!"* people gave each other gifts of money wrapped in tight little scrolls of paper and made one jug of very sweet syrupy pink and another of green liqueur to serve *Premier Janvier* visitors. It was as grave a social offense not to have the little shot glasses polished and ready on a tray in one's sitting room just as it was for no visitor to come knocking. Somewhere in the distant past someone hit on a solution to having to be in two places at the same time by electing the children ambassadors of their families, entrusting them with the duty of making, escorted by a maid or older child, the rounds of relatives and acquaintances.

In Les Cayes, it was hard to find anyone my father was not related to. Since everyone in town also knew each other by name, the visit list was quite extensive. I had long wearied of the door- to- door trek across town in the mid afternoon sun, the twins and I sweating profusely under the mop of Shirley Temple ringlets Manman had created on top of each of our heads. The limp refractory hair ribbons, sinking ankle socks and liqueur induced bellyaches added to our misery.

One particular *Premier Janvier* I toyed with the idea of forgetting the last name on the by then crumpled piece of paper Manman had charged me with. We were on a street of one of the town's squares a fair distance from our house. The *demoiselles...* at the bottom of our list: two aged spinster sisters were rarely seen away from their house overlooking the square. That was the problem. I could not be sure that they had not spotted, through the slats of their balcony's shutters, our little band as we had gone in and out of several of their neighbors' homes. News traveled fast in this small town. Our parents would be called to account for my infraction with dire consequences for me the leader. Thus motivated I dragged the twins up to yet another porch and rapped the heavy door of the house with my sore knuckles. Both women clad in almost identical outmoded ankle long dresses, gray hair pulled back from the very fine wrinkles of their light brown faces were standing in the hallway of their home at the foot of a highly polished wood staircase.

"They are here!"

I felt a pang of remorse at the two women's obvious happiness in seeing us,

"My sister: quick, quick, go fetch it!"

One sister grabbed each of the twins' faces, then mine, with both hands, fluffing our dresses, chirping out a string of questions and pulling us into a dimly lit parlor. The other one hopped up the stairs leading to the upper floor of the house with surprising agility. I felt my head start to swim and sank down into a stiff upholstered chair.

"We were prepared for weeks". The second sister had landed back in our midst with a large object cradled in her arms. Words tumbled out in a stream as the women spoke, each anticipating, and completing the other's speech. Predictably, it was: "Oh, look at the children of Solanges and Marie!"

"Look how grown they are"

"Matoutou what a big girl you are!"

"I told my sister…" the taller of the *demoiselles* was saying, "that of course you were coming".

"Yes of course" her sister echoed.

" We knew for weeks so we prepared. Ét *voila!*"

The second sister thrust the package she had been holding into my arms. The faces of both women creased in identical folds as they giggled like two conspiring schoolgirls.

"We saved this for the Bénédict girls " they chorused. In my lap was a very large tin of very expensive very rare imported Belgian cookies.

I convinced Manman to make the blue, white trim uniform dress I wore to school with two extra large pockets tucked between the pleats of the skirt. Both pockets were filled with various things that would not fit in my school satchel. Girls my age played with the dried knucklebones of goats. We called them *ocelets* and I usually had a set of five in my uniform pockets. The knuckle of a goat is a little less than a cubic inch and has four distinctive sides. One side is smooth and slightly rounded with a corresponding hollow while the other is narrow, shaped like an s and the last looks like the capital letter I. A family cook could be coaxed to save the bone from the joint of a leg of goat meat that was common enough table food. After it was cleaned of any tendon, cartilage, or meat the bone was sun-dried. In a local version of the American game of Jacks the player tosses the bones unto the floor with one hand then throws one bone up in the air far enough to have the time to position the remaining ones and gather them and the tossed one in the same hand according to a set sequence. The player chants softly to keep track of each stage of the game: "*Dos, Creux, I, S*" each times the bones are positioned with the backside uppermost "*dos*" then the hollow "*creux*", the "*I*" and finally the "*S*" side. Manman remembered sitting, with the folds of her skirt tucked under one thigh, both legs spread out straight on the stone paved courtyard of her own childhood to play the same ancient game.

Boys collected and through a number of trading activities filled their pockets with marbles. Any smooth area in the dirt of a yard or the cement floor of a porch would serve to trace a large circle for a group of boys to squat around and engage in a spirited game. Positioning one marble in the center of the circle the player would attempt to knock it out of the drawn boundary by flicking another marble with his thumb. Many a boy would forget to go home or neglect an errand simply at the enticing sight and sound of his friends flicking marbles. This game was strictly reserved for boys, as was the rolling of a metal circle balanced on its side, with the sprinting barefoot driver's stick. Any rim of a discarded bicycle, or metal band from an old barrel would be pressed into service.

In addition to the *ocelets,* the twins and I had an inexhaustible supply of rag dolls which ManLillie, our maternal grandmother, who lived in Port-au-Prince, made for us to play with. We always named each doll "*Soh*": the Kreyol appellation for "sister". They all looked alike with their cotton filled legs and feet at right angles heels touching and wore the strangest expression embroidered on their faces with black thread by our grandmother.

When our family dog *Bichon* gave birth to a litter of puppies, I was allowed to keep the one that Manman declared reminded her of a character she had seen in a movie. It had something to do with the Puppy's long legs, half straight and half curly light brown coat, and unruly whiskers. I agreed with her suggestion that I name my puppy *"Pancho"*. Only years later, as an adult, did I realized that Manman had named my dog after that infamous Mexican outlaw Pancho Villa! Meanwhile my dog was the first playmate I ever had who agreed with all my decisions and came to share my sorrows when I was punished and always loved me unconditionally. He knew my routine, and waited at our gate for me to return from school and jumped in the car when it looked as if our family was bound for an outing. If we were going away for an extended time, someone would have to tie him up somewhere in the back of the house. I worried in those times,

Child of A Mountainous Land

(although Titonton, a boy two to three years older than me who lived with us, would take particular care of him) that Pancho would stop eating, and not survive my absence.

In our home, although we had several servants, my sisters and I learned very early that we were to shun what Manman called a shameful lifestyle of calling for an adult to wait on us for things that we could do for ourselves. I had a full time job caring for and entertaining the twins and became something of a crew supervisor. The twins and I helped with the lighter chores like polishing the mahogany furniture, dusting the bookshelves and Manman's collection of figurines, leaving the care of the mosaic tile and cement floors to the adults. There was no bell in our home to summon servants, as was the rule in other households. I, and Titonton, ran errands for everyone.

In the 1600's, the original French settlers gave Les Cayes its name because of the small rocky islands and reefs or *"cayes"* that fill up the bay on its southern side. Two rivers: *L'Ilèt* to the North and *La Ravine du Sud* to its South East overflow every rainy season to effectively cut off the town from the countryside. Flooded streets were a given except at least for our own *Rue du petit Gabion* where Manman and Papa had picked just the right spot to build our family home. We kept a stock of dried herrings, cod fish and sacks of maize among other supplies to wait out the debris laden muddy torrents. Our house sat on one of the two roads at the entrance of town leading to the town market where small farmers peddled their fruit and vegetable. We, therefore, had first pick from the procession of the blue denim clad *paysans* or *paysannes* who sat astride the pack mules and donkeys tottering under mounds of plantains, sweet potatoes, carrots, beets, cabbages, avocadoes, live chickens hung upside down by their long-toed feet tied to the side of the straw baskets. Milk was also delivered to us at home from a merchant who came in daily with two large tin containers loaded in a straw harness hung across the back of a donkey. The merchants ushered in their mules and donkeys through a passage at the side of the house leading to the detached cinderblock corrugated tin-roofed structure housing the kitchen and servants' quarters. Four men carrying a large sea turtle strapped between two poles even came up on our porch once to offer their catch. The animal, to the horror of my sisters, turned its head to inspect us. Manman did not buy it.

The twins and I were warned not to give names to the chicken and other fowl, roaming for a while in our yard, that were destined for our cooking pots. My aunt in Port-au-Prince always bought a young goat when we vacationed with her family during the summer months in the mountains of Furcy. Fattening up animals for the kill was a great source of distress for my sisters and I. At summer's end when the time came for the traditional roasted goat or "*Kabrit Boukannin*" feast, we would cry for days and refuse to eat what inevitably had become our pet and dearest companion.

Preparing the day's meal for our household on several charcoal grills built into a large cement table, tied up one cook and a helper for most of the day. A charcoal filled iron was also used to press clothes that had been dipped in freshly cooked starch. In retrospect, I can see that as a family we must have looked prosperous and aroused the envy of some of the town's people. Yet, both our parents shared liberally with anyone in need. The reason we children were told to ask for only what we could eat at the dining table and were expected to eat everything that was placed on our plates was so that anything left could be offered from a serving dish to the people who came around to the cook after meal times looking for scraps.

We were taught to be especially careful to show respect for people who asked for charity. The very poor in Haiti walked about daily in search for food. People would offer to work just for a meal in payment. We had more household help than necessary because so many people needed a home. Mothers gave up their children into virtual slavery just on a chance that they would be fed and perhaps sent to school. Thousand of Haitian children known as *"restavècs"* grew up under the most wretched conditions under this arrangement; their pain mostly ignored by Haitian society and the world. Individual families tried to help but the need was always constant; so many people lacked the barest necessities. Many people chaffed under the misery of their lot and grew angry at times in frustration at the indifference real or perceived of those who lived in larger houses and looked well fed. Yet, even those who were helped sometimes would return, during better times, with a present. Our father would come home from the office with a live chicken, basket of vegetables or some fish strung along a stick. If the industrious vigilance of both our parents kept our family from sinking into the deep poverty that constantly surrounded us, it was most definitely the grace of God that shielded us from the waves of evil that could so easily engulf us.

"Yo mangé-li"

Was a Kreyol term, literal translation for "they ate him/her", I frequently heard as a child living in a deeply superstitious country, to describe a suspected unnatural death. It was common knowledge that the powers of Satan could be invoked, for a price, through one of his human emissaries a *"mové-moun"* or "bad person". My father told me once that he himself as a child lived in fear of the Satan worshippers. He grew up thinking that he lived surrounded by cannibals since no one was ever pronounced to have died naturally. In his home, there were Bibles and his folks made frequent use of its contents to chase bad spirits away. God had mercy on them since by all accounts his family neglected some of the more important Biblical principles. My mother on the other hand has a stock of stories about the many demonic manifestations she and her family had witnessed in the several haunted houses they had lived in. One incident she recalls, which occurred before she married and while she was caring for her sister's children at the family vacation cottage in the mountains of Furcy, involved a near death experience for one of her nephews, a toddler at the time. To this day, my mother maintains that the sudden illness that struck my cousin had no natural basis. Manman says that when she tried to get to a village where there was a bus going to the city of Port-au-Prince the horse she and the sick child rode on suddenly started to go off the side of the mountain pass backing unto the edge of a cliff. She was unable to control the horse as she held her nephew across the saddle with one arm. Only the timely intervention of a man who happened to be traveling on the same path kept her, the horse and child from plunging down to their death. Once in town the pediatrician could find no explanation for my cousin's bizarre symptoms. The family servants then took matters in their own hands and gave him a "special bath" which produced an instant cure. One of the most frustrating discussions anyone can have with a Haitian is one in which one tries to separate self-help measures that are in line with the laws of God and those that enlist demonic aid. My mother's attitude generally was one of accommodation: as long as the evil spirits did not overly disturb her daily routine she did not try to chase them off. She was of the opinion that the provinces because, as she saw it, of a want of sophistication, harbored a great deal more of the supernatural than her own hometown of Port-au-Prince. I lived with daily reminders of the supernatural evil.

Our cook found things imbedded in the meat she purchased in the town market that had us all convinced that some evil spirit had placed it there. There were always strange noises in the night and reports of people flying while under the influence of evil spirits. It was common knowledge that people were either forcibly or voluntarily changed into animals.

"If an evil spirit comes near you," my mother advised me, "say: 'in the name of Jesus Christ, go away!"

I took her advice whenever I sensed an evil presence, through mainly a sudden feeling in the skin at the back of my neck, and when I was not distracted by my own terrorized thoughts.

One late afternoon in Les Cayes at around sunset I remember, my parents were preparing to attend an evening social function. Manman was seated, back straight in her customary elegant soldierly pose, at her mahogany dressing table, the one with the large round mirror set between two polished rows of small drawers, her head slightly turned to one side as she held up a silver plated hand mirror. She was inspecting the twist into which she had fashioned her smooth shiny black hair. The alarm sounded. A pressed suit, the tie Manman had selected for Papa, and a crisp white dress shirt were set out on their large bed. Papa had been whistling softly in the adjoining bathroom as he dabbed a brush-full of freshly mixed shaving soap from a small wooden bowl on one cheek. At that moment, the shouting of the servants was heard from the back porch of our house. A *Loa* or an evil spirit that lived in Dieula, the maid who took care of my twin sisters, had decided to manifest its presence and the woman was running out of the family compound.

The rest of the staff, all women, had not been able to restrain Dieula so now they were all screaming for *"Doktè! Doktè!"* as they referred, to my father, to "do something!" Ordinarily Dieula was a soft- spoken self-effacing woman who was devoted to the children. She was however, like many people in our town, demon possessed. One such demon would cause her voice to change into a deeply masculine one that would growl obscenities while the woman's bloodshot eyes bulged out of her contorted face. Pancho would tuck in his tail, whimper, and head for the nearest bed to crawl under. I always kept a safe distance between her and

I when this occurred. Up until then, none of the adults had felt threatened. This time however, the tall ample Dieula was barreling through the house at a dangerous speed. Papa was left with no choice, and no time, Dieula was already out of our front gate. This was to become one of my most enduring childhood memories: my father, his bare legs swinging up and down the road, the flaps of his bathrobe and splashes of shaving lather trailing, in hot pursuit of a crazed woman almost twice his size.

"In the name of Jesus Christ go away!" I had not thought of it fast enough to try it out on poor Dieula. It might not have helped I was told. Some people have been dedicated to the devil from birth. Only that individual can renounce Satan and call on God for protection. My childhood in Les Cayes Haiti convinced me more than any theological treatise that a supernatural Devil and evil spirits exist. I have seen their power and I was afraid. Only an all-powerful God would protect me I believed.

II. Child of the Catholics and of the Protestants

"Their land also is full of idols; they worship the work of their own hands, that which their own fingers have made" Isaiah 2:8

3

The question of which priest would sprinkle me at the baptismal font caused a nasty fight between my mother and *Tante* Fifi my father's only living sister. It was a matter of honor, between the Catholic and the Episcopal Church. My mother and father were teenagers when they first spotted each other across the narrow unpaved street that separated their family homes. This was in the 1930's, a sleepy section of Port-au-Prince and relations were cordial among neighbors. Their romance blossomed from a discreet wave of the hand through a voluminous stack of letters, to their eventual marriage in 1950. She was a practicing Catholic; he was the son, grandson, nephew, grandnephew, and brother of Protestant Episcopalian priests. The newlyweds made their home in Les Cayes, the original hometown of the Benedicts and Ledans, after my mother consented to having their wedding in the Episcopalian church. Some of her friends declined her invitation to the ceremony because she, a Catholic was marrying a Protestant. In those days the Catholic Church only approved of interfaith marriages if the non-catholic converted and pledged to raise the couple's children in the Catholic faith. My father did not convert to Catholicism.

    As I was told later, my father and mother traveled back North to their families in the capital city of Port-au-Prince for the birth of their first child: and I was named Marie-Solange after one each of their own first names of Marguerite Marie and Duplessis Charles Solanges. The Haitian custom was to celebrate a first child's christening with a large family gathering that would include as many prestigious friends and acquaintances as the parents could afford to host. Many families put off having a christening called a *"Bapteme"* until they had saved enough money. This created a whole class of youngsters who lived under a cloud of condemnation since the church taught that someone who had not been christened or a *"sans bapteme"* would upon dying, go straight to hell. For the fortunate, at the baptismal reception or *reception de bapteme* after the church ceremony, the new mother often wore her carefully preserved white wedding gown, altered to a shorter length and fitted to her new figure. My mother had married late by the Haitian standards of those days and seen her younger sister and most of her friends through this ritual. I, her first-born baby, was sixteen days old. My father's business partner, a Catholic dentist, was to be the godfather. Meanwhile, my godmother, another Catholic and school friend of my mother's, had imported a long white christening gown and bonnet trimmed in all white lace with matching booties to dress me in for the occasion.

The family shuttled back and forth between their respective homes. There was, I later learned, a heated discussion. I had become the prize each side fought over. On that fateful morning, *Tante* Fifi my only aunt, on the Benedict, that is the Protestant side, whisked me off to the Episcopalian Cathedral in Port-au-Prince while my mother retreated to an upstairs bedroom in her father's house. Grandfather Georges Emmanuel Benedict, an Episcopalian minister, officiated at the well-attended christening ceremony. Heads most certainly turned and tongues wagged when certain ones took note of my mother's absence. She did not wear her white lace wedding dress on that day. There was no *reception de bateme* for us.

Back in Les Cayes, our family, with the addition of my younger twin sisters, quietly settled in the Catholic Church. Years had passed since a Benedict had attended the town's Episcopalian church founded by my great grandfather Charles Emmanuel Benedict, who was assisted by my other great grandfather Louis Duplessis Ledan. The Benedict side of the family had migrated to Port-au-Prince when my father was ten years old. Now he chose not to renew his childhood ties with the Protestant congregation. This was a very small town, a Catholic town.

Catholicism was a cover for the ordinary Haitian's real religion. "So and So is '*Mele*'" or else "*Li nan wanga*" Meant that a particular individual was keeping company with the supernatural of the wrong type and only pretended to be Catholic. Those people worshiped demons that they gave the names of Catholic saints. This practice dated back to colonial days and slavery. Africans had to hide their outlawed religious rituals from their white masters by pretending to worship Catholic saints.

Growing up in Les Cayes, I saw the physical and emotional pain of people like Dieula our maid, tormented by a force that they could not control. We never learned how Dieula had gotten that way. I was not aware of her practicing Vodoo. My parents would not have allowed this in our home. Dieula said that she wanted to become Catholic but was never physically able to walk through the doors of the church. What puzzled me was why people sought out devil possession. It was clear to me that the Supernatural was either of God or of Satan. I also realized that the two did not mix. From their behavior, I could tell that the adults around me were often confused about this. Both Catholic and Protestant dabbled in the occult albeit convincing themselves that reading cards was harmless or consulting a *Hougan* or *Manbo*, or Vodoo priests and priestesses was a matter of self-defense. People were confused about God and his views on all of this. Some people even entered into covenant relationships with demons, willfully inviting demonic possession of their bodies by "marrying" a *Loa* or spirit. The prevalent thought was that one had to enlist the help of a demon more powerful to counter demonic attacks. Time after time, history repeated itself; those who thought that a mere human could control a demon were always destroyed. The same people who told the horrific stories about some relative could be seen going down the same path. Those who practiced Vodoo without any pretence of following another faith appeared more confident in their understanding of their "religion" than those who professed allegiance to Christianity. In fact the so called Christ followers, the true meaning of the word "Christian" did not know the character of Christ and therefore could not follow Him. These Christians made up their own rules making victims along the way.

I grew up an extrovert, my mother says, playing the role of an angel throwing rose petals at eighteen months old. My speech-giving talents, having started my career at the age of three and one half were well known in the town. This caused me, at age five years old, to be thrust into the center of another religious controversy. My teacher had selected me to recite a prayer in a religious pageant. I had practiced for days and when the appointed time arrived, was dressed in my finest clothes. Word of my Protestant christening, however, had leaked: The townspeople mumbled, grumbled, and soon the chorus of their protests reached the school director:

"How could Matoutou Benedict, a Protestant child, recite a prayer to God in a Catholic ceremony?" they demanded. When the day arrived, the audience assembled in the reception hall of the *Ecole Maternelle* manifested enough of their discontent to alarm the director. She knew that the townspeople of Les Cayes would not hesitate to boycott her school and shut it down. My mother and the nun in charge of the pageant agreed on a plan to distract me with a last minute assignment while my understudy was substituted in my place. I was disappointed, but too engrossed in my new duties, that consisted of keeping a group of three years old in a straight line, to understand what had happened.

By the time my sisters and I had graduated to elementary school the pressure to "convert" in order to attend another Catholic school, which was the best available in town, intensified even though our family regularly attended *Mass* every Sunday. I had never even seen *Eglise Saint Sauveur,* the small Episcopalian Church that my great grandfather had founded, with a Parish school, in the late 1800's. I only found out as an adult that both my paternal great-grand fathers lay buried beneath the flagstones of the Sanctuary and that the backyard is filled with the tombs of their families. Most of their descendants, who still lived in the town of Les Cayes, besides us, representatives of the Benedict-Ledan alliance, no longer attended the lone Episcopal Church that had once been filled with the dreaded Protestants.

"Your father is a good man", one of the Catholic nuns at my school once told me, but "he (as a protestant), will go to hell".

The Catholic Church did not recognize my parents' Episcopalian wedding ceremony as valid. Consequently, our family did not meet with the approval of the local religious authorities. Catholics were in the majority in Les Cayes and dictated the rules of Christianity. My parents capitulated. They were "married" again in a backroom of a local presbytery and we children were " re-christened" in the same Catholic Church back room. I then was on track for the catholic "first communion" and "confirmation" rites. The Episcopalian relatives in Port-au-Prince, *Tante* Fifi in particular, fumed.

From my mother I learned that God was all-powerful, all seeing, and all knowing. I did not have an understanding of His personal interest in me. In my mind, I had to participate in church rituals in order to avoid retribution from the Almighty. The solemnity of the Catholic Mass gave me the false assurance that I was fulfilling my duty towards God. In our home, my father acquiesced to my mother's observance of the feast days and dietary rules set by the Catholic Church calendar. Manman also implemented the church's birth control method, as she told me when I reached adulthood and discussed such things. *"La methode"*, she then said dryly. "Produced your twin sisters". Women seemed to be the ones responsible for making sure that the children in a Catholic household recited the rosary and other prescribed prayers so it never occurred to me that I had never heard my father pray. I never saw a Bible until I was in my late teens and never read one until I was twenty-eight years old. My knowledge of right from wrong came from the teachings of my mother and the nuns in both the schools that I attended in Haiti.

By age ten I had memorized a list of behavior I was to confess and do penance for. There was a great number of Catholic priests in Les Cayes and I could periodically kneel in the ornate wooden booth of the church confessional to unload my sins and as I believed then, receive forgiveness by promising to recite the prescribed number of *"Hail Marys"* and *"Our Fathers"*. No one had explained to me the true meaning of Jesus Christ's death and resurrection. I dutifully lit candles placed at the feet of the statue of Mary the mother of Jesus bowing down to the wooden figure with all the reverence I could muster begging her to put in a good word for me with her son. Since I had never read the Bible, I believed the adults' explanation to me that this was not idolatry. Neither, I was told, was the homage we paid to the long list of saints whose feast days caused daylong celebrations.

"If my people which are called by my name would humble themselves and pray." Second Chronicles 7:14 (KJV) At first glance it would seem that we in Haiti were following the scriptural advice to *pray*. As with so many people, young

and old around me I prayed fervently. I asked, and asked, and asked for some things to happen and for other things not to happen. I understood that my prayer was addressed to a giver of some sort, without thinking about who that individual was. My sisters and I could discern from an early age the things we should ask Papa versus others we could petition Manman or some other adult for. My expectation varied depending on the individual I addressed my requests to. Mostly there would be a dialogue between the adult and me. Yet, I never thought that "prayer" was a conversation. I fervently prayed, at least I recited the rehearsed litanies, I was told were needed to help the souls of the dead go from purgatory to heaven. Again, since I had never read the Bible I had no way of knowing that such a place does not exist. There were enough demons showing up in my town, however, to convince me that Hell was a real place. "*Lougarous*" were known to "fly" at night when they had accomplished some mysterious rite with their human bodies. Even in day light people in our town who were demon possessed could do spectacular feats such as climb a coconut tree backward.

The outlying villages in our area all had patron saints that were honored once a year on the particular day designated for each in an elaborate ceremony involving a street procession of priests, nuns, and the pious. There was always a good number of *Vodooisants* capitalizing on the crowd's lack of spiritual discernment to mix in their own rituals. Mary the mother of Jesus was a favorite honoree. Several titles were ascribed to Mary. In turn she was known as our Lady of Perpetual Help, our Lady of Haiti, our Lady of several other places. A feast day was consecrated for each of these titles. People made vows to *Mary* when they petitioned her for something. Sometimes people dressed an ailing child in blue and white only, which were the official colors given to Mary, for several years to fulfill a vow. We offered sacrifices in our home by abstaining from candy for a certain period.

The *Vodooisants* were more prone to sacrificial giving: food, live animals and, it was rumored, humans. They were having conversations with their demons and could therefore acquiesce to their masters' demands.

I believed that the dead appeared from time to time to the living. Everyone around me, in my home and in our town believed this. Years passed before I found out the truth: that so-called dead relatives are demons who masquerade in the likeness of a human. We referred in our town to such a being as a *"Moh"*. During my childhood in Haiti, I saw one. It stood on the road where two of the women servants, Titonton (pronounced tee-tohn-tohn) the young boy who worked for us and I walked on before dawn on our way to four am Mass. Pancho was not allowed to join our party. Churches employed stick-wielding *Sacristans* to patrol the aisles during mass especially to ward off dogs.

We had been told that the *Moh* haunted this particular spot in the *Petit Gabion* area but knew that, as per local protocol concerning such matters, we should not engage in conversation with it no matter what happened. The maids in our town went to the pre-dawn church service so as to be at their post in time to awaken their employers with freshly roasted, ground and brewed coffee poured in half sized cups placed on a tray. I joined the little band of churchgoers out of a sense of piety, not to encounter a *moh*. The whiteness of the dirt road beneath our feet guided us in the dark as we walked in silence close to each other with our heads bent, huddled against the still moist air, my right hand tucked firmly in the palm of one of the adults. If anyone else traveled, there they would be going towards town in the same direction as us, unless they were not in human form. None of us spoke for fear of attracting any attention of the wrong kind. Suddenly one of the women gasped and we all turned our heads to track the object that provoked the sound. There it was, a gray opaque figure silhouetted against the blackened hedge bordering the road to the left of us.

"Give me a cigarette!" The *moh* said in a human voice.

I buried my head into the skirt of the woman closest to me. A cold feeling crawled up my ankles, legs, belly, and teeth. With my free hand, I tried to protect my ears from hearing anymore. Titonton, the boy in our midst, spoke against all caution. He was the one male in our company; it was his duty to defend the rest of us.

"I don't ... have any!" He snapped.

Church was a good place to be when fleeing from supernatural undesirables, so we must have reached our destination. I do not remember much else about that morning. That was, however, the last four am Mass I attended in Haiti.

I was born on the day of the dead. "*Le Jour des morts*" as they say in French. It was also a town holiday. On that day, the slow pace of life in Les Cayes sank to a solemn crawl as everyone attended the Masses said for various dead relatives. People flocked to the cemeteries with flowers to freshen up the graves of the departed. It was of course a special time for those who practiced voodoo who have to pay homage to their dead under the fear of retribution. Families sacrificed much needed resources, ruining their chances for a better life to do this. I thought people were actually seeing their dead relatives until I learned decades later that demons do transform themselves in the image of the familiar dead to communicate with the living. From our home's back porch with a clear view of the town's main cemetery we could see the somberly clad grieving and dutifully kneeling as families gathered in sometimes large groups the size of which dwindled with the passage of time. My sisters and I were never taken to the graves of my father's ancestors, in the small family cemetery at the back of the church they had pioneered. The rest of both my parents' relatives were buried in far away Port-au-Prince. Whether at the cemetery, at Mass, or in the streets, our town folk from the youngest to the old wore funeral clothes on November 2. This meant black, black and white combinations gray or other shades of dark cloth; the wearing of bright colors was seen as a show of disrespect. Any activity of a festive nature was also postponed. The whole town was held hostage to this somber mood.

It was however, my birthday on the town's day for the dead. I felt no personal allegiance to the dead. In fact, I did not know any dead One. As soon as I became conscious of being in the possession of such a thing, I insisted on celebrating my birthday on the anniversary of the date of my birth or not at all. In our home, Manman had started the tradition of making a new dress for anyone in our household to celebrate their birthday. We could all choose the material from Manman's stock of cloth or request a particular one from the colorful bales some ambulatory merchant balanced on her head, on her way to the town market. I proceeded to claim my privilege to select a cloth for my birthday dress. My favorite color was bright red. Therefore, each year, on the day of the dead, I wore a new red dress and had cake and kola, the sweet local brand of soda pop. Manman must have made sure that my celebrations remained within the walled compound of our home since I do not recall hearing any protests from the townspeople.

The birthday party I treasured in my memory was the last one we had before leaving the country. It was my tenth birthday on November 2, 1961. Several children dressed in their fineries came to our house. Papa had bought a new ice cream maker. Titonton packed the small wooden tub with ice and raw salt and turned the metal handle while my guests and I stood around, each one of us holding one of Manman's china cups at the ready. We had never made ice cream in our home. Ice cream vendors did not bother to push their lumbering wood carts up our sparsely populated street either, preferring instead to hawk their wares at crowded soccer games or at a town market with the multitude of other street vendors. I was also given flowers on my birthday. Manman instructed our gardener to grow a wide variety of zinnias, yellow and white hibiscus hedges, and blood red roses. There was a curtain of bougainvillea draped over the front of the house shading the open porch in a cascade of fuchsia, pink, red, and orange blooms that no one handled because of their long thorns. My guests and I toned down our impromptu games as we carefully tread on the loose stones of the garden paths in deference to our party clothes and polished shoes.

On ordinary days, usually when school was closed, my sisters, Pancho and I staked out a spot in the front garden in the area closest to the wall that shielded us from the street; in the shade of the canopy formed by the broad leafs of three young Caribbean almond trees. The same leaves fell to the ground to form a thick carpet that cushioned our bare feet tumbles. If one of us spotted the top of a particular sunshade bobbing along on the street side of our wall we would all run through the path leading to the house and scramble up the porch in time to find our shoes and change our sleeveless play clothes. Mère Saint Gregroire, the Canadian nun who was the director of our primary school would drop in unannounced. On one occasion, she walked through the front gate, clad in her immaculate silky white bonnet and floor length habit, all the way to the steps of the porch, cutting off our escape.

"Marie-Solange!" the nun exclaimed weighing each syllable of my formal name as her eyes surveyed our appearance.

"*Quelle tenue!*"

Her long white fingers reached and grasped the skin of the top of my bare arm, twisting as she pinched it to show her disapproval of our sleeveless play clothes, muttering about indecency. Adult women wore long lace black or white mantillas on their heads and would drape a longer one to cover their shoulders if wearing a sleeveless top to Mass. Girls wore hats to church and had a population of nuns, priests, teachers, relatives, and other adults to monitor and sermonize on what was appropriate Christian dress.

I caught the notion very early on that although my mortal life would end, my soul, which I believed was immortal, would live on forever. Privately I hoped that my soul, if I could stop doing bad things, would go to heaven and that I would not roam about the earth as a "*moh*" pestering the living or end up in Hell. At that time, I did not know that "*mohs*" are demons. People around me spoke about having to do things "*mohs*" demanded so the latter would find rest. It could be dangerous not to obey a "*moh*". Here local custom fused with the teaching of the Catholic Church. The living were obligated to light candles in the church sanctuary and to pay the priest to say Masses so that the souls of dead relatives would find eternal rest in heaven. The idea of Purgatory bothered me. As I was told, it was a bad place where one could linger on forever. Someone alive on earth had to do the required candle lighting or pay a priest to say Mass for the necessary number of times. Twenty years passed before I learned the truth about sin, how one really gains entrance to heaven and the finality of death. I had been misled as to who Jesus is and what His sacrificial death meant to me personally.

As a carefully taught Catholic I believed that the "host" or wafer consecrated by the officiating priest during the Mass had literally turned into the flesh of Jesus Christ Himself. The precise moment of this transformation of the man made bread into God was announced by the ringing of a bell. At that point, all in attendance bowed in adoration of the cup filled with the now sacred "hosts", which only a priest was then allowed to handle. Congregants were strictly forbidden to even touch the "consecrated" wafer. The priest distributed the "hosts" with the help of an attendant who held up a long handled shiny metal plate specifically made to catch the wafer if it fell while being placed on a communicant's tongue. The wafer was then allowed to soften up in the mouth of the individual who took great care not to chew it before swallowing the very body of God. I had qualms as a young child about being an idolater. These were brushed aside somewhat by my teachers' reassurances: it was all right they said to bow to the" Holy wafer" because Jesus himself was present in the small round piece of bread. I cherished the solemnity of the moment for years. Years later, I was to find out, that Jesus is seated at the right hand of God (Letter of Paul to the Colossians Chapter three verse one).

My father did not take communion whenever he attended a Catholic Mass, with us. Only a Catholic who had received a special course of instruction and participated in a First Communion rite was allowed to take communion during a Catholic Mass. Certain serious infractions against the church could be punished by "excommunication" in which case the offender was no longer considered a member of the Catholic Church and could never again take communion, or be married in the church. Such an individual could not even have his or her funeral Mass done inside the church walls although when asked a priest would "bless" the departed outside, on the steps of the church. The one excommunicated would be declared cut off from the fellowship of not only the church but from God Himself. Church leaders ignored the passage in the apostle John's first letter that states that if anyone confesses his or her sin He, God is "faithful and Just to forgive us our sins, and to cleanse us from all unrighteousness": First John chapter one verse nine. Ironically, even with the exclusive rules for membership, voodoo practitioners heavily infiltrated the church.

As an adult years later, I did not want to admit at first that the practice of what some are calling a positive and harmless religion was that important to the Haitian identity.

Throughout my childhood and youth, I believed the lie that Voodoo and Satanism were not one, and the same. One only has to look at the fruit of so much *voodoo* practice in the land by the people of Haiti to see the truth. This same land of exquisite beauty and fertility that Christopher Columbus described in his writings is now so scarred and plundered as to be on the brink of an ecological disaster. In the eighteenth century under its colonial name of Saint Domingue that same soil provided fifty per cent of the world's sugar supply, two third of ships sailing from France were bound for its ports and in the late seventeen hundreds, it produced as much revenue as the fledgling United States of America. At its peak, the money making machine of Saint Domingue was fed by the sweat and blood of upwards of 500,000 Africans toiling six days per week for 12 to 16 hours per day and 24 hours during harvest. The colonial Christian Church justified Slavery. The enslaved Africans saw the Church a the tool of their White oppressors. Not many slaves were willing to hear about the God of the Christians. The Africans and their descendants clung to their gods so much so that even after being cut off from their ancestors in the late seventeen hundreds, without the use of electronic recording devices, the precise drum beats of Africa can still be heard in voodoo rituals around Haiti. Did the rebel Boukman's dedication at the infamous *Bois Caiman* ceremony curse the land? How many people does it take to alter the destiny of a nation? Is one even allowed to be neutral when it comes to serving God or Satan? In the book of Deuteronomy, God warned the ancient Hebrews: *"Because thou servedst not the Lord thy God with joyfulness, and gladness of heart for the abundance of all things; Therefore shalt thou serve thine enemies, which the Lord shall send against thee, in hunger, and in thirst, and in nakedness, and in want of all things: and He shall put a yoke of iron upon thy neck until He have destroyed thee".* Deuteronomy: 28; 47-48. (KJV)

Child of A Mountainous Land

In the early nineteen thirties there was a move by young intellectuals to champion the cause of Black Nationalism which insisted on making Voodoo a necessary part of Haitian culture. Knowledge of the true God and the wealth of teachings in the Bible were set aside in favor of the corrosive dictates of a demonic culture. One who took advantage of this surge in Haitian nationalism was François Duvalier. As the future dictator formulated his political ambitions, by quietly positioning himself as a reformer who would take up the cause of the abused Haitian masses, he latched on to the people's obsession with voodoo. " We must give a traditional basis to voodoo as has been done for Buddhism and other religions". He wrote in the nineteen-thirties. Even scholars around the world decried the attempt by Élie Lescot, a previous Haitian president to eradicate voodoo practices. Many accused the church backed campaign and the removal of voodoo artifacts as destructive of Haitian culture. Not surprisingly Duvalier, as with Haitian leaders before and after him would seduce the people with these arguments. A people without God will follow anyone. The ethical values of any culture that does not stand on Biblical principles backed by an all-powerful God cannot stand against demonic infiltration.

In Les Cayes, we served God and idols just as the Satanists served Satan and pretended to serve God through service to the same idols they shared with us. A large percentage of the people in the country of Haiti subscribed to this mish-mash of service to the *Loas* who had been given Catholic Saints names. Since the 1800's thousands, some of whom take critically needed funds from their starving families, make a yearly pilgrimage to *Saut D'Eau* to worship the *Loa Erzulie*. The site of this festival is a waterfall forty miles from the city of Port-au-Prince. It is dedicated both to "*mistress Erzulie*" as well as to the "*virgin Mary*". Haitian Voodoo practitioners refer to *Erzulie* who is a *loa* identified with lascivious perverse sexuality and Mary the mother of Jesus as the same.

On the day of the *Saut D'Eau,* gathering people who bathe in the waterfall in an elaborate voodoo ritual continue their commemorative service in a Catholic ceremony at the nearby church. One of the cherished dreams of Haitians is to save enough money to go at least once in a lifetime to France to worship a statue at a grotto at *Lourdes* in the Pyrenees where Mary the mother of Jesus is said to have appeared in 1858 to a woman named Bernadette. They are not alone. Pilgrims worldwide come to *Lourdes*.

I was an avid worshiper of Mary the mother of Jesus, in flagrant disobedience of the Old Testament injunction: *"Thou shalt fear the Lord thy God, and serve Him, and shalt swear by His name. Ye shall not go after other gods, of the gods of the people which are round about you; (For the Lord thy God is a jealous God among you) lest the anger of the Lord thy God be kindled against thee, and destroy thee from off the face of the earth."* Deuteronomy: 6; 13,14,16. (KJV) My ignorance of who God is blinded me as to the true import of my actions. God's favor, His protection was not available to me because I ignored the fact that only Jesus the Messiah is the one and only intercessor between God and I. The apostle Peter gives the reason why Jesus qualifies as the only mediator between God the father and I. *"Foreasmuch as ye know that ye were not redeemed with corruptible things, as silver and gold, from your vain conversation received by tradition from your fathers; But with the precious blood of Christ, as of a lamb without blemish and without spot: Who verily was foreordained before the foundation of the world, but was manifest in these last times for you"*. First Peter: 1: 18,19,20. (KJV).

Ignorance of God has been the greatest enslaver of the Haitian people. Children are indoctrinated, the weak intimidated and the ambitious seduced in a vicious cycle of bondage. How else can so many dictators find men and women willing to do their dirty deeds? Time, and time again, one hears about the ease with which Haitian mobs can lynch a human being. That is a national sickness. How can a man stone another to death or hack a neighbor to pieces? The same story repeated itself throughout my early years in Haiti, although we would hear about it by word of mouth since the airwaves and press were censored, each time there was a failed invasion or a captured rebel group. This practice stems from a legacy that Haitians have refused to renounce from the revolutionary days to this day. Because man will not give total allegiance to the true God, he is doomed to follow the demons of greed, covetousness, and pride. Haitians have not found the wisdom to live with each other because they have looked to the wrong source.

    Our family, even though we did not know how to pray to God for protection was not a target of specific demonic activity. My parents had been told that the land they bought to build our house was situated in a bad spot, known in Kreyol as a *"Mové Katyay"*. Certain spots were known for having a high incidence of demonic activity. It seemed to me that there were more *"mové katyays"* than good ones. I was convinced that evil spirits did not respect territorial boundaries. The servants whispered about a "couple" that haunted the rose bushes in the front of our house. As for my mother, she was rather complacent about the *"moh"* that periodically appeared to her in the same spot on the property next to ours: " He stayed on his side of the wall, so I didn't bother him" she told me later. I, on the other hand remained a bed-wetter until age twelve when we no longer lived in Haiti, I think in part, because the darkness of night frightened me.

    The knowledge of the power of God and of Satan's subjection to the disciples of Jesus Christ was not yet available to me as a child growing up in a demon infested land. Fear dominated my childhood. Our last family home in Haiti had very large windows and from my bedroom, I had a clear view through the back porch, especially on a moonlit night, of

Les Cayes' cemetery. My childhood imagination fermented a steady stream of characters engaged in vague but fearsome evil activities undetected by us. Pancho would stake out a spot in the farthest corner under my bed, during the night, as if confirming my fears of the unseen. At daybreak when the welcomed rays of the sun flooded my bedroom, I often felt that I had just escaped the nocturnal malevolence of the evil supernatural world. Yet, daytime held its numerous perils. Inevitably, bad spirits infect the consciousness of even the most ordinary of people.

The schoolteachers in our town were particularly known for their bad spirited behavior in the classroom. I have firsthand knowledge of this. Two, in particular, stand out in my memory. The first was a French nun armed with a *rigoaz*, that infamous instrument of discipline made of braided rawhide with a welt-producing knotted tip that could only be demonically inspired. The tall French woman was the designated enforcer at my Elementary school and concealed a *rigoaz* in one of the pockets of the immaculate white habit she wore. I witnessed the sadistic ritual this woman performed as my classmates and I were forced to stand and watch her flog an eight or nine years old girl. Our classmate had not done her homework and skipped the assigned detention given to her the day before. *Mere St...* was called in for the reckoning. For years, the expression on the nun's face remained part of my most chilling memories. The second, infamous teacher was a *rigoaz* wielding Math tutor who abused any pupil who did not respond fast enough to her force-fed instructions. In the Haitian society I grew up in, teachers were entitled to brutalize their students. My mother, her mother before her, and Papa's mother were the rare parent who questioned their savagery. Clément Barbot, one of the most notorious executioners of the Duvalier regime, who would pull the trigger of a machine gun on a man at close range, was a former Haitian schoolteacher.

4

By 1962, as I recall the earlier years, I enjoyed the benevolent notoriety afforded by my family name. Children my age in Les Cayes Haiti ran errands under the shade of the tall flat top white-wash houses across the opened porches and under the balconies that touched each other on both sides of the *Grande rue,* the main street of town. Blue or red was the preferred color of the closely set long iron-paneled doors hung to the thick walls with black iron hinges. Time had blackened some of the walls and diluted the color of the doors of some of the less prosperous houses. Even though the street level row of *galleries* was a passageway for the public, there were rocking chairs and chairs set up by store-owners for the occasional visitor during business hours.

The top floor of the house was used for private dwellings that could be accessed from the street through the thick cast iron door past a damp cobbled stone corridor, if one took care not to step on the weathered plank covering the narrow cement-lined channel that drained into the town sewer. One would then go up a large stone staircase rising beyond the backyard water well, chicken coop, outhouse, tool shed, fruit trees of the ancient walled garden. People kept a bell suspended inside their entrance with a pull rope or one or two dogs tied up in the yard to announce visitors. At night the thick panel door would be bolted shut with a large iron hook into the wall.

The balcony doors in town, opened and closed at regular intervals unless there was a special occasion like the raucous parade of a winning soccer team with their fans spilling out of a train of cars, a religious procession, carnival bands or some other event of public interest. Since my family and I lived outside of town we would pack a large straw basket especially during carnival season with hot freshly deep-fried sugar-sprinkled *beignet*s and join friends on their balcony atop the *Grande Rue* to watch the parade below. On ordinary days, one side of an upstairs door might remain open to reveal a set of inner white wood shutters through which the curious could watch the street without being detected. Children had the duty to call out greetings to all adults, taking care to attach the proper title of *"mon oncle* or *"ma tante"* for "uncle or "aunt", *"Parrain"* or *"Marainne"* for godparents for family friends and *"Monsieur"*, *"Madame"* or *"Mademoiselle"* for acquaintances and the rare stranger. Adults also used the additional *"mon Compere"* and *"ma Comere"* to address each other if there was a relationship involving the christening of children or marriages. It used to amuse the town people to call out to me as I passed by in the streets, on my way to school or on an errand for my mother, and I always responded to their requests to recite a fable, rhyme, or sing a song. This was all before a particular point in time. Before an indescribable, something had happened to change Life on the streets of Les Cayes.

My father was in charge of the local government hospital's Dental department and worked as well in the private office he shared with two other dentists. On occasion, he and several other healthcare professionals taught science classes at the local hospital Nursing School, *pro bono*. My mother's meticulous housekeeping kept our household clear of financial trouble. Our family belonged to the privileged few in our town. For one we owned a car. My school was situated on one of the side streets near the *"Grande Rue"* in the typical two-storied whitewashed structure with doors opened to the street level porch through which came the sounds of the town.

"There goes the Papa of Marie-Solange" One of my classmates would whisper in recognition of the loud sneezing sound which my father's ancient Plymouth made as he cranked its starter in an adjacent street. Papa had bought the car one step ahead of the charcoal grill makers who cut and soldered the metal from the discards of the town's mechanics. Les Cayes had the most inventive of mechanics. The title of *"boss"* in front of the name of artisans meant that the individual was a master of his craft whether in carpentry, shoemaking, tailoring or inventing and soldering parts for cars. As artisans the *Boss* Luc, *Boss* Ti-Jean, *Boss* Dieudonne of our town were incomparable and Papa's own *Boss-mecanicien* was the best of the best. *Boss* Grimme hoisted another used engine that he had painstakingly reconditioned, up with the aid of a rope and pulley strung across a tree branch, and lowered it into the belly of the vintage Plymouth. I loved to stand on one of the car's running boards as Papa drove up our driveway and nestled most of its large body into the too short carport of our home. Its cracked brown leather back seat usually covered up a treasure trove of loose coins whenever it was pulled out to serve as a bench on a beach or riverbank outing.

I attended the best school in our town, which was run by an order of French nuns. Many of the children even from the middle class could not afford the tuition. It was a struggle financially for my parents to keep my two younger sisters and I there. French was the language used by the middle and upper class. Therefore, my classmates and I were forbidden to speak Kreyol the native language of our land in school and to adults of the middle or upper class. Class distinctions within our society maintained an unhealthy brew of misunderstanding, mistrust, resentment that would periodically erupt in hatred at any given time. Skin color, hair texture, and the ability to pronounce the French "*u*" and one's family name were major factors in determining one's place on the social ladder. Only the rich in our town could buy new imported things. We like those who were not rich, tried not to appear poor. So, when Papa paid ten Gourdes (the equivalent of two American dollars in the late nineteen fifties) for the used blue bicycle that everyone in town knew had years before been the new possession of Marie-Clemence Desrivieres, a rich schoolgirl, we hatched a plan. The damaged fenders were painstakingly straightened out and the whole thing was painted deep black. I would otherwise have continued to walk to school. There were a few students from the moneyed elite or "*bourgeois*" class in our school but everyone did the same chores refilling the small white ceramic ink-wells cradled in a hole on the top of each classroom desk and scrubbing the wooden floors with a wad of broad leaves dipped in a bucket of water. One of the activities in the school playground, which was furnished with one or two swings and a seesaw, consisted of a number of girls holding hands in a circle skipping to the tune of some childish melody or a folk song. Every child in the yard eventually joined the impromptu singing group, harmonizing seamlessly, all drinking in a brief moment of unity.

Ordinarily our family traveled to the large chaotic city of Port-au-Prince twice: at the start of the year to visit both my parents' families and in the summer on our way to spend most of the three months long school vacation in the mountains of Furcy. In those days the trip took eight to twelve grueling hours of skirting the potholes of the unpaved road, swerving around stray farm animals, fording rivers and hoping that the aged black Plymouth would climb up one particularly steep mountain pass. We were duty bound to visit the elders in our parents' families. The concept of "*salue granmoun*" or render homage to family members who in turn felt obligated to demand an account of our activities is just as ingrained in Haitian life as guarding the clan's secrets from outsiders. I disliked visiting our adult relatives in Port-au-Prince. In fact, I never liked Port-au-Prince, especially when we journeyed there in January when I was in charge of the turkeys. In recent years my mother had taken to fattening two turkeys, one for the relatives on each side of our family, and gave me the responsibility of giving them water and keeping the twins from stepping on the miserable birds as they lay, both feet tied, on the floor at the back of our car.

My sisters and I entertained each other by pointing out to the other whatever struck us as odd on both sides of the road. It might be a market woman wearing a straw hat with a brim the size of an umbrella who appeared to be floating atop a pile of produce so high that only the tip of the muzzle and hoofs of the donkey that carried the whole enterprise was visible. Little puffs of smoke appeared at times from the clay pipe the *machann* held between her teeth while both hands maneuvered a long reign to keep her mount from wandering into the path of our car.

While we speculated about the activities of the people inside the thatched roof mud-walled houses we saw in the inner country, the rivers offered the most interesting scenes. There were always women with their skirts tucked around their thighs squatting close to the riverbank wielding a wooden *batouelle* with which they pounded laundry laid out on a rock. Some ducks often floated near them with at least two or three children splashing in the same stream. In some rivers, the local men might knock down a couple of trees to dam the water to make a deeper pool upstream. The children in the water would wave at us and, we envied their swimming pool, not their chores. Two or three cows might be nearby, brought to the water by their pint size herdsmen. One child might be there to fill up a large hollowed out gourd that the *paysans* used with an old corncob as stopper, to carry water. The three feet tall, clay jars, kept in most country kitchen, had to be kept full in that way to ensure the family's water supply. Children, as soon as they could walk would be responsible to feed, water and tend to the family chicken, ducks, guinea hen, goats, and pigs. As the child grew, so did his or her chores. An older child would have to patrol a cornfield with a tin can and stick to chase off hungry birds from the tender crop. It was hard to tell who worked the hardest; These countryside or the town street children with huge flat wooden trays loaded with three times their own weights with coconut treats, molasses cookies, and bottles of various staples, that they balanced on their heads. Both in the towns and countryside, children in the lower class were at the bottom of the Haitian socio-economic system. Next up were the women, who toiled in the field along side their men folk but still were the ones seen grinding corn in a waist size wooden mortar, known as a *pilon*. At times two *paysannes* would be at the same *pilon* each clutching a long wooden pestle with both hands, both intent on the rhythm of their swaying bodies to alternate each crushing strike. The women, unless they had a young girl available were carting the sacks of charcoal and tending the fires and large cooking pots.

As busy as the people of the countryside were, they would drop everything to help a stranger to their area. This natural bent towards hospitality would prove deadly to scores of *Paysans*. Whenever there was some insurgent activity in their area, as in the *Les Irois* region in August 1958, Duvalier's henchmen beat, tortured, and slaughtered scores of them. This would be their reward for giving food, shelter, or direction to a stranger, who was on the run from the Tonton Macoutes. No task was too daunting for the *paysan*. From a car stuck in a river crossing or an overturned *TapTap*. Everyone *knew*, that with any mishap on the road it was best to rely on the ingenuity of the *paysans* with their ropes, and oxen rather than send someone to a town large enough to have the equipment to set a *TapTap* back on its wheels. I had never ridden on a *TapTap*, a large flatbed truck equipped with a brightly painted wooden structure that consisted of long benches that had straw filled seats, and back padding. Every available surface of the *TapTap* was painted with scenes of everyday life, some iconic figure or with some sayings such as "God willing" or "to the will of God". The whole thing was covered by a roof that held rolls of plastic sheets attached to the outer sides that could be unfolded in the rain and a rack to hold an enormous amount of baggage. The market women know as *madansara,* traveled this way, from town to town with their wares.

We had to press on towards Port-au-Prince, occasionally stopping to relieve ourselves in a roadside bush, as was the custom. In *Carrefour des Ruisseaux,* one of the hamlets midway on our route, we would stop for a meal at the modest establishment of one of the country's incomparable cooks. Since there was no electricity in these parts whatever we were served had to be caught, picked, or dug up upon demand. The feast would always be worth the wait. At our last stop, much closer to our destination, we would buy slabs of *douce Marcos* fudge found exclusively at that location, which all of us relished. If we happened on a vendor with a large bamboo cane basket filled with hot fresh out of the oven *patees* or codfish filled pastries, our enthusiasm for traveling through the countryside would be re-awakened. It almost made the trip worthwhile for me. Although the dust of the road clung to our skins, hair, coating our eyelashes and nostrils. At the day's end we would reach the southern entrance of the capital city through the neighborhood of *Carrefour* just as a few precariously hung electric light bulbs cast a yellowish streak from atop their thin wooden poles down on the quick moving shadows of people and cars jostling each other in the narrow streets. The smell of kerosene lamps, charcoal fires and hot grease wafted strong from the curbside army of squatting *machann fritaille* hawking their pungent wares in stiff competition with the incessant bleating of the car horns.

Geographically, the city of Port-au-Prince is situated in the central coast of a deep horseshoe shaped bay formed by the *Presqu'Ile du Nord* or Northern Peninsula, and the *Presqu'ile du Sud*, the Southern Peninsula where Les Cayes is located. With a large barrier island of *La Gonave* in the bay between it and the Caribbean sea on the east, and a range of mountains, to its North, West and South, the city was rarely troubled by the Annual Tropical storms that throughout the years have destroyed so much of the rest of the Island. Internal storms were another matter. Having replaced Cap-Haitien, which under its original name of *Cap Francais* was the seat of the French Colonial government, Port-au-Prince now inherited the tumultuous life that goes along with being the capital of the revolution prone *Republique* of Haiti.

Provincials like us avoided Port-au-Prince when things were *hot* there. On our visits, our family always stayed with my mother's side of the family on a quiet residential hill in the suburb of *Turgeau*. My aunt Christine's engineer husband, who was mostly out of the country working for the United Nations, had designed and a colleague had built their large, pink, cinderblock three-storied house. The pink wrought iron balcony railing on the second floor at the front of the house swirled down to encase a curved, dangerously steep pink mosaic staircase. There were two brown lacquered entrance doors. The door closest to the top of the stairs opened into a small music room furnished mainly with an old black upright piano while the other entrance was used on formal occasions to usher guests into the large living room and dining room. A wall of decorative cinder blocks positioned with spaces between them allowed the natural light to filter in on one side of the second floor. The family usually ate in a smaller dining room that adjoined the music room, kitchen and led to a large back porch that held a row of green painted rocking chairs. An internal wooden staircase connected the second floor to the lower level kitchen, maid quarters, garage, and back yard. The same stairs continued on to the third floor family rooms. There was enough space to accommodate my aunt, her four children, my unmarried aunt Andree, and our grandfather on the top floor, which had a wrap around cement deck that my aunt had converted into a garden of exotic potted plants. The inner rooms had mosaic tiles flooring. My sisters and I never tired of exploring the house on our visits. The youngest of my cousins was a year older than me but both he and his two brothers were quite happy to entertain us with an endless game of hide and seek or Cowboys and Indians. There was a mound of grass-covered earth under an enormous Tamarind tree that I could see from the second floor balcony or third floor deck of the house which my middle cousin Ti-less had convinced the twins and I concealed a cave where some Indians were surely still in hiding. Everyone thought that the original inhabitants of Haiti had been extinct, which is why the European invaders of the Caribbean imported Africans to enslave in their colonies. School children, nevertheless, entertained the notion that some of the original Indians had survived by hiding in the caves and mountains surrounding us. When asked, my aunt told me that she could not plant her garden on that side of the house because the ground was rocky and hollow underneath. She did not want to end up with a large rock-filled crevice next to her home, and, she added, I should stop listening to everything Ti-Less said. My sisters and I were quite content to spend our entire visit roaming around the house even without the inventive games of our cousins but the next day after our arrival started on the round of visits to all the relatives and friends of both my parents. By the time, I had recovered enough to start thinking about enjoying my stay it would be time to get back on the road for the bone-jarring trip home.

Our home in the green plain of Les Cayes with the Caribbean almond trees shading its entrance gate was a welcome sight. It shielded us from the scrutiny of our Port-au-Prince relatives. I always felt that my sisters and I never measured up to their expectations. Both sides of my parents' families seemed to disapprove of our progress. Manman had a reservoir of acerbic repartees to deal with Tante Fifi her sister in law's criticism but was apologetic towards her own sisters. Our failure appeared to stem from us simply living outside of Port-au-Prince and not being members of the bourgeois class. I felt irritated by all of my aunts. My uncles' visits were too brief and their demeanor towards me too distant to be importunate; I assumed that they were busy doing important things. Relatives rarely left the sophistication of Port-au-Prince to visit us in Les Cayes. We were settled in the tranquility of our lives seemingly forever, pretending to ignore the gathering clouds of change.

When my mother, sisters, and I went up to the Mountains of Furcy at the South of Port-au-Prince for our summer vacation with my aunt Christine's daughter and three sons, ManLillie our maternal grandmother would join us. ManLilie had powdery soft skin the color of lightly toasted cinnamon and never raised her voice. She loved the twins, my cousins and I. My unmarried aunt Andree, aunt Christine and Papa had fewer vacation days and came for a long week-end here and there during our stay as did several other relatives and friends. We all piled in the small stone cottage to sleep or shelter from the rain and wind. Unlike the rest of the country, the soil at Furcy was brick red and the air cold especially at night. ManLillie was always the first to rise. She would build a small fire in a clearing close by on the packed earth to roast the sweet potatoes she favored for breakfast, setting her coffee pot on top. Her soft face with very fine wrinkles, pulled alternately to one side and then to the other as she squinted her eyes and tilted her head. No one could convince Manlillie who was farsighted to wear eyeglasses. She gently ordered us children to step back several feet away from her so she could take a good look at us. When in town, however, she would become so excited at spotting one of her grandchildren that she would throw decorum to the wind and call out: *"Ti bout trip mouin!"* A crowd lingering on the steps of a large church after Sunday Mass or a bevy of my teenage cousin's friends would turn to look. Being called the tip of our grandmother's intestines was embarrassing. No one knew why she chose that phrase to identify us as belonging to her.

In Furcy, I loved to sit up close to my grandmother. While the boys were still outside around our nightly bonfire, after we had exhausted my cousins' repertoire of accordion tunes, late by the light of the kerosene lamp set in our sleeping quarter, I would urge her to tell one more story. Even though her tales revolved around the same theme of the supernatural, she never told the same one twice, the longer we stayed awake the more fantastic they would become. I had strict orders from my mother not to repeat the things ManLillie talked about. ManLillie wore dresses of cotton mid calf with the three quarters length sleeves denoting her status of respectable elderly woman. Maman sewed her knee length underwear and corsets to her specifications and kept her supplied with the thick stockings she demanded. In the matter of her shoes and teeth, however, a minor family upheaval would erupt. My grandmother was less than five feet tall, with diminutive feet that leaned outwardly and insisted on wearing high-heeled shoes in the style of her long deceased elders. She always appeared to be on the verge of losing her balance yet refused to wear flat shoes or use a walking cane. Each time ManLillie had worn out the heels of a pair of shoes to the point where the whole shoe would not stand straight, her daughters had the arduous task of finding a shoemaker who would meet her requirements. On the matter of clothing our gentle grandmother was surprisingly unbending. As for her teeth, every summer it was the same when she greeted Manman:

"Tell John (as she called my father) that I need a new set of teeth."

Papa would smack his forehead with the palm of his hand in exasperation when he was given the message. My grandmother would not wear her dentures and soon her gums would shrink, eventually causing her latest set of false teeth to rattle about her mouth. She would sigh plaintively:

"Marie you see, I told you that the teeth that John put in my mouth are no good!"

The rules governing childhood were few in Furcy. My cousins, sisters and I were free to roam the mountain slopes at will; lost in the world of as many adventures our minds could invent. We fished for the flannel shirts and denim pants and cow skin boots left in the cottage year round for our use. The one requirement, for us children was that, when the sun had reached its highest point marking the middle of the day, we would dip into the ice cold stream at the far end of the property to wash off the red clay that inevitably coated us from head to toe. My cousin Ti-less and his brother Jerry fancied themselves as horse trainers. Their one pupil was an indomitable colt they named *Beatrice* that had a penchant for biting and as I remember over the course of several summers, never allowed his back to be saddled. I suspected that this was convenient for the boys who obviously preferred bareback riding. The small farms on our routes enticed even Maxo, the more restrained of the boys to, using his jacket as a Matador's cape, harass a lone cow or two. The twins and I were content to hitch a ride on the back of a friendly goat or climb atop the large tombs, typical of the Haitian countryside. There were three of these structures a few feet away from the cottage when Papa Gus, our grandfather bought the land decades earlier. No inscription remained on the worn stone surfaces and we speculated on whether the people buried there had any connection to the property. The *Paysans* of the countryside were notorious squatters. Papa Gus was reluctant to evict his unknown tenants, unsure as to whom; in the labyrinth of the mountain-dwellers' relations might take offense. It was unwise to ruffle the sentiments of a Haitian *Paysan*, even with a paid caretaker nearby.

Generally, the caretakers of the property at Furcy were members of the family of *Tonton Zoulien*, a short wiry, patriarch renowned for his husbandry skills who was never seen without his machete holstered to the shoulder length, chest crossing strap of his straw weaved *macoute* or knapsack. *Tonton Zoulien* had a way with goats and raised the best in the areas. He was also the neighborhood midwife, an occupation generally filled by a female *sage femme*. His sturdy grime coated fingers were renowned to have skillfully severed many an umbilical cord. Papa Gus and the adults in our family sought out his counsel on all local matters. *Tonton Zoulien* unlike his contemporaries in the countryside who carried on the African tradition of keeping several wives, appeared to have just one. *Soh Ennay* as she was known was also referred to as *Madanm Zoulien*. She was a sturdy woman of an uncertain age. *Soh Ennay* wore the uniform heavy blue denim dress and colorful scarf headdress with a large knot at the back of her head and exuded an air of confident efficiency. We often wondered whether she had simply eliminated her rivals. The larger scarf draped around *Soh Ennay*'s hips could be tightened as a weight lifting belt, unfurled to strap a baby on one hip or twirled and rolled up into a coiled padding for her head to carry a heavy basket. Neither *Soh Ennay* nor *Tonton Zoulien* had any notion of how long they had been together. No one, including *Tonton Zoulien* knew how old he was. The title of *Tonton* or uncle was, in these parts, reserved for the very old and respected.

Our mountaintop had a forest of pine trees that hid the house from one side. Nothing grew in the carpet of pine needles beneath them. On foggy days it was easy to loose one's way around the mountain but as long as it was daylight, I did not fret, knowing that some knapsack toting *Paysan* would suddenly appear a the bend of a clay colored path to point out the right direction. The locals knew all about us and did not object to the annual invasion of city dwellers as long as the children did not trample their crops or bother their animals. Many planted vegetables on the land belonging to my grandfather and other absent property owners, in a loose arrangement that netted us some fresh produce and fruit while we vacationed there. I have never seen juicier and larger carrots than those grown on the mountain slopes of Furcy. We also had an abundant supply of milk, straight from a nearby cow. There were peach trees, wild berries bushes to pick from, and a profusion of yellow, fuchsia, white, and blue flowers that grew close to the ground resisting the strongest winds. Millions of these hardy little flowers pushed through the clumps of clay and mountain grass spreading unchecked over acres of land. The area also hosted a wide variety of songbirds, the very tiniest of which filled the air in an unending concert of melodious sounds.

Whenever our excesses would draw us back to the side of our soft grandmother, she knew just the right leaves to pick and brew to calm a bellyache or soothe a throbbing brow. ManLillie was at peace in Furcy. She greeted the wild birds and caressed the shrubs and tree limbs, her lips moving silently as if she were greeting old friends. Her familiarity with the secrets of nature had grown out of her need as a child and young woman living in a poor country. Manman had experience that poverty when her father had walked out on his family, leaving her mother to care for four children.

She was eight years old at the time. Man-Lillie, who had herself lost her mother at age three, was raised on the charity of relatives who shuttled her from home to home and never gave her a formal education. The inferior schooling given to my grandmother was common in her day since women in Haiti were barred from anything but menial work. She could only hope to marry well. One of her relatives had sized up her suitor and warned young Amélie that the dashing Auguste Toulmé would break her heart. She, nevertheless, dreamed of escaping her bleak life. Amélie was from the middle class. Unlike *Soh Ennay* and the *paysannes* of the countryside, who planted crops, bartered at roadside markets, and handled their own lives, she was vulnerable. With no one to look out for her interests, Amélie did not receive her share of her mother's large estate. Marriage was her only hope. Yet, Haitian law did not protect abandoned wives and children. Only a man's honor constrained him to care for his children once he divorced his wife. My grandfather had developed other amorous interests and neglected his duties.

At first, Amélie sold off her jewelry and other possessions and worked long hours, her calloused hands turning the small wheel of her sewing machine but to no avail. She was a righteous woman and rejected offers from the men who prey on women in her situation. Manman, her two sisters, and brother went to school often with just some tea for breakfast and with no lunch. They were starving and too proud to ask for charity. That's when Man-Lillie took the three young girls, she was afraid the boy would be treated too harshly, and left them at their father's house. Every week Man-Lillie walked from wherever she lived for however long it took to check up on her daughters and to warn my grandfather against mistreating them.

In Port-au-Prince my grandmother even after her children had reached adulthood continued to live apart from the rest of the family in a small house aunt Andree had built for her. She refused to live under the same roof as *Monsieur Toulmé* referring to her ex-husband with dignified formality, timing her visits so as not to meet up with my grandfather. Early in their marriage, my parents tried to have her live with them. Man Lillie became increasingly restless, refusing to stay in Les Cayes and insisted on returning to Port-au-Prince. She grew to be suspicious of all strangers, cooking her own meals, chasing off each of the women my aunts hired to live with her. Even though her children now provided her with all she needed ManLillie hoarded food and other supplies using them sparingly always expecting a famine to strike. As she aged, and her mental health deteriorated, her memories became a greater scourge than the poverty she had survived.

The next generation of women which included my mother and her sisters lived with the threat of poverty and no readily apparent way of protecting themselves. Society dictated the rules that changed frequently and depended on the benevolence of the males who controlled the women's destiny. Duvalierism had ushered in more changes, and more uncertainty. In our town of Les Cayes, as in the rest of Haiti at the start of the nineteen-sixties, the greedy, the covetous, the power hungry swelled the Duvalierist ranks. Others simply waited for the opportunity to profit from the misfortune of others. It was by Divine providence that the conspiracy against our family was discovered by a friend in time to allow my father to seek help. In that setting, it was difficult for my parents to find a discreet buyer for our house to finance our escape. If those who plotted to steal my father's job and destroy his life had succeeded my mother, sisters and I would have had a very different life. Most certainly, we would have joined the ranks of the poor.

Papa's family had been poor simply because his father's income as a pastor was stretched thin to sustain an extended family and a steady stream of parishioners who came around at mealtime. Amazingly, he remembers, there was always enough food to go around. He also remembers that the property owner never raised the rent on their family home for the more than twenty years they lived there. Cousins, aunts, uncles, and family friends came to die or had their wedding receptions in the sturdy house with the spacious fruit tree-lined backyard on the *Ruelle Jardine*. Sleeping arrangements divided any number of boys in one room and grouped the girls in another. Some young relatives would live there in order to attend the University in the capital city. Tuition was free at the University in Port-au-Prince. Both Papa and one brother uncle Miyou were able to train for a profession. Their older brother uncle Sonny was sent to the seminary of the Church and became an Episcopalian priest and tante Fifi the one surviving sister became a teacher and later a social worker. Protestant families were more inclined to educate their women and at least prepare them to earn a modest income.

Papa went to work at the end of his studies for the government as a dentist for the equivalent of thirty-five American dollars per month. It took him ten years to save up enough money to have furniture made and prepare for his wedding to Manman who was meanwhile busy embroidering and sewing up her trousseau. Something both my parents learned from their own childhood was to share whatever they had with others and not to steal. My sisters and I too had to be trained. Manman told me that when I was about two years old I had gone to visit a friend with my baby sitter and returned with the other child's doll clutched in my arms. The sitter explained that I had made a scene and the friend's mother had convinced her to let me go off with the doll. I was immediately sent back, after a sound spanking, to return the doll and to apologize to its owner. As I grew older, I understood that I was not to take things that did not belong to me. I also understood that it was my responsibility to feed the hungry. Both my parents were very diligent in teaching my sisters and I to share anything we had with anyone in need. So many people around us were in need. One of my classmates and I had a discreet arrangement for me to leave a small loaf of buttered bread in her desk every morning for her breakfast. Just as with my mother and her siblings in their day, this child would rather starve than accept charity openly.

5

The very poor in our town lived in shacks on whatever vacant strip of land was available in or around a town. When I was about six or seven years old there were several families living in some of these flimsy homes in the field abutting the house we were renting at the time. One family consisted of Titonton who was about ten, the mother, and one very small girl named Doucette. The little girl became ill and died. I was allowed to go see her because I had never seen a dead person before. I remember seeing Doucette lying on the family's straw pallet wearing the white dress that Manman had hastily sewed for her to be buried in, awaiting the coffin that a local carpenter was busy preparing. Two thin white ribbons were tied in a bow on either side of her neatly braided hair. The dark skin of her face was obscured by a mask of white talcum powder: This was the traditional finishing touch for a child dressed to attend church for Sunday Mass, any type of fete or party and for burial. Someone else had also donated a pair of white socks, which were probably the only ones the little girl would ever wear on her tiny feet. She had never owned a pair of shoes either and now no longer had use for any.

Doucette's mother screamed her pain, squatting on the swept dirt ground of the yard outside their home. The memory of Doucette's quiet little body resting in the darkened shack would haunt me for many years. I asked my mother why Doucette had died.

"*Lan mize.*" Manman answered. *Poverty* was something that was bad, something that killed.

After his sister died, Titonton the brother, who was already supporting his family, attached himself to our household; running errands, and working at whatever job, he could find elsewhere. It was a way of ensuring that his mother, especially and he would get at least one meal a day. He became our courier, delivering notes for the adults around town. He walked faster than anyone I knew. On school days, he prided himself on taking my sisters and my lunch to us from our kitchen to the schoolyard in town before the canteen of stacked metal containers grew cold. It was his idea, he said that it was too much for the twins to walk home and back in the middle of the day as the other students did. He always grinned broadly at our greetings and casually fanned his reddened sweat-drenched face with his straw hat. As we ate in a shaded corner of the schoolyard Titonton regaled us with stories of his latest adventures. He fancied himself a man although the length of his knee-long pants, bare feet, and his hairless chin betrayed his status as a youth. Only men wore full-length trousers in our country. Neither did Titonton wear the crude cheap sandals made out of the black rubber of old car tires that, together with the heavy denim pants and shirt characterized the *paysans* of the countryside. He whittled at twigs, and used rubber tire strips to make slingshots or kites with small bamboo strips and newspaper. At Christmas time, he could be depended on to make the traditional *fanal* a cut out cardboard lantern decorated with colored tissue paper to look like the stain glass windows of a church when a small kerosene soaked wick was lit inside the whole thing.

Titonton was also Papa's faithful assistant when the pair set off fireworks for the New Year or scouted out the terrain on one of our country outings. Our favorite spot was in Gelee, a piece of land that belonged to Papa's family that had a stream coursing through a field of broad-leaved malangas and scores of Mangoes, Avocado, Apricot, Banana and tall coconut trees. There was a dilapidated cottage a few feet from the water's edge, framed with the green *malanga* clusters, that had served as the family vacation home when Papa had been a boy my age when Grandfather Benedict rode for some six hours on a trotting horse to visit the outlying hamlets in his parish. We had to bring several cast iron portable charcoal grills and everything needed to cook a meal that included rice and beans and deep fried plantains. Titonton was in the thick of it, scaling up fruit trees that my sisters and I were not allowed to climb, loading and unloading the gear, especially Papa's blue-framed wooden deck chair that we always took with us strapped to the front end of the old black Plymouth.

At home Titonton and I would dunk the inner tube of my bicycle tire in a pan of water to search for the telltale string of tiny bubbles that betrayed a hole that we patched with a piece of adhesive rubber. Besides fixing the flat tires that plagued me he also taught me how to keep the bicycle chain greased, how to put it back when it slipped off, to straighten a bent fender, and essentially get the old bike back on the road for long enough to make it home. He was careful to obey Manman's orders not to ride the bike. It was a child's bike. His long legs dangling over a girl's bicycle would not suit his sense of dignity. Titonton dreamed of riding horses on some prairies with the movie cowboys he saw on a town square screen. My sister Tikite, the smaller of the twins and his favorite, would frequently enlist Titonton's help for her escapades and he taught her to ride my bicycle standing on the pedals because her legs were too short. I looked down the road from our home once shortly before dusk to see what appeared to be a rider less bicycle coming towards me. Just as for the time when a pack mule bolted with both the twins seated astride its straw harness atop our pick-nick baskets, there was Titonton running full tilt in pursuit. It was always interesting to hear his explanations to Manman. A day would not go by without her calling out his name in mock exasperation.

"Titonton! Where is that boy?"

Manman had enrolled Titonton in a school and scolded him about his activities there and I suspect his poor attendance record. He would grin, his light brown face reddened by the sun even under the curled brim of his straw hat forcibly shaped like those of his movie cowboys heroes. The women in our household indulged his seemingly carefree wanderings relying on him to keep them abreast of all the local news. Other than someone occasionally inquiring "*Cote-Li?*" Titonton might be at his mother's, or on the pier, watching workers unload a ship or at some impromptu crowd attraction somewhere in town. Titonton hopped on a flat bed truck once with some men gathered by government agents to demonstrate support for Francois Duvalier at an organized rally in the capital. People were coerced in participating in street demonstrations organized by the government to show popular support for Duvalier. We also had to have the flag glued to our family car's windshield and the front door of our house. There were numerous presidential orders that purported to demonstrate one's patriotism that in effect served to control every facet of civilian life. Added to these arbitrary mandates were the local Duvalierists 'own rules.

Life in Les Cayes stopped whenever the Duvalierists called for a "spontaneous" demonstration of popular support for Francois Duvalier. Crowds organized by the *Tonton Macoutes* would suddenly swarm the streets. Shopkeepers would empty out the *galleries,* pull their shutters close and all normal activities would come to an immediate end. Everyone else hid behind closed doors. Anyone suspected of non-sympathy was fair game of any mischief. One such night uncle Miyou who was a surgeon, with a skeleton crew that included Papa to assist him braved the chaos on the streets around the local hospital to operate on a man who had a piece of lumber imbedded in his belly. The lights of the ground floor operating room attracted the crowd outside. A group of men smashed through the doors and invaded the room, oblivious of the surgical set up. Uncle Miyou went on with the surgery.

"Why aren't you at the demonstration?" The loudest of the intruders wanted to know.

Papa says that he remembers his heart skipping a beat as uncle Miyou, scalpel in hand threatened to slice open the stomach of the man closest to him and ordered the crowd to get out of his operating room. When someone disappeared from our area, no one knew whether he had been picked up by a Tonton Macoute raid packed in a flatbed truck and dumped, in the streets of Port-au-Prince to listen to Francois Duvalier's speeches. As I remember these people, instead of being returned to their countryside homes were abandoned in the city without food or shelter. Some found their way back to their families. Others sought refuge in the slums that had sprouted up in Port-au-Prince. Titonton volunteered to go to Port-au Prince when the *Tonton Macoutes* approached him. It was his opportunity to travel free; he had never seen the capital city of Port-au-Prince. I had told him that it had so many more streetlights than our town.

Government employees too had been ordered by officials to show up at the Duvalierist rally to show popular support for the president. My father and his brother both worked at the government hospital in Les Cayes, which by then was lousy with Duvalierists spies who kept watch on everyone's activities. Papa and uncle Miyou decided to drive to Port-au-Prince shortly after so that they could wait out the street demonstrations at their sister, Tante Fifi's house in the larger city without anyone in Les Cayes knowing of their whereabouts. Midway through the eight-hour trip Papa and uncle

Miyou came across a group of hungry travel weary men stranded on the side of the road next to a broken down flat bed truck. With them was a familiar mud splattered boy squatting in the dirt, both hands clutching his head, sobbing.

"Titonton!"

Papa reported that for once in his life, Titonton was speechless. By taking charge of his own life Titonton at least had escaped the lot of countless children his age, who are simply turned over by their parents to serve in strangers' homes and more frequently than not are abused by their masters. With no government regulation in place to protect them and the vicious class prejudice, that feeds on their need these boys and girls were doomed to a life of indescribable misery. No one in our home physically disciplined Titonton or the young girl who was my first baby sitter but I knew of many and witnessed one such brutal beating of a young child. The boy, whose name I have forgotten, was about my age at the time, which would be eight or nine years old. He was a *restaveck* or child slave of the woman who was my math tutor. It was obvious that his very dark skin placed him beyond the natural sympathies of his light skinned mistress who nevertheless had allowed him to participate in the studies along side her paying students. One day the boy, one other older student and I were seated at the tutor's dining table with our math books and copybooks when suddenly something occurred that directed the woman's wrath towards her servant boy. The tutor was a stout masculine looking woman in her forties. Angrily she growled an order to the luckless boy, who had already started to sob, to go fetch the *rigoaz*. Our home did not have a rigoaz but I was quite familiar with the long braided rawhide switch and had seen full-grown horses respond quickly to its lightest touch.

The woman wielding the *rigoaz* had worked herself into a state of uncontrolled fury, her face frozen into a mask of hate. She swung the *rigoaz* with practiced accuracy. The other student and I fled to a corner of the room away from the vicious strokes of the whip as we watched the victim roll on the wooden floor, overturning chairs, the blackboard set up for our lesson. I felt close to loosing the contents of my stomach. Each of the boy's screams seemed to draw an even harsher blow. Then the boy's voice grew hoarse and eventually could no longer be heard as he tucked his head in his chest, trying to protect it with his arms. But the woman was still swinging at his shivering chalk covered bloodied limbs, stopping only when she fell back on a chair gasping for breath from her exertion.

I was grateful that the custom in our town dictated that children not make eye contact with adults. Thus, I was able to hide the revulsion I felt for this woman. One day the woman tutor did strike one blow to my own back with the *rigoaz* while I was at the black board writing out a math problem. The unexpected attack caused my body to freeze and stiffen, suddenly. It was as if all the air had been sucked out of my chest. I felt the skin of my back tighten along what seemed like the trail of a lit match. This woman had no right to use a *rigoaz* on me! I was Doctor Benedict's daughter! Manman had always said that if anyone dared flog her children they would have to contend with her. Did not this woman know this?

For the first time I looked at the tutor straight in the eye. She did not interfere as I gathered up my books. Even though she was much larger than me, and the penalty for fighting an adult in our society was severe, I was energized by a murderous rage that obliterated any thought of consequences. Had a machete been nearby I could have easily swung it at her head. Somehow, I left the woman's house without further damage. At least I was able to run home to my parents for protection and did not have to go back for any more math lessons. The vulnerability of the poor and especially the very poor in Haiti to the meanness of their fellow compatriots is in stark contrast to the show of piety that was the rule in most households. I grew up around very pious people. Theirs was a piety that professed to render homage to a God, the very same God who commanded that his followers love one another. I witnessed in Haiti the rigid adherence to class distinctions that condemned a segment of the population to exploitation. Very few people had pity for the poor.

III. The making of a refugee

"What mean ye that beat my people to pieces, and grind the faces of the poor? Saith the Lord God of hosts" Isaiah 3:15(KJV)

6

It began slowly. I noticed that the rocking chairs on the *galleries* on the *Grande Rue* sat immobile and empty. Upper floor shutters narrowed their slats and some doors remained shut even in midday. A sense of unease now stifled my carefree chatter. This new feeling soon trickled into and tainted the outings that I, the perennial tagalong to an indulgent father shared with Papa and his friends: the weekend soccer games, the boisterous post game parades and deep-sea fishing trips. It was as if an unknown disease had infected the laughter, the bantering, even the ornate greetings between casual acquaintances and caused it all to shrivel up and float away on a Caribbean breeze. Friendly faces scrunched up into stranger's scowls. The people who knew my every nickname, and sang along with my songs and smiled at my ditties had been spirited away.

"Don't repeat anything"

Adults told me and other children. Everyone monitored the talk of the children. There had been a lot of noise around the 1957 Presidential elections in Haiti. Graffiti in Kreyol or French sprouted up on the whitewash walls of the *Grande Rue:* the words of *"A Bas!" "Vive!"* shouted the conflicting political convictions. Discussions on the *galleries* heated up spreading to the basket and hat weavers sitting outside countryside huts, their fingers rhythmically moving to the beat of their voices. People gathered in spontaneous crowds intoxicated, so it seemed, by the fumes of yet another political revolution. The nuns at the towns' schools taught us children to pray a lot. We did as we were told. Gradually the agitation slowed. Adults warned us not to talk to anyone outside of our homes. Then there was silence in the land: Francois Duvalier, known to the world as "Papa Doc", had become president of our country. Soon after, came the whispers about people disappearing, snatched by the bogeymen or *"Tonton Macoutes"*.

"Don't talk to anyone anywhere about anything or the *Tontons macoutes* will hear and come to take you away"

This became the common admonition to all, children, and adult alike. In our culture, storytellers known as *"tireurs de contes"* invariably told scary stories about *"tontons macoutes"* in many of their folk tales. *Tonton Macoutes* prowled and did their evil deeds in the dark of night. In my mind, they were a close cousin of *lougarous* and *mohs*. This new presence, however, now identified with that legend wore the same clothes worn by ordinary men in our town yet could be spotted by the impenetrable black sunglasses expressionless faces, the particular angle at which they set their hat, and the menacing bulge of a side arm tucked under a shirt. Daytime, nighttime, any time, these *tontons macoutes* spread out in the sunlit streets of Les Cayes.

As my father explained to me later, our own town of Les Cayes, had been turned over to one particular *Tonton Macoute*. This individual was a stonemason with a primary school education who had arrived in town to work on the construction of the army barracks. By the early, nineteensixties this man had veto power over all of the town government officials including the Academy graduate military commander. Town people were jailed, beaten, and released from the town jail at the whim of Duvalier's stonemason. While the *Tonton Macoute* had usurped the Army's policing role the career officers who did not suit Duvalier's purpose where replaced by less qualified men who swore allegiance to the president. These men in turn used their own positions to harass ordinary people. There was one particular *tonton Macoute/* army captain who lived in an unpaved section in our town, who decreed that passing cars should not cause any dust to enter his roadside house. One day my father drove by too fast and was arrested by a vigilant soldier who, with his rifle cradled in his arms, escorted Papa, on foot to the town's police station. Papa was not placed in the army barracks jail. To his surprise he was quickly released: As the news of Papa's arrest spread, a woman patient of his who, unbeknownst to my father, was the mistress of the very same captain who had caused the problem decided that she did not want her dentist jailed and ordered his release.

In school, we were accustomed to have the nuns monitor the songs we sang in our playing circles at recess time. That was a given. Adults In our society directed every aspect of the children's lives, especially in Catholic schools. Yet, there was a perceptible change in the level of censorship, a product of the current political climate. "*Nous sommes trois petits soldats*" or " we are three little soldiers", a favorite chorus because it ended with a shout, very quickly with the turn of events in our world, was placed on the forbidden song list. The nun monitoring our recess time from a second floor balcony overlooking the playground would react swiftly, at the sound of our voices raised in defiant unison. Song and nervous Laughter would drift to an end as the peals of the large hand held bell drowned out our voices imposing a sullen silence punctuated by the shuffle of feet disappointed and reluctant to part with the dusty courtyard. Once inside our classrooms, no talking amongst students was allowed. We had forfeited our brief moment of freedom for a song. Schoolyard friendships were scrutinized too for any signs of a dangerous affiliation. Duvalier's spies were known to glean information from the innocent babble of children. We became afraid of each other. Except for the trip to and from school on my bicycle when I strained to keep my eyes fixed on the road ahead, both ears on the alert to pick up the slightest sound, I now stayed close to home. Yet, the walls around our family compound no longer reassured me. A shadow darker than any night I had ever known spread over our lives.

I was busy dodging the circumstances of what my life had become without much thought about the future. Some people hid within the country but increasingly there had been harrowing tales of betrayal and capture and the long silence that would follow disappearances. On late afternoons one of the adults of our household and sometimes I would step out of our gate to scan the street towards town to check if an approaching cloud of dust held Papa's car in it. After working most of the day at his hospital job my father would spend a few hours at the private clinic he shared with the now one remaining dentist. The other partner, my godfather, had already gone into exile. If the sun started to sink on the horizon, Titonton would be dispatched to find my father. Papa would pretend to be annoyed with us but was generally careful to come home before the sunset.

None of us really knew how to stay out of trouble. Those who made the invisible rules that dictated our behavior changed them frequently without informing us. We kept watch on each other against them, enforcing our own admonitions to be careful. The Tontons Macoutes could pounce on any one of us at any time. One day someone came to our house to call Papa for help: Dancles a mentally challenged man who did odd jobs for our family had been taken to the police station where the *gensdarmes* beat him mercilessly until he soiled his pants. Even though they wore the uniform of the regular army, these men were either *Tonton Macoutes* or acting under their orders. Dancles had been falsely accused of stealing. The standard procedure for those in power was to beat anyone detained and ask questions later. Duvalier's

Ton Tons Macoute militia, were a law unto themselves. It did not matter that Dancles was an honest man who would rather go hungry than steal anything. Many in town knew this man and could vouch for his innocence. Papa was able to convince Dancles' captors to release him.

Sometime before this incident, uncle Miyou, Papa's surgeon brother, had operated on Dancles to repair a double hernia. One day he came across his convalescing patient on one of the streets that led to the docks as the latter was pulling a slab-cart piled high with large sacks of charcoal. Uncle Miyou exploded in a tirade of reproach. Dancles grinned widely; his sweat soaked face creased with worry at having to balance the cart's load that threatened to crush him, apologizing and begging his doctor to understand that he had a sister who had children, they would all starve if he didn't work. His eyes filled with regret as much at having disappointed uncle Miyou as not being able to free up a hand to pull off his straw hat to show the respect he felt anyone who addressed him deserved. Dancles would work even when he had no assurance of being paid trusting with a child like faith in the good intentions of his fellow man. He was defenseless.

Our home was shaken by the news that anyone could be so cruel as to physically abuse Dancles. That incident profoundly affected me. I lived in daily fear that something similar or worse would happen to my father. Papa could be provoked into loosing his temper at the wrong time. He had come close to doing so on the day he picked up the sobbing, wounded Dancles from the Police station. Now, whenever I rode by the town police station, which I could not avoid, I would pedal as fast as I could. This practice once caused the worn leather satchel that I had clipped on the back of the bicycle to work its way out of the metal spring wire that held it just as I was riding past the police station. The *Gendarmes* of the police station wore khaki and belonged to the regular army, not the *tonton macoutes* militia, but I had started to give a wide birth whenever possible to anyone wearing a military uniform. One of the *Gardes* noticed my satchel about to fall off the bike and when I did not hear his shout blew his police whistle to stop me. The bike, satchel, and I tumbled onto the pavement, dirt, and blood from my skinned leg staining my blue school uniform. The kindness of these men did nothing to allay my fears. It took very little in those days to strike terror in my child's heart.

It was as if enemies on all sides, stalking especially my father, suddenly dogged our every step. One day, as I rode home from school on my bicycle, a pair of these self-appointed foes, face masked by the *"Tontons Macoutes"* black sunglasses, followed me in a military jeep. This was in the older part of town where large cement houses lined both sides of the street with open porches standing sided by side in a continuous shaded passage-way for pedestrians who wanted to avoid the blistering sun and piles of animal dung left by the horses, mules and donkeys that farmers straddled or drove in from the countryside. The street I rode on that afternoon was empty. Fear instantly gripped me when I noticed the two *Tonton Macoutes,* following me in the olive green jeep. The driver knew me and I recognized the man. He and his brother had attempted to have my father assassinated. The brother of this man wanted the job that my father held at the hospital for one of their cronies. Papa had narrowly escaped their plot. Now the man and another *Tonton Macoute* seated in the topless vehicle were pursuing me. I felt the row of two-storied houses flanking both sides of the street closing in on me. I do not remember seeing anyone around who would dare come to my aid. By late afternoon even though the sun still shone, the people of Les cayes stayed indoors behind the thick walls of their homes. The laughter of both the man and his passenger, as they followed me even driving unto the porch of the house I had climbed on, stung my ears. Manman, Papa, my home were quite a distance away. Quite suddenly the initial terror I had felt must have instantly subsided and given place to another emotion. That is when I dismounted the bike and confronted the men with my best scowl. The two *Tonton Macoutes* laughed louder as they drove off. A gush of tears choked my throat stopping short of spilling out.

"Don't *ever* tell your father!"

Manman said when I arrived home. We both knew that my father had been the real target of the two men's harassment. Now a simple errand under the midday sun to even the largest of the town's squares would become an ordeal for me. My sharp tongue could dispatch any opponent who poked fun at my weight. No one at school dared harm my younger sisters. People in town knew of my combative spirit, my family name... There was a shift, a change in the balance of things around me. The men who were my parents' friends and acquaintances, the ones I addressed as *"mon oncle"*, the ones who patted me on the head and even the lone stranger who answered my greeting with a nod had drifted off somewhere. I held back my tears. My mother had already taught me not to cry about a loss or any of the trials of life. Now a piece of my life was missing. I had been robbed; by a thief named fear.

Like so many of their contemporaries, my parents, both in their mid forties, were well-established, contributing members of Haitian society. Both were accustomed to working hard. For Haitians like them, family, home and country took precedence over a financially more comfortable life abroad. For five years, they had tried to adjust to this latest spawn of Haitian politics. My father had already had some narrow escapes with the new masters of our country. Francois Duvalier, who had tightened his grip on the country through extortion, torture, and murder, understood well the power of money and ambition. The most unlikely people swore allegiance to Duvalier. A good friend of my parents was shocked to hear a nephew of his declare at a family gathering that he was prepared to kill even his own mother for Duvalier. This nephew, whom the uncle promptly threw out of his house, went on to commit atrocious crimes for Duvalier including burning the eyes of a small child with a lit cigarette during one of his murderous rampages before eventually being executed himself in front of his master. Treacherous predators stalked the innocent. Duvalier played on the dictatorial propensities of the average Haitian adult to serve his own purposes.

Two men in our town, both had grown up with my father in this small community, plotted to destroy Papa through their access to the Duvalierist political machine. One of the men had a daughter my age with whom I had played when we both attended the same *Ecole Maternelle*. It was odd I remember seeing my mother exchange pleasantries with my classmate's mother at some social event and then discovering that this child's parent had simply decided that my own father should die. Papa held his job at the government hospital for twenty years. There was never any question about his diligence or integrity. Even though he was respected for his work ethics, it was no longer enough to secure his job or even his life. No one in Les Cayes and even in the rest of Haiti had the option to remain neutral. The one hospital in Les cayes belonged to the government therefore only those who demonstrated their loyalty to the government were entitled to work in it. By the late nineteen fifties, the government was dominated by the Duvalierists. Undoubtedly there were people who became Duvalierists to protect themselves and their families from the *Tonton Macoutes* and there were others, like my parents who could not betray their own sense of morality to even associate themselves with the party. Mostly the Duvalierists were opportunists who volunteered to carry out Francois Duvalier's mandate of destruction in order to feather their own beds. As an adult living in the United States, I remember the comment of an American who had lived for thirty-five years in Haiti during that period.

"Haitians are so covetous", she told me. "Someone can be smiling at you while plotting to take your belongings".

I learned so many years later, while living in the United States, the full details of the attempt against my father's life. Only then did I realize how he managed to survive and protect his family. When he found out about this particular plot he set out on foot from our town at night to avoid detection and caught a ride from a trucker on the road to the capital city of Port-au-Prince. Initially, Papa did not even know the depth of his troubles. People were so afraid of the Duvalierists that no one would help my father. To be seen even talking with an individual marked for destruction could be life threatening.

Once he arrived in Port-au-Prince, Papa searched for one of his former professors at the University who was now the head of the country's Ministry of Health for which my father also worked as an employee of our town hospital. Under the Duvalierist Regime, the rule of Law and any semblance of due process had given way to intrigue and summary dispensing of rights. Anyone who had the opportunity to know that they were under the threat of being arrested, tortured and most likely killed had to maneuver through instincts. Generally, this meant finding someone with the power to stop the mischief and willing to risk their own position in the ever-shifting structure of the government to do so. Clinging to the hope that his old professor would save him, Papa obtained an interview. The Cabinet minister greeted him cautiously, Papa remembered, shifting his weight frequently as my father started to explain the predicament he was in. At the end of Papa's narrative the Minister opened a drawer in his desk and pulled out a single sheet of paper from a file, abruptly declaring that his "case" was hopeless. In a rare move, the man slid the document he had retrieved from his desk towards Papa. It was a memo signed by Francois Duvalier the president of the country.

"*Doctor Benedict, the dentist*" it stated, Duvalier knew that there were two Doctor Benedicts in the country since he had worked during his pre political days with Papa's older brother uncle Miyou a fellow physician. The memo cited the false accusation that Papa had actively "opposed" Duvalier's government, ordered the Minister of Health to "remove him from his post", and ended with the ominous command to "do the necessary follow up". Countless people lost their lives in much the same way in Haiti. A group of *Tonton Macoutes* would arrive in a car or military Jeep and take the designated victim away to some unknown location. The Duvalierists had long dispensed with the formalities of the Haitian Judicial system. Gradually the name of *Fort Dimanche* became known throughout the country as the headquarters for torture, imprisonment, and death in Port-au-prince although unspeakable things were also done to people in the basement of the presidential palace and other police stations and military installations around the country. I do not believe that there is an accurate tally of their victims. Duvalier and his "*Tonton Macoutes*" made no claims of operating under any code of conduct. They took pride in being " hors La Loi", that is "outside of the Law". Ordinary citizens were nevertheless shocked as news of some new atrocity surfaced. The country's radio stations and Newspapers would never dare report on anything that conflicted with the information they were allowed to disseminate by the government. The "*Tonton Macoutes*" taped all the telephone lines. Even private conversations were censored.

Previously on one Sunday afternoon, my parents had been at a friend's home when someone whispered the latest bad news: Two of my godmother's brothers had been gunned down by a group of Duvalier's men in Port-au-Prince. My godmother, and Manman had remained friends, from childhood. The murdered men belonged to a prominent Haitian family; some members had served in various high-ranking positions in the previous government. Their oldest brother became a candidate in the same 1957 Presidential elections as Francois Duvalier. There were wide allegations of fraud. Factions in the Haitian Army with foreign backing had conspired to have Duvalier declared the winner. Once in power, Duvalier set about hunting down the former presidential candidates, their families, and anyone who might speak up against his dictatorship, including the people who were responsible for his victory. One of the recently assassinated brothers in particular, while serving as Cabinet minister under the previous government, had befriended Papa. Many people, including my father respected this man and his brothers. My parents, sitting in a quiet living room among a genteel group of people, learned how their friends had been cornered and riddled with machinegun bullets, in a residential area of Port-au-Prince, by a band of Duvalier's assassins. Papa let out a cry: "Doc!" He said, meaning Francois, *Papa Doc*, Duvalier, " should not have done that!"

My father had with his unguarded words instantly condemned himself. He had enemies without being aware of how or when he had gotten them. They, however, had been waiting for an opportunity to destroy him. One of the guests on that Sunday afternoon reported Papa's comments, perhaps innocently; to someone else and eventually two powerful Duvalier officials in Les Cayes received that piece of information to use against my father by feeding into Duvalier's paranoia. While in the office of the Minister of Health Papa, although he did not suspect then that his old teacher was part of the conspiracy against him, realized that his enemies would soon know that he had been alerted and was on the run. Several people he had approached had backed away either out of fear for their own safety or because their were sold out to the Duvalierists. It was difficult to know whom to trust.

Again, God intervened through an acquaintance that worked at the Presidential palace. This woman risked her own life. Not many people dared to give even the impression of disagreeing with the dictator's methods. The trouble that my father was in gave evidence of this. Yet, this woman, who's duties included making up the president's bed approached Francois Duvalier, in his bedroom, on behalf of my father. Papa was a hard working dentist who did not participate in any political activities; he was not "opposing" his government she told Duvalier. She managed to convince the dictator that the accusations against my father were false. Miraculously, Duvalier agreed, pulled out a pen, and started to scribble a note to his Minister of Health to rescind his order. At that moment, the pen ran out of ink.

" I will finish this later". The president said.

The woman scrambled to find another pen, or something to complete the order. Instinct told her she might not have another opportunity to save my father's life. Again, miraculously, a soldier standing guard at the door of the president's bedroom had a pencil protruding out of his shirt pocket, which our friend pulled out. My father was waiting on a Port-au-Prince street corner for our benefactor who handed him the sheet of paper from the window of a taxicab as it drove her by. Papa returned to his former professor's office with Duvalier's handwritten half in ink and half in pencil memo. The Health Minister recognized his superior's handwriting and the blood drained out of his facial expression. My father understood then, that the man he had looked up to, as a mentor had been involved in the whole affair. A year or so later, a Tonton Macoute friend of the Health Minister would execute the later in front of his home in a hail of machine gun bullets. Duvalier's purges of his subordinates who fell from grace were notoriously bloody. Papa never told anyone in Les Cayes how he got his reprieve and for a while his enemies backed off, not sure about his "connections" to the political hierarchy. He, however, remained vigilant to interpret the countless incidents involving the Duvalierists who ruled our town. Although Papa escaped that particular plot, he was vulnerable to other traps. Life became too dangerous for the average male in his position.

By April of 1962, our escape plan was set. It was safer for my father that he left the country ahead of us, my parents secretly decided. My mother, my twin sisters, and I would then join him in a place called Liberia in Africa. We would probably never see Titonton and our cook again or the other people who lived with us. Pancho, my very own dog would not come with us it was also explained to me. He had been my faithful companion from the time I had raised him as a puppy. Worse, he would search in vain for us, not knowing why he had been abandoned. It was impossible to explain any of this to an animal. The loss of my dog was to be the beginning of more separations to come. We were in the middle of Easter season; school was closed for a few days. I think my parents timed our departure to give the impression that our family had gone somewhere in the countryside for a vacation.

The whole town of Les Cayes commemorated the death and burial of Jesus Christ on Good Friday and Holy Saturday. Tradition imposed an atmosphere of somber reflection. There were no parties, no dancing, and no activity, no hint of an irreverent attitude. My mother made sure that our household kept the prescribed dietary rule of no meat on Fridays for the several weeks before and during the *Holy Week*. The church rituals at the Cathedral in one of the town's squares laden with incense, a multitude of burning candles and the dirge-like sound of *a capella* choruses took several days. In Haiti Easter follows the Carnival season. Holy Week was the agreed upon time for all carnival revelers to show reverence for the church at least through a show of contrition for the excesses if not outright debauchery of the preceding weeks. No meat, sweet cakes, or candy could be eaten as a sacrifice to pay for one's sins. Our cook made wonderful fish dishes in those times so that I never experienced the prescribed suffering. All gaiety was tacitly forbidden during the remembrance of Christ's death. Colorful costumes had to be put away for more sober dress. Yet the tone of the carnival parades had changed, in the preceding years, the steps of the dancers had slowed, songs lacked spontaneity, and the crowd of the *Grande Rue* was thinner. The people had moved on to the processions of *Holy week*.

Only two sets of trusted family friends knew of our plans to leave town. We ate a meatless farewell dinner at the home of one of them in the quiet mood that was as much part of us as the town's and left early the next day on Easter Sunday, before the chorus of the Cathedral's massive bells announced the resurrection of Christ and the end of mourning. My sisters and I could not risk saying goodbye to any of our classmates for fear of being discovered and our family denounced to the *Duvalierists*. We were in the midst of a brain drain that would, during the late sixties and much of the seventies see most of the professionals and educated Haitians dead, in prison or in exile. In recent months, strange faces had replaced many of the familiar ones of my childhood surroundings. There were just a few secretive goodbyes.

One Cuban woman I worked with so many years later in Miami, Florida told me that she and her family made the decision to abandon their native land because an execution wall, literally, kept getting closer to their house. After seeing so many dead bodies pass by their home and, as in the case of my own family, counting the names on the un-official ever-increasing list of victims, we all ran away from our homes.

Back in the late fifties there was the rumor circulating about Les Cayes, in hushed tones, that some of the missing people had escaped to Africa to the country of Congo, later to be known for a while as Zaire, in the part of Africa where French was spoken. We on the other hand were going to Liberia, the *English* speaking part of Africa. I spoke Kreyol and French. My father had had to learn English in order to read his textbooks at the University in Port-au-Prince when he was studying Dentistry but since the lectures where in French, he did not have to *speak* English. My own acquaintance with that language was to determine that all the texts that I saw in my father's bookcase which held the characters *"the"* were out of reach of my voracious appetite to read everything around me. There were some Americans, mysterious strangers to me, living on a hilltop outside of town that I knew to be Protestants *"missionaries"*. I never quite understood what they were doing in our area. English was the language they spoke even though they were White like the Canadian and French Priests and nuns in our town. For quite some time, I thought anyone who spoke English was White. My father had a music record, which he sometimes played, of a man who sang beautifully in English. I remember my disbelief when my father insisted that the face of the Black man I saw on the sleeve of the record belonged to the same voice that sang in that English language. This is a Black man I was told, an American, and his name is Nat King Cole. Aside from the French and Canadian of the Catholic orders and a few Arab families, everyone around me was of African or of mixed descent. Everyone I knew spoke French and Kreyol except for the people from the United States who lived on the hilltop outside of town. Now the adults around me were saying that I was going to have to learn this strange tongue. This was supposed to be my main preoccupation for the three months my mother, sisters, and I spent with our relatives in Port-au-Prince.

Our last trip from our home to Port-au-Prince even without the turkeys was weighed down, as much with the crush of the few possessions we were able to load in the car as with our silent regrets. Francois Duvalier our ruler had declared that travelers had to have his own signature on their passport before being allowed to board a plane out of the country. Professionals were especially targeted. In my father's case, he had already been suspected of being a non-sympathizer of the government. It was a time when mere suspicion became accuser, judge, jury, and executioner. The dismantling of a people and a country was well underway.

Once in Port-au-Prince, it was imperative that my father made his escape before our absence was noticed in Les Cayes. There was no turning back. He had listed a business trip to New York City as his reason for going aboard. Now he needed the president of the country's personal permission to travel outside of the country. God intervened: Duvalier's current Chief of Staff had once been the military commander of our town. Both he and my father had frequented *La Glaciere* the local tavern where men idled away many a warm night in pre-Duvalier days in hot political discussions. The former commander, now Duvalier's top general and as rumor had it himself already on the endangered list, happened to have, at the time that my father approached him, a dinner engagement with his boss in the presidential palace. No one will ever known whether Francois Duvalier recognized my father's name when he signed his passport as that of the man whose death warrant he had first ordered and then repealed in a hastily scrawled note, two or three years earlier. The irrational workings of the dictator's mind precluded reasoning any of this out.

My father's escape had been planned outside of the then current "cloak and dagger" route. A few months earlier, I had gone to visit my father's former business partner, who was also my own godfather, in the Argentine Embassy in Port-au-Prince. The scene of my godfather, who had been a Senator in the National Assembly of Haiti, standing idle among several formerly very important Haitian men, all fully dressed wearing bedroom slippers and no necktie, in the Embassy's visitor's parlor troubled me. The Argentine Ambassador, I remember appeared nervous as he reminded his guest that it would be imprudent for him to walk my mother and I to the door, as custom dictated, because of the snipers Duvalier was known to have posted around the refugee filled compounds. Foreign Embassies in Port-au-Prince remained filled to capacity with asylum seekers during Duvalier's reign of terror. A few Embassies, particularly that of the United States would refuse shelter to people running for their lives who would then be exposed to the Duvalierists. Leaving the country to take refuge abroad was a sure sign of treason against the government. In Haiti, we knew that the United States government shipped arms to Port-au-Prince and trained military officers for Francois Duvalier. Washington officials could not acknowledge the carnage in Haiti without admitting their own guilt. As an adult in the early eighties I met the wife of an American Military Attaché who had served in Haiti during the nineteen sixties. This woman told me how her husband had repeatedly reported to his superiors what he was witnessing in the country. No one in the American State Department wanted to hear about Duvalier's atrocities. As his wife remembered, the Military Attaché was transferred to another post outside of Haiti.

    One of my aunts was arrested, as she was about to step unto the Argentine Embassy's ground to obtain information for her daughter, a university student who was planning to study abroad. She was able to contact the appropriate "someone" and was released the same day. My cousin told me many years later, that she had mapped out an escape trajectory, which involved climbing down from her home into a dry river bed gorge and scaling a wall, to a house that she knew belonged to French Diplomats. She was about sixteen years old at the time. When she did go into the Argentine Embassy to see about her studies she found two former classmates living there. The girls' uncle had caused their entire family to be placed on Duvalier's hit list. They were trapped in the country. There were stories of ambushes set on the road to the airport for those who had left their hiding place even when holding a *"sauf conduite"* or safe passage document from Duvalier. Many a brave foreign diplomat risked their own lives to escort their charges in Embassy cars all the way up to the doors of out bound airplanes. Some would be exiles wore disguises. *Tonton Macoutes* had been known to stop departing planes to search them and pull off passengers. So we were relieved to see the airplane which my father boarded fly off into the sky. He was safe!

I had worried about Papa for longer than I could remember. In Les Cayes, we had no phone so when he was late coming home my mother and I worried that the *Tontons Macoutes* had picked him up. We both constantly reminded him to be careful. In a small town, however, my father's non-participation in Duvalierist social functions was reason enough to brand him an "anti-Duvalierist". By that time, I had experienced the futility of trying to remain neutral in a fascist environment. In 1963 the year after we left our home, in the wake of another Duvalierist blood-bath in Port-au-Prince, a church full of Les Cayes' residents were arrested while attending a memorial Mass for one murdered family. The elderly couple was shot to death with their servants, a visitor and even their dogs, at their home which had then been set ablaze with their grandson still in his crib. The couple's niece and her husband were my parents' closest friends and godparents to one of my twin sisters. Both of my parents would most certainly have attended that fateful Mass in Les Cayes.

My feelings about my father's departure were ambivalent in that although I wanted him to be safe I missed him tremendously. I missed the comfort of his large brown hand wrapped around mine. There was also the troubling uncertainty of not knowing how long our separation would last. I had been taught to pray at prescribed times and at that to recite ritualistic phrases addressed to a distant God. No one had told me that I could talk to Him and tell Him how I felt. The idea that prayer was in fact a conversation with God was foreign to me. Instead I poured out my child's heart into a journal I had started the previous January so intense was my need to voice my anguish. As an adult when I hear the words of the old hymn: *"oh what needless pain we bear"*, I sometimes think about that period when I first became conscious of the pains of life and how I could have cried on God's shoulder if I had known that He was available.

While living in Port-au-Prince with our relatives, waiting to leave Haiti to join my father in exile, I attempted to learn English. The new school my sisters and I attended taught English among other subjects that our provincial education had not exposed us to. Our transition from life in a rural town to the bustling hostile world of a much larger city in the middle of the school year did not go well. The other students saw us as strange and backwards. We immediately became the target of taunts. Tikite, the smallest of my twin sisters would often land in an altercation with some much larger child and inevitably involve me rushing in to her defense. My energies were focused on the almost daily schoolyard fights, not on my lessons and certainly not on the learning of English. I grew angry. One particular girl and I fought everyday for one week even jumping at each other inside a classroom. I was threatened with expulsion from the school, a disaster for a ten years old Haitian girl from a respected family. Most of the time, I played the part of the obedient well-behaved child but my inner thoughts alternated between anxiety and anger. I was separated from my father, the women who had nurtured me in our home in Les Cayes, Titonton, and I had lost my dog and my home. In our family's temporary shelter in Port-au-Prince, my mother's sisters and my grandfather were inhospitable, dictatorial, my cousins and I quarreled and avoided speaking to each other; the atmosphere in the house was tense.

My aunts and my mother made almost daily trips to various governmental offices, cajoling, bribing: wearing down employees with their persistence to no avail. There was no exit visa for a woman and children obviously en route to join a husband and father who had left the land. Lower level government employees used the situation to their advantage to line their pockets with payments for services that they could not deliver. I continued to quarrel with my older cousins. For the first time in my life communication with my father took weeks because of the Haitian government censorship of the mail. As four months passed without the necessary visas to leave the country, I feared that I might never see my father again. I felt the walls of a hostile world pressing in on me. My parents, like many others in a similar situation had taken a calculated risk when they decided that my father would leave the country ahead of us. If the whole family had applied for permission to travel outside of the country together, we might have aroused the government officials' suspicions. Stories circulated about families who had tried to leave Haiti and of the disastrous consequences when they had failed. Besides, at the time of his departure our father had no source of income, no offer of a job.

My godfather, my father's former partner who had preceded us in exile, after a stint in the Argentine embassy, lived in a remote area in Liberia in West Africa and with his own difficulties could not help Papa. In Port-au-Prince, my parents had met with the Liberian ambassador who had told them that his country needed dentists but had failed to produce any concrete assistance in securing an actual position there. A chance encounter at the Port-au-Prince airport on the day Papa left with a man who had a brother already living in Liberia, eventually led to a job as a French teacher after my father arrived in Africa. I hoped that when we were reunited with my father all would be well. Meanwhile my mind was too busy conjuring up disasters to even be curious about our trip. I felt unwanted in my relatives' house, had no home to go back to, and did not know much about where we would eventually end up. The sense of loss that had begun to hang about my world grew, intensified, giving birth to a new feeling of alienation.

In Port-au-Prince, Papa Gus my maternal and only living grandfather gave me a very old book titled *Anglais sans maitre* a sort of manual to teach oneself English without the help of a teacher. He was renowned to have taught himself several languages using his collection of *Sans Maitre* books. The one he gave me I was to find out when I tried to follow its instructions was full of archaic words. I was most ill prepared to venture into the English-speaking world.

Another divine intervention led my aunt to a contact who approached a high level government official literally as the later walked down the steps of a public building. The official used the back of our friend as a surface to lean on in order to sign Manman's passport. " This is good for two days at the most", he warned as he hurried off. One of my aunts scrambled to get our plane tickets while the other helped Manman and I pack our suitcases.

The day had finally arrived for us to join my father in Africa. I could not even enjoy the realization that we had gone past the ubiquitous pistol packing, dark-shaded *Tontons Macoutes* at the Port-au-Prince airport without incident. My aged grandfather, with a premonition that he would never see us again was in tears as he accompanied us to the last chain-link fence separating the tarmac on which those departing walked away from the ones left behind. Papa Gus' stern silvery crispness crumpled as he tried to lecture my sisters and I on how we should behave in a foreign country. He had a gift for me, as the oldest, of a silver American coin worth five cents with which he advised me to buy a cup of coffee when I passed through the city of New York. Auguste Toulme the Haitian patriot who risked death so often in the political debacles of his country had given his approval for his offspring to abandon the motherland. We were the first to go. In later years as my cousins followed one by one our grandfather had written to the young men: " Do not come back, you have no future in Haiti". There was the sound of anguish all around us in the tall ceiling hall of the Port-au-Prince airport. Men buried their faces in handkerchiefs. Women simply allowed their tears to flow down their cheeks. Children screamed as they were pulled away from the arms of a parent. People called out to each other sobbing as the distance between the exiles and their home increased.

These were different times in Haitian life. In the past when individuals fled the country, there was always the hope that they would return home as soon as the government changed. The brutality of this current totalitarian regime, left few illusions about the future, foreign Embassies in Port-au-Prince remained full of political refugees and whole families abandoned their homes to seek asylum abroad. I do not remember if ManLillie, my grandmother understood that we were saying goodbye. Perhaps she thought we had gone back to Les Cayes and would reappear again at the end of a few months. I am not sure if her worn out mind could still grasp a concept such as the length of time. None of us ever saw her again. This too was to be a final parting for my grandfather and I. My mother and sisters returned to Haiti twelve years later, he died two years after their visit at the age of ninety-four. Twenty-three years would pass before my first trip back to my native land.

On August 6, 1962 my mother, twin sisters and I boarded a Pan Am Airline plane out of Haiti and were immediately plunged into a sea of English words, right, left and everywhere. We were surprised to find out that another family we knew from Les Cayes was on the same flight as us. They had not known of our secret plans as we did not know of theirs. The mother and her three young daughters were en route to join the father in the Republic of Congo also in Africa. He was a lawyer and teacher who dodged the Duvalierists' assassins and was later recognized by the government of Congo/Zaire and honored for his services to that country.

The first stop on our trip was in Kingston, Jamaica in the midst of that Island's celebration of its first day as an independent nation. It was strange to see people walking about, talking, and laughing in obvious excitement all in an apparent communal festive mood; a contrast to the desperate scene we had just left in our own country. Later that day we journeyed on to New York City U.S.A. Each twin clutched a life size infant doll, the one toy they had been allowed to bring. The girls had received so many instructions about staying close to my mother and I that they did not dare show the curiosity one might expect of seven years old children. As for me at age ten, I had long ceased to be a child.

7

For years, I never thought back to that very long day but the emotions stirred up in me colored my perceptions of traveling. Even much into adulthood I would dread taking a plane to anywhere and going away from home. My aunt Andree gave me a book to take to my new home titled *Les Deux Nigauds*, which told the tale of two country bumpkins who leave the French countryside to visit the large city of Paris. My mother and I smiled at the misadventures of *Simplicie* and *Innocent* but our anxiety and fear level was too high at the time to allow us the see any humor in our own adventure. There was for instance the hatbox incident. Immediately upon deplaning, as it is now called, in New York City's Idle Wild Airport (now known as JFK International) Manman the twins and I set out to find our luggage. This included the hatbox that had been part of Manman's trousseau when she married twelve years earlier and had sat in the corner of an armoire untouched and untested, awaiting a voyage of importance. When our parents made the dangerous decision to leave town secretly our mother had nevertheless had her hat maker, using a dated copy of a Sears Roebuck catalogue for inspiration, produce a sizeable collection to fill up her hatbox. She had never met any Liberian lady, but she wanted to make sure the people in her new home received the right impression of a Haitian one. Haitian women of a certain social status wore hats in public. I don't remember how it happened that day so long ago, but the stitching around Manman's hatbox unraveled spilling its contents and there was a sudden avalanche of hats on the airport floor as my sisters and I scurried about the legs of the crowd trying to corral the precious headdresses. Since we did not speak their language, we were immune to the string of expletives directed at us by the people in the American airport.

Uncle *ChonChon* a cousin of my father, a kind man whose face wore an expression of mild surprise as he met us at the airport shepherded us throughout our two days stay in Manhattan. The hushed voices of Les Cayes were very far away. Even the incessant bustle of Port-au-Prince had not prepared me for the cacophonic din of this huge city. My first ride ever in an elevator had catapulted me up a twelve stories high perch overlooking a confusing, alien world. I tried to sort out the many stories I had heard about The United States of America. It is a big country I was told, full of innumerable perils. I took stock of the tall buildings, fast moving and fast talking people and herded my sisters close to our mother's skirt. There was a lot of food everywhere. I ate everything I was offered. We stayed two days in Manhattan, New York awaiting our connecting flight to Europe and then Africa. The hotel room had many new things that we did not touch for fear of causing some mishap.

By the end of our second day in New York, I grew restless. My curiosity eventually got the better of my apprehension and I decided to cross the street that I could see from our hotel room window to investigate a colorful spot that intrigued me. The large, thick French-English dictionary I had, another gift from my grandfather, was too cumbersome to take on my excursion so I looked up the English translation for some of the words that I thought I would need and set forth. I do not remember whether I did not look up the word *apple* or that in my excitement simply forgot it, yet procuring some of that fruit was the whole object of my sortie into this foreign world. In the United

States, I had been told; one can buy big, red, juicy apples. I had never tasted one of them. The apples that grew in the coldest parts of Haiti's mountains were small, sour and the imported ones were too expensive to buy. Now I had the opportunity to get one of those prized big, red, juicy apples. By then I had found out that the silver five cents coin my grandfather had given me was not enough to buy a cup of coffee which cost ten cents in this city. Manman had given me a few American coins. I hoped these would be enough to make this transaction. The roar of cars barreling down the street did not deter me. I temporarily forgot my old world where I knew each car in town and its owner. My destination with its stands of green, red, yellow, purple vegetation was alluring. It was time to put my stock of English vocabulary words to work.

" Round"! I breathed to the shopkeeper who greeted me.

"Red" I said.

The man and I gestured at each other. I repeated the English words I had carefully selected:

"red, round!"

The American's face beamed in recognition, he swung around on his heels, his hands digging into the rows of foliage lifting up a bunch of radishes.

" Red? Round? " I shook my head.

He looked disappointed but quickly went back to the bulging stands. We crisscrossed the rows of boxes, up and down the aisles, searching.

"Red?" He would say.

"Round?" he pleaded. I shook my head at tomatoes.

The man's arm would sink as I refused the sweet peppers and every red produce that he lifted up in the air. Crossing the street back to the hotel empty handed I suddenly felt the weight of the rows of waiting cars straining as if a gargantuan beast held on a leash ready to break past the thick walls of the buildings framing the pedestrian cross-walk.

The next stop on our trip was in Lisbon Portugal where we spent a few hours awaiting our plane flight to Africa. As I remember, the Portuguese airport was made primarily of wood with fans so high up in the ceiling to give little comfort in the August heat. Manman had sewn traveling outfits for all of us and the stiffness of the unfamiliar garments added to our discomfort. The twins were my responsibility. I had taken charge of them from the time that they were born and now made sure that their matching bell shaped straw hats stayed put and the life size infant dolls they each carried did not get lost. My own hat was a white-feathered contraption, long outgrown by a much older cousin that swirled from one side of my head to the other.

Suddenly a very loud, tall, and large boned woman sprang up into the little space that I had carved out in the crowded waiting room for my sisters and I. She was addressing us I realized. Her large black eyes were focused on the twins. Hers was the first dark-skinned face I noted out of the sea of white European travelers at the airport. Even though this stranger had smooth caramel colored skin, she did not speak Kreyol or French. Within seconds I knew from a recollection of the sounds I had heard on the Pan American planes that we had traveled on the past few days, in Kingston, Jamaica, and New York City that this woman spoke English. I quickly lined up the twins behind me. Our mother had wandered out of sight.

"Me"

I recited as soon as the flow of words from the stranger stopped.

"No speaking..."

She was leaning forward and I glared at her as she tried to bob her head past mine to inspect the twins,

"Engleesh!" I must have shouted.

"Ah!"

The English-speaking woman said, laughing. Another torrent of English sounds spilled out of her red-painted lips.

I realized that she was an American and possibly thought that we were too.

"Me- no- speaking- Engleesh"

I repeated slowly. Somehow, the fierceness of my desperate use of the bulk of my English vocabulary seemed only to invite the woman to bombard me with her own inexhaustible stock of words.

"Me no speaking E-n-g-l-ee-ss-h"!

The pitch of my voice rose. Another colored woman with white- framed bow-shaped eyeglasses a traveling companion to my inquisitor touched her by the elbow and said something that made the latter back away from me. My mother had also suddenly reappeared. Manman was as bad an English scholar as me in those days. She grinned at the two women and through a series of gestures was able to convince them that "me" truly did not speak English!

Up in the air on the plane from Lisbon to Dakar, Senegal our first stop in Africa, the flight attendants passed blankets around the aircraft cabin for the night. My own skin was steadily getting hotter. Manman said that I had eaten too much. She also wished that those people seated at the back of the plane would stop talking so much. I started to wonder about those voices in the rows behind us. The lights around the aircraft cabin were dimmed but my ears recognized the sound: English! I also knew whose English. Although there were several rows of seats separating us, I remained on the alert for another attack by the American woman from Lisbon airport.

Dakar was a short flight away from Monrovia, the capital of Liberia. Our father had found a job teaching French at an American College a three hours drive into the African jungle at a place called Suakoko. I remember my first sight of the African rain forest. From the plane's window, the ground looked like a thick, plush carpet with an occasional missing chunk where a village had been carved out. Particularly I remember the intense green and hot smell of the wet, red soil when we stepped out of the plane's door. It was the rainy season, which we were told lasted sixth months. This land was very different from the Caribbean. Even though I was exhausted, I realized that people were laughing among themselves and no one appeared to be whispering. I was told that the people spoke many dialects but everyone addressed us in that incomprehensible English. There were bright print cloths in the mixture of African and European dress worn by the crowd in the Monrovia airport. Our Papa was in that crowd. Tears flowed: our small family was reunited. The emotions that had traipsed through my mind from the time on Easter Sunday in Les Cayes, Haiti back in April when we left our home through the wretchedness of the previous weeks and long journey had taken their toll. By the time we reached our destination I was disoriented, in a daze, my head throbbed and my skin glowed. Manman still insisted that my feverish skin and glassy eyes were due to indigestion. The last leg of our trip from Monrovia to Cuttington College our new home in Suakoko was a blur as Papa, who had bought his first new car, a Volkswagen Beetle, sped through the copper colored clay road that parted the thick jungle bush.

Furnished housing was part of the faculty contract, which suited us since we had only been able to carry very few of our personal belongings out of Haiti and had no funds to equip a home. The house assigned to our family was a prefabricated structure that sat on stilts and had an apartment attached to it that was occupied by an unmarried physics professor from India who sang opera in the shower. All the rooms had a uniform checkered black and red linoleum floor and were sparsely furnished with a few lightweight mismatched pieces. There were no headboards for the aluminum single beds, each covered by a brown military surplus blanket that our parents pushed together to replace their large mahogany one left behind in Les Cayes. There had not been room in our suitcases for our embroidered linen and so many more things that had adorned our home in Les Cayes. In our reduced circumstances, the twins and I had to share a bedroom and were cautioned not to play outside. This is the African jungle, we were told. Yet, I noticed how the very modern stood side by side with the primitive. People carried plastic pails instead of gourds or weaved baskets into their mud huts. There were no beasts of burden. In Haiti, the women in the countryside strapped their babies to their sides whereas the African ones had theirs on their backs. Here the thatched mud walled huts were round instead of square. Often I caught myself expecting to hear Kreyol spoken. It was in the faces of the people: a woman wrapped in a multi-colored single sheet *Lapa* or a group of children waving at our car from the side of the road.

Our section of the College campus had once served as barracks to a contingent of American army advisors. The middle-aged German couple in the house to our right raised chicken. Whether European, American, African, or Asian, everyone at Cuttington College spoke English although; as I was to find out, most did not necessarily understand each other. There was a custom at Cuttington College to introduce newly arrived faculty to the campus community by having them eat all of their meals for the first two weeks with already settled families. We therefore ate breakfast, lunch, and dinner in a different home everyday as we explored our new surroundings. It was a great help for our mother who had to suddenly set up a household with no servants in unfamiliar terrain. Each family we visited had a set of advice for newcomers. We received practical tips on how to bake our own bread (the nearest bakery was three hours away) and how to protect our clothes from the heavy humidity that permeated the air six months out of the year. One hundred watts light bulbs had to be left turned on around the clock in all the clothes closets to combat the heavy mold and mildew.

The campus was self sufficient with its own electricity and water supply. There was even an Elementary School for faculty children. The twins and I would only have to walk from the house assigned to us across the college soccer field to attend the school.

This new world was multi-national. One family of four, I remember, who came from Israel seemed vaguely familiar. I could not communicate with the children, a boy, and girl about my age and noticed how the four of them remained very close to each other wherever they went. Both parents looked preoccupied, eyes darting from side to side, surveying their surroundings. They were older than my parents; must have had their children very late in life Manman speculated, she also thought that the older couple were survivors of something, called the Holocaust.

Toward the end of our initiation tour, we had a dinner engagement with the Gantu family. Dr Gantu and his wife were English speaking native Liberians. As we waited, the twins and I in our now customary huddle on a couch, it became apparent that the Gantus were waiting for additional guests before ushering us in their dining room. Mrs. Gantu had engaged Manman in a soundless exchange of gestures and grins while her husband answered their front door. There was a sudden cry of recognition from one of the newly arrived guests as she stepped into the living room. The twins and I were the obvious reason for the woman's excitement. My heart rate accelerated, leaped, bounded to a full gallop. I felt my head spin. The tall woman from Lisbon had found us! She at once immersed the whole company of adults in a flurry of words that tripped over each other as heads turned back and forth in our direction. The twins and I hung on to our position on the sofa. I warily eyed the American woman's seemingly unbounded enthusiasm. Even her quieter traveling companion had been contaminated, her eyes gleaming behind her white-framed glasses. Soon our father too joined in the exchange as introductions were made. Papa eventually remembered to translate for the twins, Manman and I, his big bass voice booming out in French:

" This is Madame Weber, your *Directrice*, the Principal of your school!"

He had more news.

" Imagine, Madame Weber has just now promised to personally teach you girls the English!"

IV. Refugee

"And she bare him a son, and he called his name Gershom: for he said I have been a stranger in a strange land" Exodus 2:22

8

According to Webster's Encyclopedic Unabridged Dictionary of the English Language, a Refugee is *one who flees for refuge or safety especially to a foreign country as in time of political upheaval, war.* Francois Duvalier and his cohorts made war on the people of Haiti for what would stretch into thirty years. There is no tally, for those who, like us had to leave Haiti. We were the ones with enough money to buy Visas and plane tickets. Others would follow in rickety, overcrowded sailboats. Many would never reach a friendly shore, thousands would be sent back. Everything our family owned had been relinquished except for a few suitcases full of clothing and my father's newly purchased Dental equipment. The country of Haiti had lost another of its industrious trained professional and hardworking homemaker. Dozens of people who depended on my parents for employment, health care, nurture, and comfort had lost their source of help. Whatever my sisters and I would become was also lost to the land. The people of Liberia smiled and greeted us with great ceremony but we were on their soil and there were specific rules of conduct prescribed for foreigners. For one all of our possessions were considered public property.

"Don't ask a Liberian to return anything he took from you" was the admonition. The locals were hunter-gatherers we were told, not agriculturalists. They also boiled a lot of fruit that Haitians allow to ripen on trees so we never ate one of any of the watermelons, pineapples or papayas Manman planted. There were no fences around the College Campus faculty and staff houses so our laundry set out to dry on a line at the back of our house was fair game for any passerby. I remember a young girl grinning at me with the customary local bonhomie while I sat in our yard on a stool in front of a tubful of clothes I was scrubbing with a washboard. She wore a red-checkered top with a distinctive pair of white buttons and white pockets that Manman had sewed for me. It was one of my favorites. Knowing the drill, I kept my mouth shut. Foreigners, I was told, could be given a "green card" on the whim of any local magistrate and expulsed from the country. One major taboo was for a foreigner to even suggest that a Liberian citizen had done anything wrong. Liberia, in 1962, was ruled by a dictatorship but staying out of trouble was relatively easier than in Haiti. There was a clear demarcation between the descendants of the freed American Slaves who colonized the land and founded the Republic of Liberia in the mid eighteen hundreds, and the indigenous people. At that point, I was ignorant of the history of the Back to Africa movement of those days. The Kpelle tribe, whose women wore the colorful single sheet *lapa* wrapped around their bodies, some wore a voluminous matching head wrap, was the predominant group around the Suakoko and Gbanga area. Another group I noticed were the tall robed Mandingo men, nomads who drove large trucks in from neighboring Guinea on the way to the Monrovia Port or walked through the open air markets with large bales of cloth on their heads. An elite made up of the Western dressed American descendants controlled the wealth and government of the country. The President of the country was reelected automatically at the end of each of his terms. No one opposed him. The Liberian constituents effectively had no right to vote for their government officials. This, was none of our business.

    The college campus; where my father had found employment as a French teacher, was in the middle of the West

African Jungle a three hours drive from the capital city. When the bush was cleared to build the College campus many of its natural inhabitants stayed on. The African version of scorpions and other insects were very large and we had to keep a constant look out for venomous snakes that particularly favored laundry baskets. Because of the snakes, we could not simply sit in the clearing at the back of the house or walk into the brush. A beautiful but lethal cassava snake, slithered into a group of children playing at my sisters' birthday party once undeterred by the noise. It was spotted in time. Someone always had to be on guard against the snakes and scorpions. Our windows were screened and we had heavy springs to snap the doors shut. There were endemic species of parasitic worms that made it necessary for us to keep the soles of our feet away from the floor; we had to wear sandals even in the shower. "What a country!" My parents would sigh. I missed the feel of the cool mosaic tile and cement floors of our house and the almond leaves carpeting of the garden in Les Cayes.

There was no bakery in Suakoko, no market with the type of food we ate. In Monrovia, the Capital city, all the restaurants used the heavy orange, distinctively fragrant palm tree oil in whatever they cooked using even more red peppers than our cooks back home. Everything was different. This was the first home I remembered living in that had no walls enclosing the surrounding property. Here we lived in plain sight of the world. I worried still about our secrets. No one had told me not to.

In Liberia, West Africa I entered the Protestant world. There were apparently no Catholics in the area. Shortly before we fled from Haiti to live in Liberia, my mother was told that *Tante Fifi* her sister-in-law had commented to someone that since we were going to an all-Protestant country, we would have to attend the Episcopalian College Chapel. A race emerged. In the midst of our somewhat clandestine travel preparations, my mother lobbied for and obtained a special waiver from a Catholic Bishop in Port-au-Prince so that my younger sisters (who had not yet attained the right age) would receive "*first communion*" in the Catholic Church before leaving Haiti. Manman made sure that my protestant aunt received a picture of the twins dressed in their all-white, ribbon-laced fineries in commemoration of the occasion.

As Manman and I worked in our new kitchen, she revealed even more secrets. One by one, she recalled the stories from her childhood, life with her sisters, and one brother. I became her confidante. My grandfather had other children whose existence my mother ignored until she had reached adulthood. One brother and sister were close in age to her youngest sister. As adults, they developed a loving relationship with each other that lasted a lifetime. Another brother, who was younger than my cousin Jerry and whose mother had died, found it harder to fit in with my grandfather as a distant parent and no sibling with the authority to look after him. Manman had a great deal of information about her family as well as my father's. She and Papa lived across the street from each other in Port-au-Prince before their marriage and it seemed that while he was busy in school and later at work, his own mother was giving family history lessons to his fiancée. Now I became the recipient of the unedited ancestral archives. When news came of the living Manman and I pored over the mysterious letters that her sisters wrote to her. Manman and her sisters rarely referred to anyone by their real name: Duvalierist spies censored the mail in and out of Haiti. Therefore my mother and my aunts developed their own coded messages, using references from their past that they hoped would be familiar to each other, inventing others over the next twelve years. They had had some practice at this since Manman' marriage and departure for Les Cayes. Writing and sending letters even within the country had always been a practice fraught with danger. We were told that the Haitian government had spies wherever there was a community of expatriates. Our family was careful not to speak about the things we had seen back home in the company of strangers.

My younger sisters with the natural pliancy of younger children were quick to adapt to our new surroundings, but I was already an adult in the skin of a ten years old. Change unsettled me. I missed our family outings in Gelee, when my sisters and I spent the day in the river in the countryside around Les Cayes, or dozed off under the shade of a mango tree. I missed Madame Trenet's, the baker who lived across the street from us in Les Cayes, fresh out of the oven molasses cookies. On the American style College campus, there were no street vendors with baskets full of deep fried *griot*, fried plantain and coconut treats. I missed the smell of the sea and gentle Caribbean breeze. When we drove three hours to the African coast, the huge waves of the Atlantic Ocean discouraged swimming. In this country, it rained torrentially for six months and then the red copper clay ground remained dry for the rest of the year. Everything would be covered with a thick layer of red dust. I did not feel the tug of ancestral roots since I was too unsophisticated to have cultivated a more romantic view of Africa. The round mud walled thatched houses were not attached to small farms and fenced off crops. There were no wandering cattle seen all over the Haitian countryside no horses or donkeys in the whole country! The sound of the people's native language sounded very much like *Kreyol*, but I could not understand its meaning. So many faces looked so familiar and yet were so foreign. I was locked into my own personal world and could not appreciate the brilliant colors and vibrancy of both people and country.

I felt a certain malaise, at my new school and the Suakoko campus. The language barrier that isolated me from my peers and the irritation caused by the teasing of my new classmates were only part of the problem. In Haiti, I had

had a very close relationship with my father, following him to soccer games or on fishing trips almost weekly. In anticipating our reunion, I had so many thoughts of the world we would share again. I hoped there would be something like our trips to *Gelee* or *Ducis*, or the long walks along the shaded banks of *L'Ilet*. Even if there were no fishing trips to *Cayes a L'eau* or *Baie du Mesle* with Papa's jovial friends surely now we would have a place all to ourselves where we could sit close to each other on a quiet evening and listen to old stories being retold. We had only been separated four months, but everything had changed. An indefinite wave swept over us even as we tried to find some of our old routine. In recent months, we had spent more and more time behind the walls of our home in Les Cayes huddling against the outside world even as we feared separation. I had yearned for "home" while in transit in Port-au-Prince even as I had forced myself to do as the adults said and tried not to think about our house on the *Rue du Petit Gabion*. Now, the closeness Papa and I had shared had been lost. The fabric of our lives was torn in unrecognizable shreds.

 I would not miss my old school with its rules, the nuns, and constant threat of falling into trouble and I was happy not to have to return to the Port-au-Prince school. What I had not anticipated was how I would feel about the loss of the familiar. It was odd not to meet anyone for days, and weeks, to communicate with. Worse, no one knew my name. I stopped myself from thinking about poor Pancho during the day. "Don't mention his name," I was told. "You will make the children (my sisters) cry." At night, I would awaken suddenly, thinking that it was because of the thumping sound of his tail hitting the floor under my bed. I did not know how to behave and who to ask for instructions on how I should conduct myself. My sisters were too young and my parents too old. It seemed to me that everyone I met assumed that I was thinking a certain way when I knew differently. In our culture children are not supposed to share their thoughts. Even when a child appeared sad or cried the adults in our world dismissed it as some sort of bad behavior. We were expert at keeping secrets from outsiders as a matter of survival. No one had given me permission to express my thoughts, and to grieve.

The Episcopalian denomination had founded and administered the College my father worked for. *Tante* Fifi, my protestant aunt, had her wish. We had no choice but to attend the only church service available to us. I liked to hear the hymns sung in the Episcopalian church service even though I could not join in since they were in English. I was troubled, however, by what I noticed was an apparent lack of reverence in the relaxed attitude of the congregants. In Les Cayes, my old home, people tiptoed in the sanctuary in silence and genuflected upon entering, leaving, or crossing from one side of the assembly to the other. Women wore head coverings and high necklines. Now that I was older, I looked at the behavior of the churchgoers within our College campus community with a critical eye. I felt that the conduct of some of the women I observed was flirtatious at least by my own provincial standards. The loss of the religious rituals of my Catholic upbringing added to the void I was becoming aware of. At that point, I did not know much about the history of race relations in the United States. In Haiti, I had been told that White Americans hated Black people. Some of the White missionaries I met in Africa reinforced my suspicions as to their attitude towards their non-White neighbors. There was a lack of sincere kindness and an abundance of palpable hypocrisy in their interactions. The foundations of my cynicism towards church attendees had been laid.

Papa and Manman were anxious about the future. As I sensed their disillusions, it frightened me. They had fought for their children and home against family members, religious clerics, official, and un-official government enforcers.

Now they were buckling under the weight of the unfairness of life. Under the circumstances, it was impossible for my father to have obtained a more equitable price for the property in Les Cayes. He had been forced to abandon his share of the dental practice as well as his Haitian government employee pension. My father's new employers did not keep their promises to him either. Although he never voiced it, I felt the discouragement of my hard-working father as he sought to establish a dental practice in the face of the obstacles set up by the same people who had agreed to allow him to practice dentistry. My father's salary at the College was not enough to sustain a family of five. Although Papa had learned English by reading Dentistry textbooks, he had great difficult at first when he had to lecture in that language. The proceeds from the secret sale of our house in Les Cayes had been just enough to pay for our plane fares to Africa and to cover the cost of a modest set of dental equipment. I was responsible enough to work as a dental assistant when school was out, on occasion wielding a small mallet to help coax a recalcitrant molar out of a patient's jaw. There was no other dentist within a wide radius of our campus. Papa treated the local people living in the surrounding areas, who did not work for the College, free of charge whenever they needed it.

We did have some paying clients. I remember a group of Lebanese traders who drove up to our doorstep in a cloud of red dust one Sunday after traveling some distance with a woman who was intermittently screaming in pain. Papa did not work on Sundays but took care of emergencies. The travelers filled up the small rooms of the office attached to our house speaking in Arabic seemingly all at once until my father walked into the room having hastily changed the shirt he had been wearing for his white work smock. There was total silence as the men exchanged glances with each other, then an eruption of more Arabic broken by a mournful shriek from the woman with the toothache. Apparently, no one had told these people that this dentist, living in the middle of an African jungle, was a black man.

The coded letters my mother's sisters in Port-au-Prince wrote to her took weeks to reach us. News filtering in was distressing during the sixties as politically motivated assassinations and repression escalated in Haiti. Some events were shocking enough to earn a place in the back pages of the American *Newsweek* or *Times* magazines. We clung to the faint hope that the world would do something about the savagery of the Duvalierist regime. My mother wondered aloud why the Pope was not "saying anything" about so much killing. Among the names of " the disappeared " were an increasing number of people we had known. The husband of a close family friend had been led away to his death in front of their nine years old son. Duvalierists were insatiable in their lust for blood, money, and power. People in the spread out community of Haitian exiles in Liberia were wary of each other. There were reports of reprisals in Haiti that proved that Duvalierist spies infiltrated Haitian groups abroad. Something said or done on foreign soil could spell doom for a relative back in Haiti. We worried about family members left in the old country.

Eventually we heard that Edouard my mother's seventeen years old nephew who had been "picked up " by the *Tontons Macoutes* had also vanished.

I remembered the last time I had seen Doudou, as he was known in the family, an exuberant handsome very black skinned then sixteen years old with a charming grin, revving up the throttle of his motorcycle in my aunt's driveway to the admiration of my sisters and I. He was the oldest of my uncle Adalbert's children and the apple of his eye. Doudou and a group of friends, the youngest of which was twelve, had somehow encountered a group of Duvalier's armed thugs. For years, my uncle Adalbert was made to believe that his son was alive in one of Duvalier's dungeons. As for thousands of other fathers, he had no recourse and was powerless to help his son. Someone eventually told my uncle that his son had been executed shortly after his capture. Uncle Adalbert never recovered from his grief in the thirty-five years remaining to his own life. Even those who survived the Duvalierist prisons, no one knew which prisons or how many were incarcerated, remained scarred physically and emotionally. Several of the ones I would meet across the years in exile harbored deep in the recesses of their eyes the taint of memories that they dared not reveal to any man. A sense of impending doom was to cling to me whenever I thought of my old home of Haiti for many years to come.

At the College campus Elementary School in Suakoko, the other students, especially two older boys, a tall lanky Black American with his friend a Liberian boy ridiculed me whenever I tried to speak. Even though the mood I was in tended more towards silence. My Haitian upbringing was at odds with the rest of my new world. The situation was even worse than at the Port-au-Prince school a few weeks earlier. I was now in a mixed school after seven years in an all girl school and had no verbal ability to deal with the teasing of non-Haitian boys. No adult appeared to notice the teasing of the boys or my growing anger. The immersion method of learning English was not successful for me. No one with the exception of my immediate family spoke a language I could understand. The suspicion and the fear I had picked up in my former home hung on to me, unwanted yet too familiar to be shaken off. I scrunched up my face in a defensive scowl that became permanent. The American and Liberian boys laughed at me at every turn. I could not understand what they said but was furious at their obvious teasing. By the year's end, our teacher gave me a few lines to read in a Christmas play. I had no idea what the English words meant. No one spoke French at the school. My attempts at reading the script had my tormentors rolling with laughter at my expense. The teacher removed me from the play. I felt humiliated.

The school placed me in the fifth grade because I was almost eleven years old, and the twins in the first grade, but for the two years that I spent in the Suakoko elementary school, no one taught me English or anything else. There was a wide difference between the French and American systems of Mathematics. My parents were unfamiliar with the American version and did not have any French material to continue my instruction in the subject. In Haiti I had had to have private tutoring, to keep up with the Math taught in my class there and was now somewhat relieved that the whole matter had dropped out of my life. By the time, I had learned enough English to be required to study Math, it was too late, and I never understood the subject ever again.

No one my age lived close enough for me to interact with. My classmates in fact the entire student body, with the exception of a few very young children all lived in a hostel on another American Mission campus. They came to and left from school in a bus. Their parents were Christian missionaries somewhere in Liberia. Several black American children and one Liberian all seemed to be living in perfect harmony with their white friends. I did not fit in.

"Fix your face"

Papa told me one day. I was surprised that he and Manman had noticed; I had not even realized that I walked around with a tight and angry expression on my face. I took up a new pastime retreating from the outside world into myself, spending hours daydreaming. At school one teacher monitored several classes in the small Elementary school. Since there was no uniform required of the student body, we even wore sandals with our casual clothes. The curriculum was a correspondence course geared to American children living abroad. Besides the United States, students came from other nations around the world but seemed to have mastered enough English to participate in the classroom.

Three American girls at the school did not laugh at me. It took me a while to notice that their smiles were friendly. I was hungry for a smile in my direction. For so long, it seemed to me, that no one liked me. My face relaxed when Gabrielle, Jeannette, and Margie were around. The other students appeared to tease me less in their presence. At times, they gave me small presents; an eraser, a piece of candy wrapped in colorful paper, or a length of ribbon. I treasured each gesture. We could not communicate in words but the kindness of these three girls had reached into my cage with a soothing touch.

For the first year, I was left to my own devices at school. I had access to the College Library and its foreign languages section. No one at school noticed the French book I hid inside my English Textbook while the other students wrote in their notebooks. The second year, a new teacher, a tall red bearded Texan whose bow legged strides reminded me of the cowboys I had seen in movies, took an interest in me. He started to look at my assignments and writing an "A" or "B" letter in the margin of my notebook. In Haiti, students were graded on a scale of ten to zero but I had learned that in this setting an "A" was a "ten". I never understood what the textbook or the assignment book said. For some time, however, fearful of appearing idle I had taken to scanning the questions on the assignments and then looking for words that appeared in both the questions and Textbook. When I had found a match, I would rewrite the entire paragraph from the textbook in the space provided for the answer. In Haiti I had had to recite, lengthy passages memorized the night before for the daily classroom recitations. Here no one quizzed me. Gone also was the threat of corporal punishment. The kindness of the new teacher, however, motivated me to start translating my assignments. He even gave me an individual project: a report on my native country of Haiti that I wrote and read aloud in French to the other students seated in the classroom. The teacher led the applause from my reluctant classmates.

I read as many books as I could borrow from the College's library and even (hiding in a brightly lit clothes closet) my father's collection of the French classics that I was not allowed to read, because of their adult topics. My father bought my sisters and I a box full of Children's English classics from a European mail order store at around the time that I had run out of French books to read. I then embarked on my first English book, a novel titled *Lorna Doone* that I read from cover to cover using an English-French dictionary to look up all the words on the first few pages. As I penciled in the French translation in the margin of the pages I used the dictionary less. At home, we kept 100 watts light bulbs lit in the clothes closets because of the extremely high humidity of the African rain forest climate. This made for a perfect reading spot, especially at night while the rest of the family slept.

In Liberia, we no longer had live-in servants. Local men hired out to cook for families, which my mother never grew accustomed to since in our culture only women belonged in the kitchen. Girls were also expected to take care of not only their younger siblings but also the children of neighbors. My mother was offended when people offered me money to baby sit. Neighbors are supposed to help each other out she felt. She had spent her life before her marriage raising her niece, nephews and babysitting an endless stream of children. Word of this somehow reached the campus community so my free services were in high demand. The twins were too happy to have more playmates. Again, because I was a Haitian girl and the oldest child, household chores filled the rest of my days.

9

In 1964, when I was twelve years old, my parents, noticed that I was not getting an education at the campus Elementary School. I was still unable to communicate in English. They announced that I would go to England to a boarding school. I did not want to leave my family. Even though another Haitian girl a year younger, whose father worked with the United Nations at a neighboring compound, was to be my traveling companion, I was apprehensive about taking a trip so far from my family. Our destination was a Catholic convent school located in a small village in the English countryside so once again I was Catholic. Brick walls and the gray skies hanging low over that first winter in England after the bright colors of Africa stirred up an instant dislike in me for my new surroundings. The school was, as some of the English novels I had started to read would say, a "gloomy and cheerless place".

The nuns I had known as a child in Haiti, with the exception of one sadistic Frenchwoman, had generally been polite if not always kind. There was an aura of mystery about these particular women as they glided across the classroom floors in their immaculate white habits. They had servants so appeared rested and could enforce a strict discipline for the schoolchildren and remain serene. One did not have to live with them. The English nuns in contrast, worked from sun up to sundown tending vegetable gardens, raising chicken and rabbits, carrying buckets of coal to fill the heating stoves around the compound in addition to teaching in the school. Most of them were past middle age so the one nun who appeared to be in her mid thirties did most of the physical work. This same woman taught math, and was in charge of making sure that our group of ten to fifteen girls remained within the bounds of the activities prescribed for us. Whenever we saw her approaching us, my new companions and I expected something unpleasant to happen. It was as if the folds of the nun's worn, black, patched up habit were laden with ill will towards us.

Now that I was living with a group of girls my own age I was ill at ease. The language and cultural barrier was even more acute. The oldest girl among us maintained an air of superiority and had a small retinue of followers which included my younger Haitian traveling companion, who spoke English fluently and had from her extensive experience living in various countries better socializing skills. At twelve years old, all of my very brief friendships had been prescribed, monitored. My accent whenever I attempted to speak in English made people laugh which easily offended me. I was alone.

Although I could cook, sew, wash clothes with a wash board, iron them, diaper, bathe and feed babies and braid the hair of small children, no one had taught me how to untangle and braid my own hair. One of our servants in Haiti or my mother once, we moved to Africa, had always wrestled three long, thick braids from my coarse mane. In the Haitian culture, children have to have permission from their elders to do things such as play with one's own hair. Cutting some of it off was unthinkable even though we could see that women and girls in Africa with the same hair texture as mine wore their hair short in what was being picked up then in the United States as an "Afro" hairdo. We were Haitian, that meant scalp close haircuts for the boys, and braids for girls deemed too young to wear their hair hot ironed straight. At around the time boys were allowed to exchange knee length pants for full length ones girls could take off their ankle socks and hair ribbons. I had by age twelve reached up to my adult height but the twins and I continued to wear our matching outfits and ribbon laced hairdos. Shortly before I boarded the plane for Europe my mother took me to a hairdresser in the city of Monrovia and for the first time in my life had my hair straightened with a hot iron. She also gave me a pair of stockings to wear on the trip. I had never worn stockings either and had a terrible time keeping them and the two makeshift garters Manman had made out of two thin elastics from sliding down to my ankles whenever I walked. Once at the school I was issued a uniform outfit, at least I was dressed like everyone else around me. Except for my hair, that is. The Rainforest climate in Liberia had dispatched the hairdresser's labors before I even left town. More humidity awaited me in England causing my hair to shrink into tight impenetrable curls. Soon I simply learned to ignore the odd-shaped tangled wad on top of my head.

One of the students at the convent school was particularly curious about me. The girl, a year or two older than I, had long, platinum blond loose curls and clear blue eyes with a hint of pink on both cheeks. Her pale skin made me almost think that she reminded me of a doll until I noticed that she was not pretty. After one of our short holidays, she returned to school from a visit to her home in the English countryside with a book to show me. It contained derogatory remarks about my hair, my lips, my skin, and my race. This girl had searched for and brought a book authored by some racist and sought to prove to me that I belonged to a race that was inferior to her own.

I had lived in predominantly Black societies in Haiti and Liberia. The College president my father worked for and the majority of the professors, including my own father were

Black, so were the presidents of both countries and all of the professionals whom I knew. In fact, the only authority figures I was aware of at this stage in my life, who were White were some of the nuns and priests in Haiti and other foreigners I had read about in newspapers or were colleagues of my father at the African College. As a child, one of my first recollections was of the respect the people in our community had for both my parents and their families. Even though the world pointed to Haiti as poverty ridden and primitive by the industrialized world's standards, the average middle class child growing up in the mid sixties in our country was taught to be very proud of our culture and of the Black race.

I did not communicate all this to this young racist but with my limited English told her that my father was a dentist and a college professor and then asked her what her father, whom I knew was a manual laborer did for a living. She kept her distance from me after that. Years later I remember watching a Black activist in a Television interview in the United States and remember her comments about how she reacted to racists attempts to make her feel inferior. This woman stated that her parents had raised their children with so much positive reinforcement about themselves that by the time she encountered racist views it was too late for her to begin to feel inferior. Her own sense of self-worth had been set. As for me, I had started to develop an intolerant view of bullies.

Once a week the whole student body at the convent school filed two by two, in formation, through the village in which the school was situated to the nearby Catholic Church to attend "confession". There was a chapel in the school and the parish priest came to say Mass at 5:00 AM, every other morning. We the "boarders" as we were known, did not have to leave the compound to attend the required Church rituals, which included saying the Rosary while on our knees every afternoon. The nuns at the school had confiscated most of our personal possessions. We lived every single day in uniform, sat on back less wooden benches to eat the meager portions doled out to us, in enforced silence three times a day. Our last meal was the traditional English " tea" which the nuns had pared down to a half a slice of buttered bread and one teaspoon of jam. A woman teacher who bought overripe or mostly rotten fruit for us administered our pocket money. We were never taken to a store so I quickly understood that this was yet another scheme to extract more money from our parents. Since our mail, even to and from our parents was read none of us had any recourse to complain.

We heated water for our water bottles to warm our beds and slept in thermal underwear and blankets in the winter. The nuns told us that it was too dangerous to leave the gas heater turned on in the dormitory during the night while we slept. Even the English girls who were used to the climate were always cold. The youngest lay teacher a woman in her early forties, who came in from the village to teach English, kept her beige sheep skin-lined coat and matching boots on to protect herself against the cold draft in our classroom. We were allowed to heat up one pitcher of water to wash ourselves with in the morning before attending five am Mass. We wore the same hounds tooth pattern wool uniform dress, gray wool stockings and gray wool sweater everyday. Once a week we were issued a clean detachable white collar and were allowed to heat up more water to hand wash our flannel underwear. In my Haitian home, I would be punished for not taking a shower and changing my clothes daily. I won a seat close to the potbellied stove in our classroom when I developed a painful swelling condition the English call *chilblains* in my fingertips and toes. The one benefit of this experience was that I became cured of bed wetting after the very first episode.

Wetting my bed had been a great source of anguish to me for as long as I could remember. Our maids in Les Cayes had tried all manner of folk remedies to no avail. When I stayed with relative in Port-au-Prince and in Furcy, I always had the use of a plastic sheet to protect my bedding and enough people around to wake me up for nocturnal potty trips. My chamber pot was always close by. In Liberia, I was the laundress and could count on the twins' loyalty not to divulge my secret. Sneaking a chamber pot and plastic bed sheet past the vigilance of an English Convent Boarding School nun was, however, another matter. At first, I tried not drinking any water (the only available drink) after our late afternoon "tea". Waking up, once I had tucked myself under the flannel sheets with the hot water bottle, proved to be my undoing. The wood planks of the old house creaked under my weight as I felt my way in the dark, past my classmates' beds to unlatch the door of the dorm in order to reach the refrigerated closet toilet down the hallway. I was afraid of the dark.

When it happened, I steeled myself into adopting a composure that robbed my roommates of the fun they could have had. Instead they had to contend themselves with a few muffled sounds as word of the source of the stench emanating from my rolled up sheets spread around the rows of closely set metal beds. The expression on the face of the nun in charge of my dormitory group was grim. She escorted me down to the cellar and left me there with a bucket of cold water and bar of soap. My teeth were shattering and my hands soon grew numb. There was no washboard or clothes wringer. Washing and wringing ice-cold water from a set of flannel sheets in a dank cellar was an experience I was determined to avoid from then on.

I set out to maintain the distance that already existed between the other boarders and I. It was well known that I could not *speak* English. My understanding of the language, however, had grown immensely during the past few days after my arrival in England. Many of the words I had so far seen on the printed page had become recognizable thanks to the English's pronunciation of their language. When I heard the *t* sound in *butter* instead of a *d*, the printed form leapt back to memory. I loved to read and noticed the similarities, (thanks to the Norman conquest of the early Britons) between a very sizeable number of French and English words.

After resisting it, the learning of English became my solace. My companions and I were not allowed to read our textbooks outside of the scheduled classes and homework sessions. The books remained in the classroom. Most were dull, antiquated and in worse condition than those, I had left in Les Cayes. For one, all of the few illustrations were black and white sketches, even the textbook for Botany. An old woman who was in a perpetual state of irritation, as she mumbled on at length, wagging her crooked finger at the rows of twelve years old girls, taught that subject. This woman was also our art mistress. Each student had a small tray of watercolors, one, or two thin brushes, a jar of water, and a book with picture outlines that we had to fill in. Our teacher, I soon understood had an idiosyncratic dislike for the color white. She inspected each of our paint trays to make sure that, as she had instructed, the small container of white paint had been dug out and discarded. I had lived with people who splashed uninhibited strokes of vibrant colors on wood, cloth, metal and created, an enormous variety of the most whimsical objects, simply for their own pleasures. One of our neighbors, shortly before I had left Suakoko had taught me to calculate proportions in sketching the human figure free hand. In my two years of self-study in Suakoko, I had read an entire bookcase of the French classics and had a broader frame of reference for my imagination than any adult suspected.

I yearned for the end of each of my school periods and for the arrival of the sheep skinned clad English teacher. As she paced about the classroom or perched on a tall stool, reciting, with the prowess of a seasoned Thespian, *The Charge of The Light Brigade,* or *The Destruction of Sennacharib,* I hung on to her every word. That was my introduction to Tennyson and

Byron and the nineteenth century poets. There were streaks of gold in Mrs. Clarke's shoulder length light brown hair and a certain quality to the tone of her voice that elevated her moderately stout frame, her country garb and gave credence to her depictions of the characters we studied. She was disappointed by her students 'lack of interest, their refusal to learn the poems she assigned, but cheerfully moved on into another recitation. I never had the courage to tell her that I had memorized every line of Robert Browning's *My Last Duchess*, or that I privately spoke the words of *"O my Luve is like a red, red rose, That's newly sprung in June; O my luve is like the melodie, That's sweetly played in tune"* and other verses penned by Robert Burns, out of earshot. The memory of my Christmas Play failure at the Suakoko School was still fresh. I was, however, beginning a love affair with the sound of English words.

During school vacations, a chartered bus would take us boarders out of the Convent grounds for the same outing: The Wipsnade Zoo, to look at a sad group of wild animals languishing in metal cages. At school attending Mass, every other morning, and saying the Rosary, every afternoon was one of the methods used for keeping us occupied. There was, in the student dining room/recreation room one large locked closet, which contained the entire collection of books available for casual reading. I soon found out why no one took the trouble of enticing the nun who monitored our activities to unlock the book closet. The books were so dull that most of the worm infested pages remained un-separated, just as they had left their publishers. By that time, I had taught myself how to read English, sufficiently well. Reading had long become a way for me to escape my surroundings.

I felt trapped and increasingly angry. As the oldest child in a Haitian family, I had been expected to obey rules and comply with restrictions and mostly never questioned their necessity. I had, however, also been very busy when not sitting at a classroom desk. Never had my life, both in Haiti and Liberia, been so regulated by meaningless, fruitless routines. Compliance with the Duvalierists most arbitrary rules had the purpose of, as I saw it staying out of trouble in order to protect my family. There was no useful purpose for me to be in this place. I was angry with my parents, convinced that they were punishing me. With no books to feed my imagination and with no skills or opportunity to interact with the other girls around me, my daydreams took on a sour note. In my family home, besides my household chores I had always had time to myself to sketch, or write (I kept a journal form age ten on) or read. I was not looking to be entertained with childish games. My childhood had long slipped away unnoticed. Boarding School, however, right after the easygoing atmosphere I experienced in Suakoko and Liberia seemed to me to be an unreasonable imposition.

The monotony of my daily life and forced inactivity tortured my mind and gave me time to mull over my discontent. For the first time in my life, I noticed that I was unhappy. Rain or shine even during flooding season in Haiti when there were no eggs to be bought, my mother always made me a birthday cake called a *massepain* that we cut after family and friends had sung *"Bon anniversaire"*. In Liberia, we had eggs so Manman made real cakes for my eleven and twelfth birthdays. This year there was no celebration, instead my thirteenth birthday ushered in a period of deep sadness. Stern-faced strangers prescribed every moment of my life. I lived in a virtual fishbowl whishing that I could sit on the floor or even in an armchair instead of the backless benches that we were restricted to. Haiti and Liberia were both far away. My younger sisters too were far away. They had been my constant companions since their birth. I ached for the sound of their voices. So much of my previous daily routine involved them. I knew that they were too afraid to irritate our parents with questions about when I would return. We had no telephone contact. Our mail to and from the convent was opened and read by the nuns, I could not feel free to communicate with my family. It puzzled me that my parents would allow these strangers to censor the letters we exchanged between each other. I felt isolated.

The weight of my loneliness increased daily. So did my anger. I wanted to strike out at my parents. One night, I climbed out of the school dormitory's window, intent on ending my life. I did not think about the eternity of Hell. In my anger, I wanted to deprive the nuns of the power to control my life. I did not write a suicide note. No one, I imagined, would care about what I had to say; my parents would probably lie to my sisters about my whereabouts. The thought that I would enslave my immortal soul to an indescribably horrible and inescapable fate never crossed my mind. I had almost drowned once as a child in Haiti in the river at *Gelee*. Right before Papa had pulled me out of the water, I had felt such peace. Everything around me had been blue and quiet then as I drifted into unconsciousness. There were times when I had thought with regret that I should have been left alone in my watery grave and allowed to slip away. Yet, eternal peace is only found in heaven. Had I died then I was surely headed for Hell. I noticed, however, how close the ground was to the second story ledge of my dormitory window, I surmised that I would just hurt myself if I jumped down and went back to bed. God was still watching over me.

Up until my convent school experience, I had been a devout Catholic, following my mother's lead in participating in all the required rituals and had a deep sense of awe of God. I knew the stories of ancient Biblical characters like Noah, Abraham, Isaac, and Jacob, even Jonah and King David without really knowing the *real* story of what their relationship with God meant. It was those same stories that caused my misgivings about the attention and homage I was encouraged to give to the statues of dead "saints". I had a small French book of instructions for a child attending Mass that contained some excerpts from the New Testament without reference to their source or their context. My youthful mind was open to receive faith but no spiritual food was forthcoming.

At the Convent school, the meanness I witnessed in the nuns on a daily basis placed them, in my mind, in a different category of religious leaders. I soon became aware that they were lax about things like the dietary rules and prescribed feast days while emphasizing the ones that served their purposes. It served their purpose to have the entire student body kneeling in the Chapel to say the Rosary every afternoon. We attended the 5:00AM Mass every other day again because it was convenient for their schedule. One nun could monitor the whole student body during these periods of enforced silence. We took our meals in a long dining hall that doubled as our recreation room. I never saw any toys for the younger students, anything in the field in the school compound. My school in Les Cayes, Haiti at least had a set of swings and a seesaw. Later I wondered how this English municipality in 1964 would allow a school to keep scores of girls age three to sixteen penned up with no daily physical activity other than walking around a walled compound and playing tag. I was in the group of older students who had a later curfew than the younger girls. After our homework was done, we played cards sitting on the same backless wooden benches around the same rectangular tables we ate our meals on. This, I thought, must be what a Women's prison or a Reformatory institution must be like. My parents as so many others in Haiti, dreamed of having their children educated in Europe, and believed that girls were better educated in Convent schools. They had also been reared not to question religious authorities, so their main advice to me was to stay out of trouble. I, however, was in crisis.

The Convent school rules inevitably collided with my earlier training as a Catholic. I had been taught and sincerely believed that to take communion without having confessed to a priest and received absolution from the same was a mortal sin. The nun's routine was to escort us through the village to the local parish church for the regularly scheduled "confession" every Saturday afternoon declaring that no one would sin again and would remain in a state of "absolution" until communion time at the Sunday morning Mass. They had a rule however that *every* one, including all students without exception, would receive communion at *every* Mass. Mass was said by the priest who came over to the little chapel within the school compound every other morning. My sins, especially the secret ones were many and I could not remain in a state of "absolution" with just one chance at confession, for an entire week.

I do not remember how many times I was punished for simply staying silently in the pew, not taking communion. My explanations were ignored. I did not want to commit a mortal sin: that is taking communion without being in a "state of absolution". I remember that I was sincere in my convictions. By then years of attending Catechism classes in Haiti had taught me to differentiate between relatively minor and what, according to Catholic doctrine, were mortal sins. Murder was a mortal sin, so was taking communion in an unworthy state. For all my shortcomings, I had a deep reverence for and feared God. The ritual in that English school chapel was identical to the countless ceremonies I had participated in my native Haiti even to the Latin phrases which the priest and worshipers recited. Even after my two years-long excursions into the Protestant church services, the solemnity of the Catholic Mass had not diminished for me. I had never taken communion in the Episcopalian services my family and I had attended in Suakoko. My mother had out of earshot of my Dad instructed my sisters and I to abstain because it was not "the real thing". My father took communion alone in the Protestant service. As he had abstained when he attended a Catholic Mass with our family in Haiti, we were the ones not participating in the Lord's super. Now the English nuns were ordering me to take communion when I had told them that I was not in a "state of absolution" which was a requirement of the Catholic Church for everyone who participated in the sacred rite. I was shocked at, what I saw as, the sacrilegious attitude of the nuns. Yet, they were my leaders in matters of religion.

Although I had never read the Bible, I knew about the Ten Commandments that God gave to Moses the ancient leader of the Jewish people. I also knew that I could not obey my superiors when they commanded me to sin. I was also, however, under the assumption that I had to receive forgiveness for my sins through a man instead of simply addressing myself directly to God in the name of His son Jesus. This conflict caused me much anguish, further fueling my ever-present anger. With no one to speak to about it, I poured out my feelings in my diary.

The six or eight other girls who shared a dormitory and I had no privacy and knew full well that the nuns routinely searched the small crate that served as a bed stand to hold the very few personal items we were allowed to keep with us. Keeping my small transistor pocket radio, a tiny flashlight and a copy of a *Georgette Heyer* novel that by now my only friend Margaret, a girl who attended the day school smuggled in to me, had taken months of daily vigilance. So many things were forbidden to my companions and I that we were caught in an intricate web of subterfuge to maintain some measure of personal freedom. My life had so far been spent in countries ruled by dictatorships, even though I experienced more freedom in Africa. This brand of fascism at the convent school, especially because it controlled every aspect of my daily routine, particularly irritated me.

During the first few months at the convent, my diary too had never been found. Now I deliberately placed my journal, written in French, which I knew the English nuns to read although they never attempted to speak that language to me, behind the flimsy curtain of my nightstand crate. I poured out my feelings about them, filling up pages of my notebook with the most venomous script I could muster. Predictably, my notebook disappeared within a day or so. I braced myself for retribution. There was no remorse on my part. I felt good about striking at my enemies even if they pretended that nothing had happened. The nuns' facial expressions remained unchanged.

The nun in charge of my group of students addressed each one of us in the same cold stern voice. She did not usually join in our idle chatter during our recreation time. Instead, she sat on the bench at one end of the long table, arms folded inside her sleeves occasionally nodding to sleep for a brief moment. This was the end of a laborious day for her. None of us ever dared engage her in conversation. We were compelled to occupy our recreation time by playing Dominoes, Parcheesi, Chinese Checkers, and a variety of card games. I developed an intense dislike for any form of board games. Most times, I longed for an armchair and a good storybook. I do not remember any real competition among the board game players. No one was allowed to simply sit out this tedious routine. Sometimes while our nun on guard slept someone in our group would try to entertain the others by miming some absurdities. Often the reluctant players would simply lean on their elbows on the plastic coated table, head propped in idle hands, allowing their minds to drift. My own mind was soon preoccupied with speculations about the punishment that would be meted out to me. Solitary confinement, even in the dank rat infested attic I had spent two weeks in for contracting the measles some months before, would be worth the satisfaction of having hurt my jailers.

Two days passed without anything being said, then three, one week, two; nothing. By the third and fourth week, I was anxious to be called in for the show down. I had seen how the slightest hint of criticism against any of the school staff was always met with swift retaliation. Although they did not use corporal punishment, the nuns were quite resourceful disciplinarians. I could not believe that they would content themselves with simply confiscating my notebook and I was right.

One evening as our group of girls lined up outside the dining hall for our customary walk to the dormitory, the nun escorting us motioned me to stand aside. My companions filed past me without a glance; I had not confided in anyone about the diary. I wondered about the unusual timing. Punishments were not generally administered, late at night, the earlier in the day, the better so the offender would have the most number of hours to reflect on her misdeeds without the solace of sleep. *Sister*, as the nuns were addressed, did not utter a word as she stood next to me. A substitute nun appeared from one of the doors in the hall to accompany the remaining girls for their bedtime routine. I was to be handled personally by the nun in charge of our group. She kept silent. We walked toward the front parlor of the convent, which I had never seen, stepping in the dimly lit room where I immediately recognized the tall black-clad figure of the Reverend Mother, directress of the school.

The Reverend Mother stood stiffly erect in spite of the much-wrinkled skin of her face and gnarled hands. Aside from the white bonnet, lining of the thick black head veil that framed her face every part of her was shrouded in black cloth that swept the polished wood floor. On a rare occasion, she had addressed us as students to deliver a stern warning or other. Once she had lectured us, brandishing in one hand a newspaper, which she repeatedly stabbed with her crooked index finger. It was an article with the picture of a woman wearing what was being hailed as a modern trend: a nun's habit with the hemline a few inches below the knee and head covering showing the wearer's hair. The reverend mother, her face contorted with fury had declared that such an abomination would never be seen in her convent. Now she greeted me with an icy stare.

"Your father has sent you a ticket to fly home to Africa", She said.

" You will be leaving in the morning".

My heart sank. This is not about the journal, I thought. Something must have happened at home. Did someone in my family die? I knew not to expect any trace of sympathy in this place even if something bad had happened to me but wondered about the palpable malevolence of the nun under what I thought must be tragic circumstances. No, someone did not die in my family. The expression on the Reverend Mother's face was one of pure hatred. Her eyes half buried in the folds of her wrinkles locked unto mine as she told me her reason for summoning me to her parlor: she was expelling me from her school. My journal had been mailed to my parents with instructions for them to immediately send me a plane ticket to fly home. I understood then why it had taken so long for me to find out about the confiscated journal. Mail between England and Suakoko took weeks. I was to spend the night in a separate room far away from any of the other students so that I could not infect them before leaving in the morning for the airport.

"You are a virus!"

The Reverend Mother hissed as she dismissed me from her presence. I was torn between the relief that I felt about finally leaving the convent school and worry about how my parents were reacting to the fact that I had been expelled from school. My parents had refused to listen to my pleas to leave and would suspect that I had deliberately set myself up to be sent home. In truth, I had not thought that my punishment would be that severe. The stigma attached to being expelled was more than I had bargained for. I was not given a school report card although the school year had almost ended. My solo trip from Europe back to Africa was very long. I never again kept a journal until I reached my mid-twenties when a College Course in America required it.

In Suakoko, my parents to my surprise were sympathetic when I told them about the conditions at the convent. The Haitian girl I had gone to school with soon returned at the end of the school year and corroborated my story. Her parents decided that she would not go back to that school. Papa, however, applied to another convent school in England for me to attend in the fall. I begged to go to Dakar in nearby Senegal where I could resume my studies in French. My father was adamant; I was to finish my education in English. I think my parents were beginning to plan our eventually moving to the United States instead of returning to the still-troubled Haiti. At that point, I did not want to see England and another Catholic nun ever again. I also dreaded the thought of going to school although I still loved reading. Three years had passed since my studies had been interrupted. Even if I learned enough English, I was afraid that I would be far behind any other student my age. The thought of being labeled as backward filled me with dread. For months while in England, I had thought about killing myself; having concluded that life was not worth living. God had, however, provided Margaret an English girl my age a day student at the convent, to befriend me. She lived with her parents in the village in which the school was located and smuggled gifts of batteries for my contraband transistor radio and would replace my reading flashlights and *Georgette Heyer* novels whenever one was confiscated. Most of all It was her sense of humor, I remember, that kept me from drowning into my despair. Like the three young American girls at the Suakoko Elementary school, Margaret had thrown me a lifeline.

Neither one of my parents realized the impact that my first Boarding school experience had on my life. I had gone off to school, a devout young girl with deep religious convictions and returned home a cynic. No one around me noticed the change. Clear however, in my mind is that this was the turning point in my spiritual life. From then on and up until my late twenties I viewed everyone who practiced any religion as self-serving hypocrites. I also had a baggage of misinformation about God from my earlier childhood. What did all the rituals I had carefully participated in Les Cayes and in the Chapel at Suakoko do for me? It was then that I decided, at the age of thirteen, around about my ill-planned suicide attempt that I would become "independent" of religion and therefore God.

My father's application for me to another English Catholic Boarding school was immediately rejected because of my expulsion from the Convent School. I remember that I was standing at our kitchen sink with a towel wrapped around my newly washed hair peeling potatoes when the rejection letter came. It was during the rainy season when everything around was swollen and damp even inside the house where clotheslines sagged with wet laundry. I even remember the red shorts and white blouse I had on that day. My father became very angry and said some harsh things to me. I

"Was trouble!"

My father said. My mother said nothing. A large lump of sadness settled into the pit of my chest. No one wanted me. I did not want any Boarding school in a far away inhospitable place to want me, but once again, I no longer had a home to return to.

V. A Single Blue Suitcase; Well Traveled.

"As a bird that wandereth from her nest, so is a man that wandereth from his place."
Proverbs 27:8(KJV)

10

It cost several English Pounds the sales clerk in the store in Yeovil, Somerset, England told me. She could see from my uniform, my skin tone, and accent that I was one of those foreigners from the Park School For Girls.

"It is a very strong suitcase" the English woman said slowly, "It will not break easily".

She instinctively simplified her vocabulary, taking care to enunciate every word, to the basic information needed to secure the sale. The English sales clerk was right, I could see that the thick plastic sides of the suitcase were unbending. Manman had told me to buy a very strong suitcase, even if I paid a lot of money for it. I liked the color of the suitcase, a shade of blue that pulled towards gray. It reminded me of the blue uniform worn by the Pan American Airlines Stewardesses on the plane I traveled on the first time I left home. The mirror-like gleaming silver toned hinges and clasps on the hard plastic case at the front, back and sides were strong. Inside, the lining was of a lighter shade of soft blue satin with a matching zippered pouch. There were two sets of darker blue sturdy ribbon straps with shiny silver metal buckles to secure my belongings from within and keep them from being tossed about.

The Park School for Girls in Yeovil Somerset was a vastly different English Boarding school from the Catholic Convent School I had attended the previous year. It was run by a Protestant denomination. As a Boarder, I attended Church services twice every Sundays in addition to Sunday school and must have heard passages from the Bible read, but my heart remained closed. If a gospel message was preached, I never heard it. Each time I sat in a sanctuary of any sort, I immediately separated myself from my surroundings by plunging my mind into an elaborate daydream. I did attend a Billy Graham Evangelistic Crusade in London, watching the event on a large projection screen, and remember being touched by the message but no one followed up with me and I quickly dismissed the experience.

My new all girls school, allowed me to experience the fellowship of girls my own age who came from various cultural backgrounds. There was a good mix of other girls of varying skin tones, some of whom had as incomprehensible an accent as mine. For the first time in a long time, no one laughed at me when I spoke in English. My fear of falling behind academically was unfounded because I had a wealth of knowledge about a variety of subjects. This was the fruit of my insatiable reading habit. It also trained my mind to understand new material and retain information at a faster pace than most of my peers. The study of Mathematics, however, remained my Nemesis. The school had a small Student Magazine and I felt encouraged enough to submit a funny piece for publication about a visit to the dentist. When it was published, there was congratulatory amazement all around. Everyone thought that I did not know English. In truth I read and wrote, English better than most of the other students because I read a good number of English books since I did not have any French ones available. I also had some recognition from my peers for my artistic talents thanks to Nicole one of our neighbors in Africa while I lived there, who was French and taught me how to sketch.

At my new school, I also played sports for the first time. Once a week, in accordance with the English school system our entire student body had the exclusive run of the town's swimming pool for various activities. For a short time, I joined the Diving team until a bad jump convinced me that I was not focused enough for that particular sport. We even had three tennis courts right on the grounds of our "house". The student body was housed with one adult in several buildings that were named for various British heroes. I lived with about twenty other girls in "Kingston House" one of the residences of the Boarding school. Two or three girls shared a bedroom. Classrooms and the dining hall in adjoining buildings had a modern heating system. Everyone was entitled to two tub baths per week, there was a sink with hot and cold running water in each room, and we had more than enough to eat. It was a huge improvement from the Convent school of the previous year. For one we were allowed to go out for walks outside of the school compound. In addition, as a member of the older students, I could go shopping with a companion for two hours in the town shops every Saturday morning.

During the two weeks vacation at Easter, the school rented a house at the Seaside resort town of Sandbanks for the students, like myself who could not travel back to relatives or home. One teacher would serve as housemother and bring some members of her family along. We lived in an ordinary house and walked barefoot in the sand, and mingled with other vacationers in our own everyday clothes. Side trips to the surroundings enlivened our days. Old castles and historic areas were my favorite haunts. I developed a new appreciation for England.

We were at the height of Beatle mania in Europe. The Common Room in Kingston House had a large table pushed against a corner wall that had a mountain of black round forty-five inch playing records of every song the Beatles and other popular Pop groups produced. A student would buy the latest hit song, play it incessantly, and then toss it on the common pile. The record player played nonstop. We sang along and tried within the confines of our school uniform to imitate the fashion of the time, rolling up the waistband of our skirts (at least when outside of the school) to make them look like the then fashionable "mini" skirts. While some of my classmates complained about having to trim their hair above their eyebrows instead of being allowed to have it hang over their eyes in the current Beatle fashion, I was content.

Even with the day students, our class size averaged ten to twelve students. The individual attention I received from several teachers in those three years was to make a profound impression on me. Our art mistress was a very creative, easy going long legged young woman who looked like a model with her mini skirt and long brown haircut Beatle style. She was the only faculty member dressed in fashionable clothes. The loft above an old stable served as an art studio and became one of my favorite places. One Christmas we made dozens of large papier-mâché colored balls for a garland trellis we hung across the ceiling of the school's dining hall.

We traveled on buses to play in Field Hockey matches against other schools and they came to play on our turf. Both teams always sat down to a civil "tea" after the games. Mostly our teams did not bring home any trophies but I enjoyed the events. Our coach was one of the most cheerful and kind individual I have ever met. Often when I think of the words "encourager" and "constructive empowering" our coach comes to my mind. She did not condone slothfulness, but I never saw her being unfair or rude.

In fact most of the teachers were nurturing: There was my Math teacher who invited me to stay with her and her family after school was out and I was waiting for a visa to move to the United States. Another teacher shepherded my companions and I, to unusual field trips made memorable by her enthusiasm for history and the countless stories she had about the Battle Of Britain she witnessed in her youth. This teacher had maintained her shapely diminutive figure and an entire wardrobe of elegantly tailored vintage skirt suits with matching accessories. Grey hair pulled neatly in a bun or a sweeping nineteen-forties hairdo framed her small face that frequently glowed in the retelling of a cherished memory.

As an adult, I have reflected on the importance of teachers in the life of a child. The women who taught at the Park School for Girls in the Town of Yeovil England deposited something in me that withstood the onslaught of the negative forces I was to later experience. It was to the patience and skill of a retired teacher in Yeovil that I owe my entry into the world of English speakers. For four years, I had taught myself with books but had failed to communicate intelligibly in English. I was still afraid of ridicule and said as little as possible. I was told that a retired teacher, who lived in an apartment across the street from the school grounds, had offered to tutor any of the foreign students who needed help learning English. She was a very short large-boned woman who looked to be in her seventies with soft silk-like hair, the color of white daisies. As with several of the older teacher at the Park, she spent a good deal of time living in her past but was very efficient in using up our hour-long session to correcting my diction. Her method was simple. We read aloud taking turns, from one of the English Classics and discussed the story, the author, and anything that related to them. There was a reassuring, soothing quality to the lilt in her quiet voice. She never laughed at me. No one else was around to mock me. I read aloud and eventually spoke fearlessly. Every Friday for about a year or more I ran (she was a stickler for time and scolded gently when I came late) up to my tutor's "flat", as English apartments are called, with my hair still wet from the weekly session at the school swimming activities. There I would find a large cup of tea poured out on a tray with two cookies or English "biscuits" for me to refresh myself with before plunging into the world of Dickens, Shakespeare, and others.

I do remember buying a bouquet of white daisies once for my Tutor when she broke her arm but am sure, to my chagrin, that I never fully expressed my appreciation, in the insouciance of youth, to this precious woman. There is no price tag for what she did. What she gave me was more than English lessons. I was like a toddler taking her first steps into a new world. My parents, with their love and nurturing, had laid an important foundation that had started to erode under the baggage of self-doubt I had accumulated in recent years. The three blond American girls at the Suakoko Elementary school, Margaret my one friend in Yeovil, Mr. Rudholm, the red-bearded teacher from Texas and now this genteel English woman helped me at a crucial time in my life. When I graduated from Nursing school several years later in the United States, my Class Year Book, enumerating the talent for which each graduate was distinguished, had next to my name the words "good diction": a belated tribute to the labors of Miss Philips, my English tutor.

Many times in our English schoolgirl talks some of my classmates, from India, Bahrain, Persia, China, the Caribbean, other parts of Europe, and Africa had reflected on the future, anticipating the struggle that cultural expectations would foist on us once we left our school. In England we wore uniforms, competed with each other on equal footing, incorporating, without articulating it, the multi-textured fabric or our diversity into our own individual consciousness. I for one had stopped being just a Haitian girl. No one was around to remind me of the ancestral taboos. There had not been one pronouncement of *"Ca pa bon"* within earshot. At this school, the older students enforced discipline for the whole population with minimal adult intervention according to a well-established code of conduct reflecting the broader Democratic English society around us.

This was also, a Christian community. The teachers and staff were truly righteous people. They modeled courtesy and kindness to us. Even though they insisted that we speak the "*Queen's English*" and followed the school's rules I was not troubled by the requirements. We were taught by the leadership to scrupulously respect each other's differences. I remember that when the school served beef at a meal, there was a choice of lamb for the Hindu students, if the menu featured pork; something else was made available for the Muslim students. Arrangements were made for each student to attend a religious service of their denominational choice on Sunday morning. I chose to go to the Church of England because I was expected to attend a service, privately I considered myself to be without any religious affiliation. Sunday evening the Christian students were taken to a worship service at the Brethren Fellowship affiliated with the school. Whatever church service I attended I kept myself entertained by daydreams or read a hidden book. I looked forward when the time came at whatever assembly I was in, for the sermon and the invitation to sit in silence, when I could allow my mind to drift into the fanciful recesses of my imagination. No one ever asked me about my personal spiritual beliefs. One of my school friends gave me a Bible but it remained at the bottom of my blue suitcase. I do not remember ever reading it. There was a Sunday afternoon class on religion, which I found tedious, but life in general was pleasant.

By this time, I had grown accustomed to being separated from my family. When I went home to Liberia for summer vacations I was seen as an English schoolgirl by my parents. My sisters had made their own friends and moved about the Suakoko compound unconcerned with the outside world. The brief letters we wrote to each other were not enough to sustain strong ties between us. The closeness we had known in Les Cayes had been lost forever. I was emotionally estranged from my family. Even if we had remained in Haiti there would have come a time when we would have been separated. That was how Haitian parents who had the means to educate their children saw things. Older children especially had to be educated in Boarding Schools. The English had a parallel philosophy. When I lived in England during the nineteen sixties it seemed to me that a large number of children were sent, even at a very young age, to spend most of their lives in Boarding Schools. At vacation and as well as school opening time I would travel on trains filled with uniformed children and youths traveling to and from schools all across England. Some tugged at steamer trunks and other assorted luggage. My strong blue suitcase acquired a dent here and there but never broke.

My new friends and I corresponded by mail whenever the arbitrary summons of adults kept us apart. Prickles, Bob, Gail, Janet, and Shari were my first true friends. If we quarreled, I have no recollection of it. We shared confidences, books, dreams, and separation from our families. We were on cordial terms with the other boarders and several of the Day students but forged a special bond between the six of us. Priscilla a.k.a. *Prickles*, a brown haired English girl, the youngest in our group was the tallest and a stand up comedian. We both shared a second floor room in the concrete Victorian style house overlooking the well-tended gardens of the school, with Elizabeth, an Indian girl whose nickname was *Bob* and who had grown up in Bahrain. *Bob* loved horses and her very traditional Indian family was distressed by the way she ignored her untamed, long black hair and her preference for jodhpurs over saris.

Our other three friends were a year older and in a more advanced class. Olive toned and black haired Golshar or *Shari*, at least while she lived in England, was from Persia. Janet had very white skin, although she spent her summer vacation in Tanzania with her Scots missionary parents, very clear blue eyes, and deep black hair. Gail too had long black hair, she was a Chinese from the Caribbean island of Tobago. We all spoke the Queen's English except for Janet who defiantly held on to her Scottish brogue. *Prickles*, was the goalie for our field hockey team. She would enlist *Bob* and I to paint her protective leg pads with shoe white the very night before a game, mumbling every time that she didn't know why she had allowed our coach to talk her into playing that position. Her impromptu monologues enlivened our afternoon walks and none of our teammates took her studied air of despair seriously: she was good-natured about letting the hockey balls in while guarding the goal during a match.

There was always a great deal of civility all around whenever we played another school's Field Hockey team. Our main rival was a school housed in a large castle surrounded by beautiful gardens. Although we always lost to their team I loved the trip deep in the countryside on a chartered bus and the obligatory post game tea for which we had to change out of our culottes and mud caked cleats. They did the same when it was our turn to host them in our own much plainer dining hall. Playing sports was always a social occasion for us even the mandatory early pre-breakfast jog, rain or shine, around the park that gave our school its name. My small group of friends and I joined the Judo Club, played tennis on one of the several courts on the school grounds, and feasted on the generous care packages that came from Gail's family in Tobago. We also painted ambitious watercolors, followed the fashion trends and latest Pop artists, at a distance at least, taught each other the latest dances, and entertained each other as only carefree teenagers can. I do not think we felt pressured to excel at our studies. Class sizes were small and the teachers interesting enough to keep us motivated. Since this was an all girl school, there was none of the tension of having to compete with boys. There was also no need to contend with each other for the attention of boys.

As I became older, I started to keep up with some of the other teenagers I would meet on summer vacations with my family in Liberia. Sometimes when I changed planes in

Amsterdam, Geneva, Paris, Las Palmas, or Dakar or waited at the airport in Monrovia for my familiar blue suitcase to be pulled from the belly of a plane I would run into an acquaintance. There were at least two or three other Haitian families in Monrovia with children studying in Europe or in French speaking Senegal. I could count on at least one dance to go to during the summer. The boys spoke French in the courtly manner of their elders both in Africa and in Europe. I noticed that the presence of boys complicated things. It was awkward at times for me: vacillating between wanting to be noticed and fearing rejection. Encounters with the opposite sex were brief enough not to ruffle the tranquil pace of life at the Suakoko compound. I was free to read as many books as I wanted while awaiting the start of the school year. My sisters had their own activities and we did not pressure each other by trying to merge our separate interests.

In 1967, my sister Tikite became very ill. It was a terrible time for our family. Papa was in Africa to finish out his contract with the College while Manman was in the United States with the twins and had rented an apartment in Brooklyn New York. I was far away in Europe. From the sparse letters my parents wrote to me I gathered that the plan was for us all to settle in the United States. Both my sisters were enrolled in school there. Then Tikite became sick. Manman, who had not learned to speak English, could not understand what the American doctors were saying. Papa was a three hours drive away from telephone communication out of Liberia. He flew back to New York. Some of the medical specialists told my parents that my sister had a brain tumor. Tests were needed. My sister's long black hair was cut off and half of her head shaved. She remained alert the entire time and was greatly distressed. In those days, hospitals did not allow children to visit and Tikite could only see her twin from a several stories high window as Pepe stood outside on the grounds below. Pepe confessed to us later that she had thought that she had caused her sister's illness because of something she had said. She was afraid to discuss it with anyone at the time.

In the midst of all this news came in from Port-au-Prince that ManLillie, our maternal grandmother whom Manman had not seen in five years had fallen from off her porch and lay in a coma. Anyone returning to Haiti had no guarantee of being able to leave again. At best, there was a possibility of being detained for months, possibly years. Manman had to chose between her sick child and dying mother. ManLillie who was drifting in and out of consciousness had been calling for her. From her hospital bed, my grandmother counted off my two aunts and my uncle Felix and knew that her fourth child, Marie was missing. Papa told me later that it was the only time in all the years he had known Manman, that he saw her cry. Although she could not attend her mother's funeral in Port-au-Prince, Manman wore the traditional all black mourning clothing for a year to honor her memory. Papa Gus too wore the black widower's armband and wept at his ex-wife's funeral, insisting that she be interred in the Toulmé family crypt.

"I don't know what I have done to Amélie that she won't even talk to me ".

My grandfather had said some years earlier to one of my aunts. He obviously did not think that his repeated extramarital affairs, walking out of their marriage, leaving her and their four children to starve were "something". Man Lillie had consented nevertheless to allow him to escort her at the wedding procession of both my aunt Christine and later my mother's. Now once again Auguste Toulmé wanted to observe protocol and at his insistence, my grandmother was laid to rest in his family vault.

Several weeks passed before I received the news of my grandmother's death. She and I had never corresponded. At least I never received a letter from her. There was one photograph of her in my family album, seated in a black and white pose with her characteristic squint. I must have written to her while we lived in Les Cayes, as custom dictated, to thank her each time she sent the rag dolls she sewed for the twins and I. For a long time now, since moving to Africa, there had been no more dolls from the gentle Amélie.

Tikite did not have a brain tumor. A new physician providentially came on the scene and rescued her. My sister was forcibly transferred to another more efficient hospital and set of doctors. They diagnosed her condition as Meningitis, a severe infection of the brain and treated her with the appropriate antibiotics. When she improved enough to travel, the whole family returned to Liberia. I joined them there within a few weeks for the summer vacations my blue suitcase packed mainly with books that I had no room to store at school.

Manman was very quiet that summer of 1967. In New York, she had come so close to her family, talked on the phone with them and yet had not been able to see them. My aunts and her resumed their arduous coded correspondence. Haiti seemed even further away. Manman spent her mourning period in isolation. There was no one to proffer visits of condolences. Customs in Suakoko differed; no one noticed her deep black dress. Now more than ever, she wanted to leave Africa. I on the other hand thought that my family had resettled in Suakoko. Throughout that school year of 1967-1968, I imagine that we were following the routine of recent times. Once school ended, I expected to fly out to Liberia for the summer vacation. By then, I had made a life for myself at the English Boarding School.

In the summer of 1968, I received the news from my parents that I was to join them in the United States of America. Six years had passed since we had left Haiti. The thought of moving to New York City filled me with foreboding. I had followed the story of the Civil Rights movements in the United Sates and seen the scenes of the Chicago

Police's intervention at the Democratic convention, and Viet Nam war street protests. Dr Martin Luther King Jr. the civil rights activist had been assassinated earlier in April. If living in the Haiti of François Duvalier was dangerous for a non-Duvalierist, so was living in the United States for a non-white, I thought.

Papa was having trouble with his employers. He was no longer allowed to practice Dentistry in Suakoko on the College campus or at the nearby affiliated Community hospital where he had helped set up a Dental department. The sister of the Liberian College's president, a new graduate dentist was given the position at the hospital, which had been promised to Papa. Obviously, people would prefer to be treated by a more experience dentist. Papa was ordered to close his private practice. His salary from the College as a French teacher was inadequate and he did not have the connections as a relative new comer or the assets to set up an independent practice in the Capital City of Monrovia. The smaller towns in the rest of the country were too isolated and too small to allow for a lucrative dental clinic outside of a government controlled one. My father's former business partner from Les Cayes (my godfather) had settled in one of these small isolated towns and struggled to make a living until he finally died of pneumonia in a Monrovia Hospital. Manman and Papa decided to take their chances in New York City. They were both forty-nine and fifty-one years old and once again did not have enough money to move our family's belongings. The collection of books I had started a few years earlier and replenished on summer trips was left behind in Africa.

Instead of the roundtrip ticket to Monrovia Liberia, I received a one-way passage booked for New York City U.S.A. My parents had characteristically forgotten to fill me in with the details of their plans. Now they had relocated our family to New York. Another detail they had left out was the procurement of an immigrant visa to the United States for me. It was relatively easy for people living in the calm under populated country of Liberia in 1968 to obtain permanent visas to the United States. The quota for those like myself living in England, however, was much more restricted. I found this out at the end of the school term. Much of my summer vacation was spent going back and forth between the empty school in Yeovil and the American Embassy in London. The monotony was interrupted by the two weeks I spent visiting the English countryside as a guest of one of the school's teachers and her family. I would have to stay in England for months, I was told.

On one of my trips to the American Embassy, a vice-consul who had done a tour of duty in Haiti sympathized with my situation. He telephoned me one evening to tell me that someone on the waiting list for visas had cancelled and he had placed my name in that individual's stead. I suddenly had the prized green card to permanently reside in the United States of America. It appeared, from the short cryptic letters my mother wrote to me, that our family's finances were severely depleted and that we could no longer afford to have me stay in Europe. The Headmistress at the Park School offered me a grant to help pay my tuition but I felt that it would still be better to rejoin my family. I had never wanted to live separated from them. Circumstances had forced me to adjust to Boarding school life and I would miss my friends and would have to leave most of my books behind. My weathered blue suitcase had black scuffmarks that I had not tried to clean. There were some scratches and irreparable dents in the darkened blue hard plastic exterior. Inside, the soft pale blue lining was intact except for one corner at the top with a dropping stain left long ago in Suakoko by my sisters' tyrannically inquisitive pet African ricebird that loved to monitor my actions. There was no one to watch me pack for this trip. The other school boarders had left weeks before. Only a few books from my collection fit in among my sparse wardrobe.

The idea of living in the large city of Brooklyn frightened me. My friends were ending the summer vacation with their families in various parts of the world and would soon return to the Park School for Girls in Yeovil England without me. My boarding school days ended just as I had grown accustomed to them and gained enough confidence to make friends. On the train from Yeovil to London, the traveling clothes I wore no longer distinguished me as an English schoolgirl. It was the wrong time of the year for uniforms and tasseled berets. I struggled with my heavy suitcase, loading it on the taxi that I took to Heathrow airport. There was a surcharge for the extra weight in my one piece of luggage. I had the equivalent of one American dollar left in my purse. That sum was enough to rent the earpiece required to hear the sound of the movie the airline showed on the eight hours flight.

The familiar sight of London quickly faded as the plane gained altitude, and I kept the shade of my window down to avoid looking at the endless stretch of the Atlantic Ocean. My limbs ached as the tedium laden hours crawled on to the New World. The rehearsed voice of a Stewardess eventually crackled over the loudspeakers announcing our arrival at Kennedy Airport. I pulled up my window shade. From my seat I saw the September sky below as we neared the land; a foreboding mass of battleship gray clouds shrouded the tall buildings of New York City.

I had been called to yet another foreign environment and lost another part of my life forever. Papa and Manman met me at the airport and took me to our new home in one of a row of identical brown brick buildings in the Flatbush area of Brooklyn. Our apartment was on the sixth floor. The smell of cooking permeated the elevator and the nondescript linoleum covered hallway. I noticed that we did not exchange a greeting with any of the people we encountered on the way. Papa pushed on an electrical buzzer set in the middle of a heavy black metal door at the end of the tunnel-like hall.

There was a clicking sound on the other side of the door as the shutter of a peephole opened and closed. Suddenly I was face to face with two strangers. In the year that had passed since I had seen my family, the twins had grown with astonishing speed. I barely recognized my sisters. They were both slightly shorter than I and had gained a lot of weight.

The difference in my sisters was more than in their physical appearance: Tikite, possibly as the result of her life threatening illness the year before, had lost her fiery disposition. Her tone of voice was subdued, her manner uncharacteristically shy. The girls had changed homes twice in less than two years after six years of roaming about freely on the College campus in Suakoko. My little sisters had grown up. Absence had drawn a distance in our relationship that hung like a weight between us in the small rooms. We now had a television set in the living room of our home for the first time. We spend more time with it than with each other. After a four-year separation, we had seen each other for a few weeks every nine months to a year, we had all changed, and I did not feel comfortable with my own family.

Even as I had lost track of our family routine I noticed an important change: in New York neither one of my parents attended church, so my sisters and I no longer thought of Sundays as "Church Day". God had become even more distant to me. I had stopped praying and avoided church of any kind, timing my arrival at weddings, christenings, and funeral services to mingle with the departing crowd. In New York I did not feel inspired to sketch or paint the slabs of cement and brown bricks that I saw from our apartment window stretched out, for as far as the eye could see. The twins had learned to cook so I did not revert to my old occupation of housekeeper. There were no sports activities to participate in that I knew of. Everything cost money. Gail, *Prickles*, Janet, *Bob*, and *Shari* did their best to keep me informed about their vacations and activities at the school back in England. My own answers to the letters I was receiving from Europe or Africa grew shorter. In spite of mutual promises to remain friends, forever, the passage of time overcame our best intentions. Again, I was disconnected from the familiar. I had lost contact with my native culture. Yet, a large community of Haitian expatriates lived New York City. I started to gradually learn about being Haitian from observing them. There was of course criticism from those who thought I had lost my roots. Some things inevitably *had* been lost. I could no longer express myself in the French spoken by the average educated Haitian girl of my age. Even my Kreyol was not as smooth initially.

11

The old suspicions festered still among the Haitians living in New York City in the late sixties. My mother especially wanted to know the family name of anyone we met. Each new acquaintance was scrutinized for their educational and social pedigree and especially for their relationship with the Duvalierist regime back in Haiti. Many former collaborators and even some notorious enforcers of Duvalier had joined the community of exiles when they had fallen out of favor with their boss or his heirs. The brother in law of one of our close friends had gunned down two friends of my parents in Port-au-Prince and committed innumerable atrocities. This murderer, and scores of others like him, was at large in the exiled Haitian community although we never encountered him.

"*Pitit ki moun ou ye?*" (Whose child are you?) Haitians asked when introduced to each other at a wedding, christening, or first communion party. Haitians believe that bad blood reached down through generations. Parents with youth of marriageable age were wary of unwittingly contaminating their lineage with a "*move Moun*" an appellation that no longer designated voodoo practitioners only but now included the doers of bad deeds under the Duvalierist regime. In an average conversation, the typical elaborate exchange would skirt around the attempts of one speaker to uncover the other's secrets as both used layers upon of layers of subterfuge to hide. This made for some very confusing encounters. Some individuals with an uncertain past would stir clear of their Kreyol-speaking compatriots, insisting that they came from some other Caribbean island even as their speech and mannerism betrayed them.

When a group of Haitian men felt secure that there were no "traitors" in their midst however, there was no end to their discussions. The theme never varied: "this is what is wrong with Haiti, Haitians, Americans, Politicians, Haiti, Haitians, and if it was me I would..." Somewhere in a room, even with the pulsating sounds of a *meringue*, playing full blast in the background, the partygoers would argue. Rare was the woman who stepped into these discussions. Their voices were too soft to be heard above that of the shouting men. Whether in French or in Kreyol, neck veins bulging, arms and hands gesticulating with the ardor of a dramatic actor in the throes of an Academy Award performance, the oratory pugilists were a wonder to watch. The problem was that none of them knew how to exit a scene. In a home with a strong-willed matriarch, any chaos would be instantly reined in with a firm:

"*Allons Messieurs, ca suffit!*"

There now gentlemen, that's enough! Letting the guests know that enough had been said. In situations were things degenerated unchecked there might be a dramatic finale culminating in a breach. At that point, the aggrieved male guest would call out to his wife to gather the children for a ceremonial exit. Only then would the women spectators realize that they had just lost their own friends and the children, their playmates.

One lively family, whose parents were old friends of my own, brought me up to speed about a few more things Haitian. From the boys I learned how to dance the Haitian *meringue* while their sisters reintroduced me to some of the food I remembered from my childhood. The older girls had already settled or were in the process of settling into marriage and motherhood. My own head was filled with romantic ideas about the opposite sex. I did sense however that I was not free to behave the way most sixteen years old in new surroundings, whether Haitian or American did. Even by Haitian standards Papa and Manman, who continuously referred to the pronouncements of her own father, held on to very conservative ideas.

My mother and the Kreyol speaking older women I met in New York City told me stories. For the first time I started to think about the implications of these anecdotes. I was starting to associate myself with their past and current lives. More secrets became known. Manman was now also voicing her disillusionment. Even though she had waited for the right husband, her life had not turned out as she had expected. She had fought straight-backed as ever to fulfill her duties as a homemaker, wherever that might be. Now the recurring theme of her advice to me was that I should not get married. At least, not until I had received an adequate level of higher education.

"Men will disrespect you if you don't have a paper (meaning a diploma/degree) in your hand". She said grimly.

In New York City, my mother and some of the friends she met up with from Haiti were experiencing a revolution of sorts. Even though they worked in garment factories, and did not speak English, these women were earning money and developing an autonomy that imperceptibly redefined their roles. The time was ripe now for men and women to engage in open and sincere discussions; something that cultural taboos had not prepared either group for. Marital as well as parent-children relations were deeply affected by the uprooting of the family unit from the old country and transplanting to a new land yet no one discussed it. I became aware of a double standard of behavior in the Haitian culture that arbitrarily ascribed roles to the sexes. Worse, I discovered that I was locked into the wrong sex. There were many inconveniences to being a Haitian woman. In New York my compatriots worked outside and at home while their men lounged in front of that new addition to the Haitian home: the television set. Outside of Haiti, there were no maids for the middle class and the women had to take up that function as well as help financially support the home. Yet families tried to maintain the same household customs, down to the cooking of the time consuming rice and beans, deep-fried plantains, marinated meats, served on starched, and ironed table linen. Had I not gone to Boarding school in Europe I would have continued with my routine of household chores and unpaid childcare services. Now I was beginning to shock some Haitian matrons who eyed me as a prospective daughter-in-law by saying that I had already kept a home, raised children, and was not eager to jump into the cycle that they were into.

Many Haitians I was meeting had emigrated directly from the country having held out under the Duvalierists longer than our family had. Others, however, had started to come in from the Congo and other parts of Africa. I heard many a tale of shattered dreams. We were all starting to identify with a sense of collective homelessness. In times past Haitians who had served a few years, about the number of years many of us had abroad, went back to the home country. Now instead of going home Haitians still circled the globe as more exiles joined us.

My father was always away at work and we rarely saw each other. I did not find out until late into my own adulthood that his first job in New York City had been as a janitor. He was in his mid-fifties and had been a respected Dentist and College Professor. Papa did not settle down into menial jobs and was able to eventually resume his career as a dentist, after a stint as a dental lab Technician, and an Inhalation Therapist. The drive to provide for his family would not allow him to just sit and mull over his problems. His philosophy was unaltered: He expected to work hard.

"If something is for me, then it is mine" he would say, meaning that he would never try to obtain an unfair advantage over any one to meet his own needs.

In New York, we shed the last vestiges of life, as we had known it as a family both in Haiti and in Liberia. Even in Africa we had stopped setting the daily dining table with formality, reserving one white embroidered table linen which Manman had salvaged from her abandoned trousseau, for the Sunday meal and for birthdays and anniversaries. The faculty housing at the Suakoko compound in Africa was furnished more for convenience and economy than fashion. Our home in New York reflected the meager conditions of our family's finances. Everything was made of Formica, plastic and thin brown cloth. It was shabby compared to the custom made set of furniture that Papa had saved years for back when he was a hopeful suitor in Les Cayes. All that had to be left behind with our house and other furnishings in Haiti. The windows of our Brooklyn apartment remained closed to shut out the winter cold. We could not get rid of the sour staleness of the air around us even with frequent bursts of artificially scented sprays. Because of Papa's work schedule, we saw him less and less at our meal table. Now that Manman worked outside of our home, the constancy of her presence no longer cemented our family unit. This pattern was repeated al around us within the community of exiled Haitians. Many families either left or sent their children to Haiti to grow up with relatives. This was a common enough practice within the country itself. Papa had several cousins who grew up in his parents' home in Port-au-Prince. The difference with the New York families was that the children were much younger, infants at times, and the distance from home too long to sustain a meaningful relationship. Everyone believed that this arrangement was for a short time and was harmless. The actual result of this way of life was to foster a disjointed family unit and irreparable damage to the parent-child relationship.

After I had been in New York for a few days, Papa took time off from work to enroll me in a private Catholic Girls school. Both he and my mother refused to listen to my protests. Haitian parents still held to the illusion that getting a good education meant attending a Catholic school. Since my parents could not afford to send my sisters and I to private school, they were both willing to do what ever it took to send at least one child, their eldest. Neither understood how much I had grown to resent nuns and priests. I felt trapped. The sheer number of people in this city intimidated me. My immediate world was restricted to our own family of five and two other Haitian girls who lived in the Building next to ours. Once again, I was feeling uprooted, and lost. I then convinced myself by the time I turned seventeen years old, that I was shy. Groups of people made me feel uncomfortable. Although I weighed about 110 Lbs, felt fat and unattractive.

The nun at the Brooklyn school did not welcome us in spite of Papa's habitual deferential manner towards anyone in a religious outfit. Old memories flooded in as I scanned the dark paneled interviewing room. It was all too familiar. Even though the woman sitting behind the heavy brown desk wore a dark blue head cover and dress that were cut in a more modern style than the black voluminous habit of the English convent nuns, who had expelled me from their school, I was suspicious. Nuns are all the same I thought. Predictably, the questions were directed at my father. Papa was at a loss to explain what the papers I had brought with me from my last school meant, yet the nun appeared to have enough of an understanding of the British school system to evaluate my record. Since I had successfully taken some 'O" level examinations in Yeovil, she concluded that I only lacked a year of study before I could earn an American High School diploma. We were therefore surprised to hear her say that I was to be placed in a class in her school that was two years away from graduation. There was no more room in the Senior year class for a new student, she explained, so she had decided that I should start school in the Junior class. The expression on Papa's face was comical.

"*Sister*, are you saying that the only reason you want to admit my daughter in a lower class and hold her back one year is because you have too many students in the senior class?"

He asked incredulously. That was the last I heard about enrolling me into any Catholic school. Just as the school year started I found myself at Erasmus Hall High School on Flatbush Ave Brooklyn, the largest school I had attended in my life. It was also my first experience in a public school. Most of the school day was spent walking through its long crowded halls going to and from classes. Besides a course that I took in American History, and another in Biology and Economics I learnt nothing new. The woman counselor in charge of helping graduating seniors at the school with career plans never interviewed me. My own "guidance counselor" a very distracted white man who never looked up from the stacks of papers on his desk at me dismissed my original interest in becoming a journalist or an architect. Several years later when I reviewed my High School grades, I realized that with proper direction I could have gotten a four-year College scholarship. By then it was too late to salvage my dreams. The cares of adulthood had snared them.

I remember standing one morning, in the bedroom of my best friend at the time, in a Brooklyn New York apartment. My friend was lying on her side on the top shelf of a bunk bed, her head resting on a folded elbow. The back of my shoulders, I remember, felt the cold of the unpainted metal frame of the bed. We had grown up my friend and I, as small children in the same town in Haiti, and separated as both our families fled from our homes. Her own family had spent years in hiding while in Haiti during the Duvalierist reign, and now we were reunited at age sixteen. In New York City, we had renewed our friendship.

She had already lived there for several years and understood the city, so it seemed to me, quite well and promptly took me under her wing. I had arrived at my new home to find both my parents so overwhelmed by their own problems that I was left alone to maneuver around this very large, frighteningly strange city. My life until then had been spent in small communities in Haiti, Liberia, and England where I had attended small private schools. My friend got me registered in the huge American Public High School we both attended and shepherded me through the morass of paper work, interminable hallways and fashion dos, and don'ts. I admired her determination and razor sharp mind. We turned seventeen a few days apart, and soon were three quarters way through our Senior year with graduation within reach. Unlike her, I was still very much ill at ease with the bustle and restless pace of life around us.

I lived in the next apartment complex of brown brick buildings. One other girl our age who lived nearby in another building identical to ours walked to school with us as we rendezvoused in the bare gray cement courtyard linking our homes. Our schedules never allowed us a glimpse of each other again for the whole day once we crossed the school's threshold into the labyrinth of crowded halls. Each one of my classes was held in a different classroom with a different set of students. As Haitian born girls, we could only visit each other at our homes for a prescribed length of time when the adults in our families gave special permission. This was reserved for particular occasions. We had phones in our homes for the first time in our lives but could not run the risk of offending an adult caller who might later complain to our parents that they had been greeted by a "busy" telephone signal. Therefore, the bulk of our confidences were exchanged as we walked in groups of two and threes or rode on the public buses and waited at the Transit stop.

I stood that spring of 1969, with my back propped up against my friend 's bed searching for something to say. The light of the early morning partially shut out of the room by the drawn curtains of a window mingled with the darkness to cast a gray hue around us. No one else seemed to be up in the apartment. It was Saturday; we did not have to go to school. Some weeks earlier, I had attended a counseling session for graduating students. The classroom was full. A woman counselor sitting at a table in front of about fifty of us called out my name, eyes searching to and fro through her large black framed eyeglasses until she spotted me in the crowd. I do not remember what I said in response to her questions, but she immediately assigned me a profession. I do remember asking about one of my own dreams, and her curt reply: "No" the record showed that I did not have the grades needed in Mathematics to go to a college and pursue a degree in Architecture. Therefore, she said I should go to a two- year Nursing School. My real dream was to be a Journalist. However, I had heard that one had to be very good to earn a living at it and I doubted my abilities and had no adult in my world with whom to discuss this. In England, at the Park School, my roommates Priscilla, Elizabeth, and I had dreamed of traveling the world: I would be the Journalist, *Prickles*, the photographer for my articles and Elizabeth would raise thoroughbred horses. For the brief time, since leaving Europe, that *Prickles,* and I had corresponded I had learned that she at least was in Art School. Both of us had lost track of *Bob.* I wondered at times whether our friend had discarded her jodhpurs for the trunk full of gorgeous saris her family had shipped to her from the East.

As a foreign graduate professional, my father did not have a license to practice Dentistry in the States and had taken up another profession for less pay. My parents were expecting me to earn some sort of credentials to start working soon so that our family could buy a small house in the suburbs. Papa had joined the Association of Foreign Dentists in New York. Some of its members had powerful allies lobbying the State legislature to remove the two years Dental School Course requirement for a foreign graduate to sit for the Dentistry Boards. Meanwhile my parents were ready to invest one thousand dollars of their savings to get me in Nursing School and then hoped I would get a scholarship to finish the program.

My friend here had better plans. I had repeatedly heard about a relative who was a successful professional who was interested in mentoring her and of a multitude of other prospects for a very bright future. She had very good Math grades. Often she regaled me with apt descriptions of the yet to be lived adventures. I marveled at the intensity with which she met each day head on and charted the course of her own life.

Now this gray, still, Saturday morning my friend lay silent under her bed sheet. The fiery staccato of her eloquence uncharacteristically locked in her motionless form. She barely acknowledged my presence with an occasional grunt. It had been a very long night. I was called in to see her as her family had brought her home from a hospital. Her mother said that maybe I, who seemed to be her daughter's confidante, might know why my friend here had swallowed the entire contents of a large bottle of pills.

In Haitian circles, one did not discuss emotional pain. If wearing a sad expression were considered bad behavior in a child, an adult doing the same would likely be seen as socially inappropriate. My paternal grandmother died a few months before my birth. She and Manlillie, my maternal grandmother, by all accounts demonstrated the signs of an overburdened soul. It embarrassed our family that the two women did not suppress the outpouring of their pain, for longer than they had.

Years later when I thought about my friend it struck me that it was odd for her family to ask me, a confused seventeen years old if I could tell them what was wrong with their daughter. No one seemed to think the hellish childhood she had lived could have led to her desperate act. She was the oldest child, a girl, in a Haitian family. In the small town we both grew up in everyone knew about her parents' very public marital fights, her father's alcoholism and notorious womanizing and dangerous political activities. Frequently the whole family had to go into hiding when her father was on the run from the Duvalierists. My friend had been the actual parent in the house. People marveled at how well she took care of her younger siblings and admired the serious expression of her face. She and I never discussed it but I could imagine what her life was like in Haiti and even after the family moved to New York City.

12

I walked along the metal railing bordering the Brooklyn sidewalk on my way from the Subway train station carrying the same blue weathered suitcase that had held all of my worldly possessions the previous fall. A year had passed since my coming to the United States. The weight of the suitcase bruised the palm of my hand. This was the first time I had enrolled myself in school without anyone's help. There was the nagging thought that I had made a mistake. I was afraid that I was wasting the thousand dollars check that Papa had given me. Our family was trying to save money to buy a house in order to move out of our dismal apartment. There was the ever-present feeling pulling down my thoughts that I had forgotten something, and that I was about to squander my father's money.

At my High School graduation ceremony on June 24th 1969, I had looked in vain for a face that I could recognize among the large assembly of students. This was supposed to be a special time, a festive time. At least that is what I thought from what I had read in books and magazines and from conversations I overheard in the school cafeteria. I felt like an outsider looking in without knowing what I was missing. June 24th was also the second anniversary of Man Lillie's death and Manman, still in exile, had not yet been able to visit her grave in Port-au-Prince. Both my parents were buried in their own disappointment: my mother who for the first time had to work outside of our home was unhappy with her job in a factory as a seamstress, Papa was mostly absent. We all hated living in our sixth floor apartment.

My mindset in 1969 was one of confusion and frustration when it came to making immediate choices for my life. As the oldest child, I felt responsible for a now ill-defined burden. It was apparent that I needed to do something with my life that would help us all. I was allowed to co-sign for the mortgage on the house we wanted to buy in the suburbs of Queens New York on the strength of my future earnings. At seventeen years old, I was once again very anxious about life.

The luggage and my steps grew heavier as I approach the Nurses' Residence of the Methodist Hospital of Brooklyn School of Nursing. Groups of arriving students and their families were unloading boxes, lamps, bookcases from several cars parked along the entrance of my new home. People milled around the lobby, and elevator and the floor to which I had been assigned a furnished room. There was a lot of animated talk, even laughter. A reception had been set up with refreshments for visiting families in the common area.

"Did your Mom and Dad bring you?"

A new student who introduced herself as coming from Vermont asked. Another girl and her family had flown in from Wisconsin. Suitcases and boxes filled up the halls. This was a big day for everyone.

I remember the interview to get into Nursing School. The first instructor-interviewer a friendly woman of Italian descent set me at ease so I was taken aback by the second interviewer's obvious animosity towards me. We had never met before. In the sheltered English Christian community I had lived in before coming to America, people were polite. I never experienced the racial tension that was to rack English society in later years. At Methodist Hospital School Of Nursing, I was the only Black in the class of forty-four students to be admitted straight from High School. Blatant, unprovoked hostility from a stranger was a forgotten experience for me especially so many years after living in Haiti and the English Convent school. The two other Black students who enrolled in the same class were already Licensed Practical nurses and appeared to know instinctively how to conduct themselves. Even so, during our two years at the school this same instructor, a slim, fashionably dressed young woman with translucent blue eyes and frosted blond hair styled short to compliment the contour of her delicate face, always treated the three of us Black students more harshly than the rest of the class. We tried to avoid any confrontations with this woman. The three of us became adept at exchanging warning signals with our eyes. I for one dreaded having to answer any questions from this woman since she never passed up an opportunity to humiliate me. At the entrance interview, she had insinuated that I was not very bright because my High School Science grades were not as high as she thought they should be. I had in fact scored lower than average on the general pre-Admission Exam for those subjects, but in the top percentile of applicants in the Academic topics.

"What will you do if we don't admit you to Nursing School?" She asked.

I told her that I had already applied for a job as a Dietary Aide to deliver food trays to patients in a hospital.

"Is this what you plan to do for the rest of your life?"

She asked with obvious disdain. At that point, not realizing how much I did not want to be a Nurse, I told this woman that I was going to work and save money and keep applying until I got into a Nursing School. For two years, I could feel her watching me expecting me to fail my courses. For the two years that I lived at the Nurses Residence in the Prospect Park section of Brooklyn, I did not see myself as an adult. The Nursing Instructors demanded a strict account of our time through scheduled classes, patient care duties and indirectly by way of a voluminous assortment of daily assignments. I hated Nursing School. Under the constant threat of being thrown out of the program, life was tense. Because my heart was not in it, I had to study very hard to keep my head above water. Therefore, even though my family lived a two hours train and bus trip away, I rarely saw them.

In Nursing School, there was none of the camaraderie I had enjoyed in my last English Boarding School. Even though I knew of the race relations problem in the United States, I was disappointed now that I was finally fluent in English to find myself an outsider again. The two other Black women students were older, one of them was in her forties and married, and did not spend much time at the Nurses' residence. I was the youngest at seventeen of the group of twenty-two that eventually remained from the original class of forty-four women and the only foreigner. Both in Suakoko and in England I had eventually interacted easily with people from various ethnic groups.

I did not yet understand the American culture. The entering students immediately paired off or formed little circles. I did not invite myself to join any particular group for fear of being rejected. I kept to myself. Then one evening I heard the sound of Black comedian Bill Cosby's *Chicken Heart* monologue through the wall of my room. The owner of the record player who lived next door to me had a keen sense of humor. She did not want to become a nurse either and was a good companion until she too left the program.

Within days, we were made aware through the second year students that only half of us were expected to complete the Nursing program. The school had a reputation to uphold we were told. Exams were structured to be much harder than the national average to ensure that a high percentage of those who made it through to graduation would succeed in the New York State licensing exam. The hostile instructor from my entrance interview did her best to discourage me and to goad me into leaving the program. The school had decided to close its doors after our Class. We felt the added pressure because all of our course credits would not transfer to another Nursing program if we were to fail out of this one.

A sense of duty to family kept me motivated to finish Nursing School. I had realized by the end of my first three months there that I had made a serious mistake. This was not my field. It involved mostly "work" and very little "play". My family had spent their last thousand dollars and I felt obligated to make good on their investment.

The format of the testing at the school precluded any grading based on the instructors' bias for the most part. There was, however, always the danger of receiving a poor evaluation for the work done during the clinical assignments, that depended on the judgment of the evaluator. I managed to stay out of trouble until the very last semester in the program.

The hostile instructor was in charge of my last clinical rotation in the program. A poor evaluation from her meant that I would not graduate. I had no illusions about her feelings towards me and took great pains to try to surpass her expectations.

As it happened a young woman who had been admitted to my assigned unit whom no one suspected was pregnant, had delivered a baby during the night shift and tried to drown him in a toilet bowl. Another patient alerted the Charge Nurse and the baby was rescued. By divine intervention, my assignment had been switched at the last minute; I would have been the one dealing with that situation instead of another more experienced nurse.

This young woman patient was unmarried and faked the symptoms of a blood clot in her legs (more sophisticated diagnostic tests became available in later years) in order to be admitted to the hospital when she went into labor. Her family did not know of her true condition. The unit staff therefore took all precautions to protect this woman's secret. She herself would not admit to having just given birth to a baby, even though she signed papers to release him to the Social Services Department for adoption.

The protocol in 1971 was to wrap a thick "binder" around the chest of a newly delivered woman who is not nursing her newborn baby to avoid a condition known as *engorgement* of the breasts, which can be very painful. I attempted to use the binder, as the protocol for "Post Partum" required. The patient refused to wear it and told me that she would ask her family to bring her a support brassiere instead. This was an alternative to the protocol and since the girl was very obese, which is why everyone missed seeing her pregnant condition, it seemed like a good idea.

I did not pressure my patient to wear the binder. When her family came to visit her, they would see the thick binder under her gown and ask questions. I was also trying to hide the truth from them. On the following day, the girl "forgot" to ask her mother to bring the special bra and yet would not wear the binder. At this time in my life, I was reserved, unassertive and somehow did not do the right thing.

When I finally mustered enough courage to report this to the hostile instructor, who was in charge of this rotation, predictably she saw a wrong motive on my part. "You're Catholic!"

I remember the Instructor's accusatory tone as she sat at the Nursing Station with one of her legs propped on another chair, her cold blue eyes inspecting me from head to toe.

"You think this girl sinned and should be punished."

She added. I in fact I had thought that the young woman patient had had a psychotic breakdown when she tried to kill her child and sympathized with her fear of her parents, and had taken care of her as best I could. As for my religious beliefs, I had not been to any church for years or to a Catholic church in seven years. I quickly realized that the instructor had been waiting for such an opportunity to harm me; she continued to insist that I had deliberately given substandard care to my patient.

Several times in my childhood I had been accused of doing something that I had not done. In Les Cayes when I was about seven years old, a woman from our neighborhood who had never used indoor plumbing was allowed in our house by one of our servants to use our toilet and had caused it to malfunction. I was immediately accused of breaking the toilet. When I protested my innocence, my father doubled up the electric cord of an old iron and gave me a severe beating. This was to teach me to tell the truth. Long after the welts on my skin had faded, I seethed at the memory of the injustice done to me. Another time my mother, convinced that I had broken a certain doll and was lying about my guilt whipped we with a belt. I remained angry about both incidents for decades.

While in Nursing School during one of my infrequent weekends at home my twenty-six years old cousin, who lived in my parents' house and I had been stranded in Manhattan at a party and because of some problems with telephone lines had been unable to call home to say that we were staying overnight with friends. My father refused to believe that I had tried to call even when my cousin corroborated my story.

During the week and on the week ends that I did not go home neither one of my parents had any idea as to whether I slept at the nurses' residence or not. I had traveled alone in Europe, Africa, and the States for four years and had had any number of opportunities to deviate from my expected route but did not. At that particular time, I was also very angry with my father for fairly pushing me into going to Nursing School. I was angry with the Nursing instructors for the unrelenting pressure of their demands. The record of past wrongs bubbled up from the recesses of my memory. This latest accusation of my father provoked me to a level of anger I had never experienced. I reacted with such violence that it frightened me. The episode however marked a turning point in my life, I was no longer afraid of being misunderstood. I decided then that I was not the problem. No one had the right to accuse me of things that I had not done!

Now I looked at the woman instructor who had the power to do me harm simply because she felt superior to me and I hated her with every ounce of strength I possessed. Ugly thoughts churned inside of me. I had an explosive temper but had held it under control so this woman had never heard the tone of voice I used that day when I felt threatened. Looking at her straight in the eye I allowed all the hate I had felt from the very first day I had met her to pour out as I told her between clenched teeth that I was going to get my Diploma even if I had to go all the way to the President of the United States. Although she did not give me the grade that I deserved, she did not give me a failing grade either and we were both able to avoid talking with each other for the remaining few weeks of school.

Of the twenty-two who "made it" through the school two graduates missed passing the New York State Nursing Boards by one subject each. My classmates and I passed the "Boards" on the first attempt, with high scores, which was quite an accomplishment. Yet, I never felt a sense of satisfaction and was not looking forward to working as a nurse. We had job offers at the hospital we had trained in and I felt obligated to accept. After two years of intense study I needed a vacation but the new employee orientation session began the day after our graduation ceremony and I was afraid to be "jobless" so started to work right away. Our family had by then moved to Queens a suburb of New York City. My prospective earnings as a nurse had been factored in when I had co-signed for the mortgage on our house. I had lived in the Hospital School of Nursing residence and occasionally, when my mother gave me transportation fare, took the subway train and bus to visit home for a weekend.

Moving to the suburb of Cambria Heights in Queens into our own house was something of a victory for our family. The house set in a neat row of a tree lined street was very old with yellow shingled exterior, difficult to heat up in the winter and very hot in the summer but it had enough space within its small wallpapered rooms to fit us all comfortably. There was a fresh new smell on the inside. It had a basement; two floors, an attic, as well as a chain linked fenced front and backyard with more trees. One large cedar pine filled up the small patch of ground in the front. Manman immediately planted a row of flowers in this her first garden in the years since we had left Haiti. Family and friends started to pour in from Haiti. At one time, we had three of my cousins as well as a younger half brother of my mother staying with us. We lost track of who had keys to the outside door. Now with the school of Nursing closed there were rooms to rent at the Nursing Residence for any of the new graduates who worked at the hospital. I could keep the same room I had used for the previous two years. My father vetoed the idea.

"Why do you want to leave your home?" He asked. "This will set a bad example for your younger sisters".

I had been away from home since age twelve, except for my senior High School year, and did not feel that I had a home. In fact, my parents had drifted apart. My father especially, spent a lot of time away from home. Once again, I slid back into the adult child relationship, bowed to parental will, and settled in the attic of the house in Queens with an older cousin.

My contribution was now paying the mortgage for the family house but I was very unhappy with my job. My work consisted of two weeks on the day shift alternating with two weeks on the twelve to eight am one. I spent four hours everyday commuting between our home in Queens and the hospital in Brooklyn on the bus and subway train. The night shift however was the most taxing. By the time I arrived at my subway stop at around eleven thirty pm the damp cavernous Seventh Avenue station was deserted and I would look over my shoulder for the long walk from the platform up and out through the dark streets, afraid that I would get accosted and attacked by some lurking criminal. The story of Kitty Genovese, the young woman who had been stabbed to death on the streets of New York within earshot of several witnesses was fresh on my mind. So was an incident that occurred while I was still a student at the hospital.

One winter evening, shortly after dusk another Nursing student and I had heard a woman's voice screaming beneath the widow of the room we sat in. We saw the scuffle on the sidewalk involving a woman and a man. There was no time to pull on our coats. My companion and I recklessly ran down the nearest flight of stairs. By then, the woman had slumped to the ground and her attacker had fled. The other student and I made a quick assessment of the situation. The woman was talking, she had been mugged she said and her attacker had stabbed her with a knife. There was a large gash in the sleeve of her coat.

At least two pedestrians brushed past the three of us on the sidewalk. I was in my stocking feet, the other student wore a bathrobe and bedroom slippers. No one came to help. We were half carrying the sobbing woman between us as we headed towards the emergency room of the hospital. Later someone in the Emergency Room telephoned the Nurses Residence to tell us that the woman had not been injured. The thick padding in her winter coat had deflected the knife, protecting her. I became afraid to walk alone at night on the sidewalks of Brooklyn.

It was hard for me to stay awake on the train home when I started working at the hospital as a graduate nurse. I wound the straps of my purse around my folded arms when I sat in the overheated passenger car for the long ride. One morning after a particularly exhausting night shift, I was awakened from a sound sleep by a blow to the head. A man leaned over me and was in the process of prying my arms loose to release my purse when the lurch of the train had caused him to accidentally hit me. The train had arrived at a stop. We stared at each other in surprise before he bolted out of the car's open doors with me in pursuit. The loud *whoosh* sound of the train engine releasing steam jolted me back to my senses and I jumped back into the car barely squeezing past the closing doors. My heartbeat raced. I then realized that my purse was on my arm.

I had a long wait for the bus home. When it was time to switch to the two weeks Daytime tour of duty I had to be at the bus stop by five am in the freezing dark of the winter morning earlier than the rush hour with its crowd of people. The hospital had no parking for its nursing employees and was situated in an area of the city where it would be impossible to find a spot on the adjacent streets even if I had a car. I lived too far or was in the wrong job.

As a new Graduate I was at the Staff Nurse level on the hospital floor during the day, but on the night shift rotation I was the "Charge" nurse because I was the only Registered Nurse scheduled, displacing a more experienced Licensed Practical Nurse. This nurse bitterly resented my presence. She did her best to make things difficult. The rest of the staff especially an orderly, who was a known drunk were just as uncooperative. I worked on a forty bed chronically understaffed surgical unit. Instead of proffering help, my supervisors, contributed to my problems. Some say about the Nursing Profession: "They eat their young"; an observation that I agree with.

As a new nursing graduate I was a target for the bullying of older nurses, both Black and White, who felt compelled to demonstrate their superiority through pointing out my shortcomings at every turn. That was part of my initiation rites into the Nursing profession. I refused to fit into the mold these women, there were no male nurses on those particular units, had decided I belonged. New graduates were supposed to accept the worst shifts and worse assignments and be continually criticized until another new graduate came in to replace her in that role. My non-compliance with the unwritten rules of the Nursing pecking order drew enough fire on the Day shift that I should have preferred to work nights. The night shift was, however, staffed by the angry LPN, her accomplices the drunken orderly, and disappearing Nurses Aides. Someone in the Nursing hierarchy had determined that an inexperienced nurse should be in charge of a mutinous crew to care for people who had experienced a major surgical procedure a few hours earlier. The unrelenting pressure of my working conditions made me regret that I had stuck it trough Nursing School. Other twenty years old were having a better life than mine.

VI. Liberated daughter of a troubled people

"All we like sheep have gone astray: we have turned everyone to his own way..." Isaiah 53:6

13

In February of 1972, five months after graduation from Nursing School, convinced that I had made a wrong career choice, I enrolled in night school at the City University. Its Queens College campus because it had parking was my first choice (by then I had learned to drive and had bought my first car). This was my chance to meet people outside of the medical field. For the first time in my life, I felt that I did not have to give an account of myself to anyone. Tuition at the City University was free. I also did not have to declare a major course of study for two semesters so I registered in a modern dance class, and a history, anthropology, art appreciation courses; I was in school for my own personal enjoyment. I also joined the International Students Club and the Political Science Club. Unlike Nursing School were attendance was closely monitored, I could decide to skip class or attend the lectures as I pleased.

The Freshman English class that I enrolled in shortly after my arrival at Queens College reawakened an earlier passion in me. I started to write again. Aside from letters to my parents and to older family members and friends who only understood French, I wrote in English. Like Joseph Conrad, I preferred to write in that language rather than in my mother tongue. The fount of vocabulary words and the flexibility of English suited me best. French was too exacting. Besides, I had not been tutored in the latter since I was ten years old and now found that I expressed myself with greater ease in English.

I took several creative writing courses taught at the College by a French woman author who also wrote in English. She taught me to clean up my style:

" Keep it simple Marie-Solange! Say what you mean."

There were several very good writers in the class including a brilliant young Haitian born woman, whose name I do not recall. At Queens College, there were people from all occupations, all ethnic backgrounds, and a variety of ages. I felt unsure of myself in the first year or so and reluctant to plunge into the class discussions but I loved the atmosphere. It was somewhat like the ethnic melting pot I had experienced in my English boarding school days. At the same time, my work setting was forcing me into adopting an assertiveness that I might not have sought out otherwise. Finally, I was enjoying life in New York City and could even tolerate my nursing job. I was beginning to dream dreams about the future.

There was always a "prince charming" in my dreams but as the list of my requirements grew, he would develop larger than life clay feet. My sisters, who were three years younger, and I did not even broach the subject of dating with our parents. I for one had already decided that I would meet my own beau somehow differently than the traditional Haitian courtship rules prescribed. Manman and Papa had waived at each other for years across the balconies of their respective homes on the Ruelle Jardine in Port-au-Prince, Haiti so many years before. They had never gone out alone until the day before their wedding. We had, my sisters and I been fed an inexhaustible list of acceptable and unacceptable "decent female" behavior that did not equip us to deal with the realities of our own world.

Shortly after my arrival in America at age sixteen my heart had been set aflame by a very handsome Haitian male sporting a perfectly trimmed afro hair cut, white turtle neck sweater and a most charming smile set in my direction. This was 1968 in New York City: my family and I had renewed our ties with our ancestral roots in the middle of a Haitian community where the word "boyfriend" ran a close second to the word "leprosy". Therefore, for about two years this particular young man and I smiled at each other, danced together at family parties, but never mentioned our interest to anyone, especially to each other. Meanwhile he indulged in the typical Haitian male practice of flirting with other girls, never noticing that his smile had started to loose its glitter. When he decided that it was time to declare his sentiments it was too late. I had started to examine my life and evaluate my options. The double standard applied to male and female in our community troubled me. As a child, and later an adolescent I had never questioned my role, and did household chores and took care of younger children. In those days, with the custom of extended families and paid household help the work was shared among several women. Back in the old country, the women of my mother's generation and social status remained in their homes. In America, women had to work outside of the home to help support the family as well as do all of the housekeeping. The older men insisted on staying out of the kitchen while expecting their traditional time consuming meals and all the frills of a Caribbean lifestyle. Young men of marriageable age felt obligated to follow the example of their elders; oblivious of the change that had taken place in the consciousness of the young women like me. Therefore, I said "no thanks" to my would-be Haitian husband.

I did not want to remain a nurse. After nine months of commuting, four hours a day and switching between the mandatory night and day shifts, I sought out a hospital day job that did not require shift rotations. These were rare for new graduate nurses who were expected to pay dues to the profession by working in the most undesirable positions. Because my social life evolved around weekends, I was not ready to spend most of my free time away from people who were of the same age. The four-hour commute chipped away more time. I felt isolated. After a meticulous search, however, I found a day only job. My new position was on a forty-bed Orthopedic patient care unit in a private hospital, owned by a group of doctors, less than one hour's drive from my home. It had free parking. I also had a guarantee of having every other weekend off.

There is always a hidden hugely negative side to every nursing job and I soon found that the workload and lack of ancillary support in this one was so much more than I had imagined. Every other week off was a draw for any hospital to attract young single newly graduated nurses. To achieve this however, the administration staffed the weekend shifts with a skeleton crew of two nurses, two assistants, one Medication nurse, and a Charge nurse. The floor Charge Nurse had to process physician orders, answer the phone, since there was no "Unit Secretary", and oversee the work on the unit. In addition to distributing medications to forty patients from stock bottles, the Medication Nurse maintained an accurate inventory, completed pharmacy forms, walked to and from the Pharmacy on another floor to deliver and pick up medication. Frequently we had no Charge Nurse on the Weekend and one individual would have to function as both Charge and Medication nurse for the shift. The 500 beds hospital had maintained its credentials with the main hospital accreditation body in the United States. Therefore, after I had received an all too brief New Employee orientation in July 1972 I was shocked to find out that there was no Inhalation Therapy Department in the hospital. A contracted vendor delivered Oxygen tanks and supplies; the floor nurse, administered the respiratory therapy treatments. There were no Dietary Aides, the kitchen Staff delivered the stacked up food trays on a large cart to the front of the elevator doors of each unit for the Nursing staff to distribute. We had to pick up the used meal trays and stack them back on the Kitchen cart. The Nursing Staff transported patients to and from other departments for diagnostic tests and Surgical procedures, and there was no Intra Venous Team to assist with the care delivery to the mostly bed bound patients. Patients who remained on the Orthopedic Unit did so because they were immobilized in a traction apparatus, with weights suspended off the end of their beds or in a body cast, which extended from their chest to their toes. Others were recovering from recent surgeries such as a Hip Pinning. There were patients in need of intravenous therapies, wound dressing changes, assistance with meals, use of the bedpan and repositioning in bed in addition to other treatments. Anyone with a simple broken bone of an upper limb was discharged home. The bulk and weight of the equipment used on an Orthopedic Care Unit challenged the strength of the most physically fit of us. By late afternoon, I would arrive home exhausted and sink in an armchair, barely able to unlace my shoes to prop up my burning feet.

    The unwritten rule on my new unit was that one came to work an assigned shift regardless of any personal problems. An illness would have to be totally debilitating to allow any one to be absent. This was a good team except for one woman, with a particular mean streak in her, whom I discovered much later had been a Christian at the time. Whatever an individual assignment, no one took a meal Break or left at the end of our shift if a team member needed assistance. Our problem was that our unit shared the same floor, on the other side of the elevators, with an Obstetrical Unit that had a severe moral problem. That unit had seen its population of patients shift from mostly women who came in to give birth to teenagers from the Midwest and other parts of the country in quest of a Late Term abortion. New York State was one of the few States in 1972, to legalize abortions. Our privately owned hospital quickly restructured its Obstetrical services to meet the growing demand of the local physicians and out of State clients. Because so many of these abortions were Late Term, meaning that the women had past the time when a Dilation and Curettage procedure could be used to terminate the pregnancy, the Saline injection method had to be used. The Obstetrical Staff were used to the occasional situation when a patient would be brought in from the Labor and Delivery Suite to their unit after giving birth to a stillborn baby and would mourn with the grieving mother. They would not have seen the actual event. Saline Abortions were a different matter. I had never seen one in Nursing School. It involved the injection of a highly concentrated salt solution into the uterus of a pregnant woman and then waiting for the baby to die and be expelled through the vaginal canal. The Staff on the Obstetrics unit now attended the birthing of scores of small dead bodies. Several workers, citing their religious faith requested transfers to other units. Those who were refused transfers, left the hospital and the remainder frequently reported being sick rather than work on their assigned shifts. In response, the Nursing Administration regularly raided our unit to staff what, in our eyes had become a Death Ward.

I was a feminist, so intellectually I was for a woman's right to chose the termination of a pregnancy. When it was my turn to be "floated" to the unit next door, I marched off with only the thought of how I would need to organize my day to complete my assignment. The nurses who had been there before me had warned me that I would most probably be assigned the most difficult patient on the unit, an elderly woman recovering from a gynecological procedure who had multiple bed sores requiring extensive wound dressing changes. I already knew her room number. It was on the way down the hallway to the unit's Nursing Station where I had to first report to the Charge Nurse and pick up the rest of my assignment. Sounds of pain behind the closed door of one of the rooms I passed caught my attention. I pushed the door in and pulled the privacy curtain around the bed of the patient who was now shrieking. Something was missing. As a latecomer, I had not heard the morning Report from the outgoing shift's staff and briefly wondered that a woman who was obviously in labor was not being monitored more closely. Why was she here instead of the Labor and Delivery Unit? The patient was young, about fourteen or fifteen years old and was lying on her back with knees bent and spread apart. As I pulled off the bed covers I recognized the large pool of clear fluid on the absorbent pads placed on the bed and saw the characteristic bulge from the patient's bottom. A dark crown of hair was already protruding. I yanked the call bell off the wall of the room to alert the staff at the Nursing station that I needed help.

In Nursing School during my stint in Obstetrics I had assisted, more as an observer in several births and actually seen one patient deliver her baby in a hallway as I was wheeling her bed towards the Delivery Room. Something that I was not quite sure of was missing in this situation. My sense of foreboding grew when the baby's head started to come out. I had noticed that the mother was white and very young. As I gently cradled the head with my bare hands (gloves were not readily available in a patient room) my heart sank. The baby's shoulders, torso, buttocks, and legs slid out in the correct order but the skin had a dusky hue as if it had been dipped in soot. This was an emergency! A trickle of sweat dripped down my forehead, stinging my eye.

"He is not breathing!"

I whispered to the floor nurse who had just reached the bedside, conscious of not alarming the mother. There was a lack of urgency in the movements of my colleague. Her eyes locked mine. The tone of her voice was quiet and firm.

"Go get some towels!"

I opened my mouth to ask where the emergency equipment was to resuscitate the baby. The look in the nurse's eyes stopped me. Suddenly, I understood: this baby had been killed. The saline solution caused, I noted that it was a girl, the odd color of her skin. I did not hold on to any religious affiliation, but my Catholic childhood memories came flooding in. I worried about the soul of the dead baby I had touched with my bare hands. We kept her out of sight of the girl in the bed. Her small still body in a wad of white towels reminded me of Doucette, in Les Cayes, so long ago; the only other dead child I had seen. That family had been too poor to afford a church funeral. Surely, a priest must have gone to their shack to anoint that dead child. A priest would be called, I remember, to baptize a dead child who had not lived long enough to be taken to a church. I had not been involved in any church ritual in close to a decade. Anyone could perform the ceremony, I was told, if no priest was available. I sought out an opportunity, as I helped the other nurse clean up the girl and her bed. Then, when no one was looking, I released the few drops of water I held in my closed fist over the baby's head and quickly whispered:

"I baptize you in the name of the Father, the Son and the Holy Ghost".

Since I had never read the Bible, I did not know about the finality of death and that the soul of this infant did not need my help to get to heaven. My useless actions would have drawn a reprimand from my superiors, but no one saw me.

I was soon reprimanded for something else. In yet another effort to increase the profits of its shareholders, the hospital administration decided to close down its Central Supplies Department. That department was responsible for ordering supplies and maintaining an inventory of items needed by various Patient Care Units. This allowed the nurses especially, to order supplies either through a written order form or by telephone from one central location. We were now receiving bulk shipments delivered to our workstations for us to store in whatever cabinet space was available. Our Head Nurse started to add " restocking" duties to our assignment sheets. Each individual patient care assignment was heavy even on weekdays. Therefore, when I noted the order from the Head Nurse to clean out some cabinets and shelve several cases of Intravenous Fluid bottles, I balked. I had no time to give all of the nursing care that my patients needed, I told the Head Nurse, and could not complete the extra assignment. She reported this to our Nursing Supervisor, a Caribbean born woman who was particularly ill disposed towards me.

Within a few weeks on Staff at this hospital, I had noticed that, although we had never exchanged more than a few words, Mrs. Pope the supervisor found it difficult to address me in a civil manner. There were nurses from the former British colonies, particularly the Caribbean, whom I met occasionally who appeared to disapprove of me on sight. She was approaching middle age, with many years of experience and training and was in a Supervisory position so her attitude baffled me. Possibly some of my compatriots had offended this woman. Haitians tended to irritate other Blacks in New York City because of their insufferable pride. It might be that she resented me because of my lighter-skinned coloring. I had faced that type of problem before from dark-skinned Blacks.

"I thought you were the most stuck up girl around".

A very dark-skinned Black young man had told me at the hospital I had worked in previously. I was a new graduate nurse and had just given him a bed bath as he recovered from surgery. His comment surprised me. We had worked side-by-side several times over a period of more than two years, he as a Respiratory Therapist and I as a Nursing Student and later Staff Nurse. Clearly, I did not behave as others expected. For one I did not engage in the easy at times, flirtatious banter characteristic of young New Yorkers my age. I was from a different culture. In this instance, I had proven myself. The man thanked me for the care I gave him and when he returned to work adopted a brotherly attitude towards me whenever we met. With Mrs. Pope, my supervisor, there would never be a change of heart. As with the hostile White woman instructor in Nursing School, nothing I could do would meet with her approval. I could not physically work harder. My co-workers, our Head Nurse, and her assistant knew it. Our orderly shook his head when he would find that I had lifted a heavy patient without his help.

"You are too young to break your back missy!"

Our head Nurse belonged to a class of people I had noticed, in passing so far. In retrospect there were wall to wall individuals in that category who peopled Haiti, Trujillo's Dominican Republic, Liberia and other Dictatorships and as I was to learn later; "Corporate America". One such member of the class was on my Nursing School faculty. She was Black, the only fulltime instructor at the school and possibly the first in the hundred plus years history of that establishment, and very insecure about herself. This woman and I never had a private conversation until she gave me a failing grade on a term paper. I requested an interview with her and immediately sensed her discomfort. She was always nervous and defensive during her lectures, vacillating in response to questions from the mostly White students (we were only three Blacks in a class of forty-four women). At first, I pitied her and took great pains to treat her with the utmost respect, which was natural for me as a Caribbean bred English educated student. This Nursing instructor interpreted my behavior as a sign of weakness. She may have thought that treating me harshly would demonstrate her power and boost her confidence. I, however, was not inclined to be anyone's sacrificial goat. At our private conference, I politely listened to her lecture and lame excuses for the unjust grade that she

had given my paper. When she stopped talking, I played my trump card. The other students and I knew her greatest fear.
" I am going to complain to the school administration."
My quiet words threw my teacher in a panic. Her eyes widened and her face blanched to a grayish hue. She snatched up the paper that lay between us on the table, crossed out the failing grade she had first written and rewrote a much higher grade than it deserved. I felt very sad as I walked away.

Manman had drummed into my head so many lectures about integrity and was so vigilant about nailing it down into my sisters and my consciousness that I did not know how to behave differently. We also witnessed both our parents repeatedly demonstrate that principle. At times, we saw what it cost them to do this. Their parents, who in turn had received instructions from the previous generation, had indoctrinated them. I remembered how shocked Papa and Manman would be each time they learned of one of their acquaintance's failure to live by that tradition of personal integrity. "So- and so", meaning a dead ancestor of that individual, "would drop dead from indignation if he was alive to see this! " They would say.

Those who had repressed the traditional teachings or rejected the tenets of probity recognized each other. They sought and nurtured each other. The same individuals produced and sustained the dictatorships of Francois Duvalier, Rafael Leonidas Trujillo Molina who orchestrated the massacre of thousands of Haitian workers in the Dominican Republic in 1937, and so many more killers. It was now my turn to experience first hand, and away from the protection of my family, the moral failures of the human race. On this, the second position of my nursing career, I am sure that my Head Nurse did not think of herself as lacking in integrity. She probably rationalized her behavior. So many people say they have no choice when faced with the decision to harm someone or face an uncomfortable alternative.

Over the years, I have observed that unscrupulous people in positions of power seek out unscrupulous underlings to promote as middle managers. Many unscrupulous middle managers fall in the category of the weak, the fearful, and the insecure.

I believe cowardice is learned. Manman never allowed me to become a coward. My Head Nurse was hand picked by our employers for her ability to serve up her staff to be mistreated. She was very pleasant, mild mannered and appeared to be sincere in her appreciation of the people under her supervision. We responded by doing everything she told us to do, demonstrating our loyalty to her by not complaining. Our unit was known for working harder than our counterparts around the hospital. When I joined the staff, I was young, physically and morally strong enough to ignore the rumors; some were starting to wonder why our Head Nurse allowed our staff to be "floated" to other units so frequently. This created a chronic shortage on our own unit even as we individually faithfully came in to work our assigned shifts. We suspected that we were the hospital administration's guinea pigs. Our Head Nurse volunteered us for or at least never tried to protect us from more projects than we could handle. I had at first thought of her as a mentor. Aside from one Haitian doctor who was doing his residency, the physicians with privileges to practice at the hospital, and the owners, were White. Our leader was an experienced, knowledgeable, and skilled, nurse who was an excellent teacher and manager, but she was Black. She feared for her position. My youthful impetuousness made no allowances for her past history and personal situation. I did not know those. It appeared to me that her professional reputation was well established. People at all levels sought her advice. She had worked for and deserved her position. Her insecurity turned her into a coward.

One morning my Head Nurse simply called me away from my assignment to tell me to report immediately to the Nursing Director's office. I took the elevator down to the Director of Nursing's office to face the Director, her Assistant Director, and Mrs. Pope the Department Supervisor. There was no prior notice of this meeting except obviously to my Head Nurse. She was my direct supervisor and either had chosen or been told not to accompany me or to brief me on what was to come. I felt betrayed by her. My interrogators were concerned about my poor performance, I was told. None of the three women were interested in anything I had to say. In fact, I was not allowed to speak. I felt like a child ordered to report to the reverend Mother's parlor back in my Convent School days. My immediate supervisors, the Head Nurse and Assistant Head Nurse who could have vouched for my competence and performance were not at the meeting. The words *Kangaroo Court* flashed across my mind. Mrs. Pope, the Supervisor particularly remembered observing me administering *"Pericare"* to a patient without following the proper procedure set by the Hospital's Policy and Procedure Manual. After the incident with the restocking assignment, I had bumped into the Supervisor on several occasions as I went about my work. The woman would stand quietly behind the privacy curtain in a patient room to spy on me. I also knew that she was questioning my co-workers and the patients assigned to me.

    I realized that one day I would slip up and give this woman the ammunition she needed to harm me but felt powerless to stop her. The protocol for *Pericare*, short for Perineum Care called for the nurse to place the patient on a bedpan and squirt water from a squeeze bottle between the patient's legs. One day as I bathed an uncooperative, disoriented woman who was recovering from a hip pinning surgery, I was unable, because of her weight, to slip the flat shovel shaped bed pan under her hip as she lay in the bed. The Unit staff was just as busy as I was and no one was around to help me. Even if I had seen the supervisor hiding behind the curtain, I would not have sought her assistance. Supervisors walked around in their crisp white uniforms with a clipboard and were unapproachable in that sense. I modified my technique to clean the patient without the use of the bedpan. The patient had a tube known as a Foley Catheter in place to drain urine from her bladder. I used the same technique to clean her perineum as I would have if I had been removing and replacing the catheter. There was no harm done, I thought.

The issue of cleaning up and stocking cabinets with Intravenous Fluid bottles had been linked, without any mention of it, to my ability to perform my duties as a Registered Nurse. The Director of Nursing placed me on probation: I had to be closely monitored by the Head nurse, Assistant Head Nurse and Charge Nurse. I was no longer deemed trustworthy enough to be assigned Charge Nurse responsibility. On our unit, I was third in line for the Charge Nurse duty on a shift whenever both the Head Nurse and Assistant Head Nurse were absent. Both these women trusted my professional judgment and we all knew that the Disciplinary action against me had nothing to do with the performance of my nursing duties. Fear, intimidation, cowardice, those familiar ingredients of a dictatorship were just as ugly in Haiti, Liberia, the English Convent School as in the Queens New York Hospital.

There was no additional pay for being in charge of a shift and that assignment invariably held more headaches since it meant that both the Head Nurse and her assistant were not on the unit to handle administrative or clinical problems. It was also impossible, because of the workload to closely monitor any nurse on our unit. No one had a definition of what that meant. The Nursing Supervisor wanted to keep me on a short leash for her own reasons. I was angry. *This, after all was the United States of America, these people cannot treat me this way.* I thought. My first impulse during the meeting was to turn in my employee badge to the Supervisor and walk out of the job. That was what I knew Mrs. Pope wanted. Instead, I made a mental review of the Calendar. In New York City, the usual length of vacation time for nursing employees was four weeks after one year of tenure. I had taken a two weeks vacation at the end of my first six months at the Hospital and was due to receive another two weeks of paid vacation time if I completed another six months. As the Nursing Director wrapped up her disciplinary speech, I was silently adding up the days and arrived at the exact date that I would turn in my resignation without jeopardizing my two weeks vacation pay.

One Sunday sometime later, the Medication Nurse on our shift became ill and left after she had prepared her tray of Medications but before she could distribute them to the patients. The Assistant Head Nurse who was in charge of the shift, and would now have to take up the Medication Nurse's duties in addition to her own, promptly began to vomit and was sent home by the Nursing Supervisor. This was a relief supervisor on duty, who had just started to work at our hospital on weekends. Mrs. Pope had the day off. We had barely served breakfast. I had stocked up a cart with fresh linen and other supplies and was making my way from the farthest end of the unit with my Nursing Assistant. On days when we had twenty patients each, we teamed up to give "AM Care" to as many patients as we could before the dreaded call would sound from the elevator area that the lunch trays had arrived.

I was told that the Nursing Supervisor was asking for me on the phone at the Nursing Station. The Supervisor told me that I was now in charge of the shift, and yes, it seems that I would have to "pass meds" and no, she could not find another nurse to help and pick up where I had left off. I retorted that I had not been the one to pour out the pills from the medication Stock bottles into the tiny paper cups labeled with the name of each patient on individual cards. Therefore, I would have to set up another medication tray for the forty patients on the unit. Did she know I asked her that the only other Nurse on the unit could not administer Blood Transfusions? And that a new patient recently admitted on our unit was bleeding from a condition known as Esophageal Varices, and needed Transfusions in addition to having his stomach flushed through a tube with an ice cold Saline solution? I would have to care for this patient personally. Another Staff member was informing me that several patients were asking for pain medication. By then the whole floor had missed their morning dose of Librium or Valium. The physicians routinely prescribed these tranquilizers for most of the patients who had to spend hours in bed and were immobilized by plaster casts and various contraptions. Yes, the supervisor replied she knew all this, and that I was on probation and not supposed to be in charge of a shift. She, however, had no choice.

"I need a *Blakemore* Tube".

I said trying to focus on my most urgent problem.

"The man with the Esophageal Varices is bleeding and his doctor has just walked in and ordered the *Blakemore*, we do not have one on this unit." I explained. With the closure of the Central Supplies Department, various items were stocked on different floors around the Hospital. She was new to the hospital, the nursing Supervisor told me, and the only Nursing supervisor covering the entire hospital, and did not know where she could find a *Blakemore* Tube. The *Blakemore* Tube is a stomach tube that has a lining that is filled with ice water to compress the Esophagus, or tube like section that connects the throat to one's stomach. This particular patient had tiny blood vessels all along the soft tissue of his Esophagus that had weakened and started to bleed. I had been hooking up Blood bags to his Intravenous set up, observing the required protocol and monitoring procedure in addition to helping the other nurse assigned to him to wash out his stomach. Now, I had to inform this man's physician that I could not locate an essential piece of equipment needed to stop the patient's bleeding.

Doctors in this particular hospital were especially boorish in their interactions with the nursing staff. I had already had a couple of surgeons scream at me for something or other. I braced myself for another unpleasant episode. This physician however did not lose his temper. To my relief he calmly stated that he was going to drive to another hospital to borrow a *Blakemore* Tube. His manner told me that he understood what was going on in our hospital. The life of his patient was more important to him than useless posturing.

Later that day I had the switchboard operator call up the Nursing Supervisor on the pager system. Her response was a surly grunt. I began once again to catalogue the reasons why I needed another nurse to come to our unit to help me. There was no Intensive Care unit bed available for me to transfer the patient who was bleeding, and whose condition was deteriorating in spite of the insertion by his physician of the *Blakemore* Tube. His care required most of my attention. None of the patients on the wing I had started out with had received their "AM Care". I could not keep up with the situation, I told her on the telephone.

"Miss Benedict", the Nursing Supervisor interrupted: "A good nurse always manages".

I mentally drew another chalk mark on my calendar. The day on my timetable to leave this job was drawing closer. In a file at home, I kept the resignation letter I had already typed. I had not even looked for another job and had a negligible amount of money saved. At home, I had been paying more than my share of living expenses in my parents' house and now felt no guilt about taking a Sabbatical. Since I knew that my parents would not understand my feelings, I did not discuss any of this with them.

At first, I had taken seven college credits per semester but felt an urgency to complete my degree. My plan was to get out of the Nursing profession. I needed to both work and go to school. So far, work was sapping all of my mental and physical strength. There did not seem to be any reasonable hospital job for a relatively new nurse. I did not want to work on another hospital Patient Care Unit even if I had to earn a lower salary.

I did not want to remain a nurse because I rarely felt a sense of accomplishment. On most nights, my brain would keep me awake rehashing the whole shift I had completed in minute details. I would make an inventory of all the things I had left undone. So much of what I had learned in Nursing School had not prepared me for the realities of a busy understaffed Patient Care Unit. In the hospital I had trained in there was a separate set of people to deliver and pick up meal trays. Spoon-feeding an elderly patient took at least twenty minutes. What happens when there are four patients needing that simple task on one nurse's assignment? Six others who need to be bathed in bed? How often did someone who cannot use their hands crave for a few sips of water and suffer the indignity of laying in his or her own waste for over an hour? Instead of feeling that I had improved the condition of a patient, I mostly felt that I had contributed to their pain and discomfort. In this hospital, there was no Respiratory Therapy department. Setting up the equipment, mixing up the medication, and making sure that the patient was following the instructions on how to take the treatment was time consuming. So much of Nursing is preventive care. I felt frustrated that I could not give the back rubs, reposition the patient, exercise her limbs coach him to expand his lungs, keep his dentures clean, boost her ability to heal!

14

My first encounter with death was in Nursing School. I had to accept that the amiable grandmother sitting up in her bed with her eyes wide and mouth open had died because she was too ill to benefit from our care. We had been taught in our classes to maintain the appropriate distance, not to cross the professional line between patient and nurse.

"Focus on the patient's need"

I tried to do as I was told even as I made a mental note not to work in Pediatrics or in Psychiatry. The innocence of a sick child and the tragedy of mental illness, I found caused me unbearable sadness. Receiving bad news about any patient was also very difficult. Several time we had patients on our unit who were diagnosed with Cancer. Usually these patients would be transferred to a Surgery or Oncology unit since ours was an Orthopedic floor. Mr. S a Black school principal requested to return to our unit after his diagnosis of Cancer each time he was re-admitted for treatment. I took note of his race because I realized that in the United States, in 1972 it took much effort and persistence for a Black man to become a Principal in the Public School system. He, and his wife and two teenage daughters knew each one of us by name. We silently mourned with them as his condition deteriorated and I was relieved when they decided that he would return home to die.

Another patient I cared for was a surgeon who had had a double barrel colostomy, a procedure where both part of the large intestine (after it has been cut in half to remove a diseased section) are pulled out through the skin of the belly for the contents to drain in a specially fitted pouch. The staff usually did not like to care for doctors or nurses fearing the additional scrutiny of one knowledgeable of the health field. A sick colleague would discover our shortcomings and might cause problems with the administration. Initially this man was too ill to be aware of what was going on around him. The fellow doctor he had allowed to do his surgery had pioneered the questionable practice of using un-sterilized gauze to dress his patients' wounds. I was told that this surgeon gave antibiotics in anticipation of infections and then insisted that anyone caring for his post operative patients should use clean but un-sterilized dressings which were stacked on an open cart for dressing changes. This was also touted as a cost containment measure. Sterilized and un-sterile dressings were distinguishable by a special blue string and I was told that this particular surgeon would retaliate against anyone he found disobeying his orders. No one knew whether the colleague and now patient of this man had any knowledge of this practice. I had lived in third world countries. Manman and Papa had taught my sisters and I to respect germs long before I had gone to Nursing School. This practice disturbed me but there was no one to voice my apprehension to.

The physician patient in our care developed a horrible infection that almost killed him. He was conscious by then and never complained as he lay with his flesh rotting in front of his eyes. The smell was overpowering. I had never met this physician before his illness and was inspired by his courage. Everyone on Staff became involved; we could not allow this man to die on our watch. Some of us wondered why he had not requested to be transferred to another hospital where surely more sophisticated treatment was available. There was a collective sigh of relief on our unit when our patient started to improve and eventually was discharge to his home. Shortly after, I saw his wife speaking with our Head Nurse at the Nursing station. She did not appear upset so I concluded that there was no problem with our patient. He must have asked her stop by to thank us; there is probably a box of candy at the station for the staff, I thought. Our Head Nurse looked bewildered as she escorted her visitor to the elevator. She came our Head Nurse told us, on behalf of her husband to arrange, for the entire staff to have dinner at a nearby Polynesian restaurant. I had been to that restaurant and knew that it offered a very good and expensive cuisine. The restaurant had been instructed to reserve a reception table for two separate times to allow for the coverage of the hospital shifts. Everyone on our staff would be able to participate as this couple's guests. The physician sent his regrets that he was still too weak to join us for dinner but wanted to express his gratitude: we had saved his life.

I treasured that couple's gesture and that of others who sent flowers, candy, or Thank You cards. These times served as a buffer against the feelings of hopelessness I felt so often while working on that Unit and in other Nursing positions. Private duty Nursing was not an attractive option for me because of the low pay and fluctuating assignments. In retrospect, I should have tried to find better mentors in the hospital field who could have directed me to a workable niche. After a year on the Orthopedic unit, I was tired. I wanted to spend more time on my studies. Going to Queens College was the best thing I had done in years and working on a day shift allowed me to continue to attend the evening classes from 6:20PM to 10:00PM.

My mother was predictably upset when I stayed home for an entire month after resigning from the hospital. She also disapproved of my short "afro" hairstyle. For years, I had straightened my hair with chemicals and worn it shoulder length. I slept late and refused to go to any job interview unless it was for a Monday to Friday Day shift position outside of a hospital. Eventually I saw an advertisement for a very low paying position in a clinic for a Registered Nurse to "triage" in-coming calls or walk-in patients. The outgoing nurse was pregnant and planned to spend time raising her family. "Its crazy here!" she said. I could tell that she had been away from the hospital scene for quite some time. I accepted the position and soon found myself in charge of a Medical Center of eight physicians that included a Surgeon, an Obstetrician-Gynecologist, a Pediatrician, and a very eccentric Allergist. It was a demanding job but with a different type of stress. For one no one was lying in bed waiting for me to complete a string of chores before I could get around to give them a bath. There were no confused elderly patients getting out of restraints, pulling out their Intravenous devices. My creativity was challenged as necessity forced me to train a variety of individuals to function as Medical Assistants, Phlebotomists, Electro Cardiograph technicians, and Medical secretaries. All the instruments used in the Center by the Surgeon, the Gynecologist and others had to be cleaned, autoclaved, and packaged. So much of what I had to do had not been part of my training in nursing School. It served me well to have helped in Papa's dental practice so many years before in Suakoko. This was also my first experience doing the payroll for twenty people. The Center supervisor and I were the only two of thirty employees who were not Union members. This might have been problematic. In fact, there were continuous Labor Relations issues with the other Centers that were part of our group. After I had been on the job for about a year a Black woman, who had been with the company for years and worked her way up the corporate ladder, was promoted to supervise the Center. My other supervisor was a scholarly, courteous, mild mannered Director of Nursing who spent most of his time in his office at one of the larger centers. He and I had a very good working relationship.

Within about a week of her arrival, the new Center supervisor called me in to her office. She had been observing me, she said and wondered how I was able to do all that I did on a daily basis. The two white males who preceded her had delegated an appreciable amount of their own work to me. I had never suspected it. For instance the payroll... In her experience, she said, she had never seen a Center nurse work as hard as I did. She then proceeded to remove several of my most taxing duties from me. This woman, I also found was an expert at Labor Relations. "One hand washes the other." She would say. In our Center, she treated our employees better than their Union Contract required, earning their trust and respect. Her practical common sense approach and her integrity made her a very effective manager. She taught me many invaluable lessons in the two years that I worked on her staff.

In those days, I took twelve to thirteen college credits at night and spent most of my weekends studying but I was happy. My Haitian friends had taught me the steps of the native dances. I loved to dance. Every birthday, anniversary, christening, first communion, wedding, was an opportunity in the Haitian community living in New York City to dance. From the very old to the very young, we all danced. I went to at least one party or to a dance club almost every weekend. Even during the years I worked in a hospital, I would sometime make it to the patient care unit from a party just in time to change into my uniform. Most girls my age went to dances to meet prospective husbands but I was already in love; with the music and scouted the crowd for the best men dancers. In Haitian dance with convention dictating that the male leads, a good partner is essential. Dancing was also a way of pushing back the sadness of Haiti and Haitians. The usual live band of those days played too loud to allow one to talk to one's partner, keeping each blissfully ignorant of the other's shortcomings. It was exhilarating to come and go as I please. I very rarely got drunk at parties, because I wanted to remain in control of every aspect of my life at all times. When my mother took a trip back to Port-au-Prince, I did not accompany her. Even though Francois Duvalier was dead, the Duvalierists were still very much in control of Haiti under his successor son. I did not want to risk loosing the life I now had in the United States. After twelve years, the government in Haiti still restricted the movements of its nationals. I held a Haitian passport and was now a nurse. We had heard of young professionals being detained there in the government's belated attempt at containing the exodus of its trained workforce. Everyone knew that Duvalierist spies prowled the exile community's salons eager to find something to use as bargaining chips back in Haiti. Manman had to go back. Her father was now over ninety years old and she wanted to see him one more time.

"When is Matoutou coming back?"

Papa Gus would ask about me. The twins, both were sixteen and high school students, traveled to Port-au-Prince with Manman. By my twentieth summer, it appeared to me that most of the young men and women of my generation who had the financial means to do so had left Haiti. The State University in Port-au-Prince set up arbitrary barriers to admissions that often prevented the best students from obtaining an education there. The ones fortunate enough to get into the university then had to contend with the capricious demands of a hierarchy that was controlled by the Duvalierist regime. Most of my extended family members were among the expatriates living in several places in the United States and Canada.

Some of my cousins had settled in Montreal, Canada after completing their studies there and I drove up from New York to visit them several times during the summer; which is how I met Julien. It was a small family party with the usual dancing and I noticed, sometime during the course of the evening after I had danced several times with him that we were attracted to each other. He was soft-spoken, courteous, appeared to be physically fit, well proportioned and neatly groomed. We exchanged phone numbers and corresponded by telephone and letters for a few weeks until he came to visit me in New York. We were both working while attending school and had planned our schedules carefully in order to meet. By then, I was experiencing the first stirrings of a love relationship and he, from his beautifully penned letters in impeccable French was professing his affection for me.

Manman was outraged when I told her that I was going to pick up my friend from the airport and drive him to the relatives with whom he would stay for the weekend. Men are supposed to pick up women and not the other way around. She forbade my sisters to speak about any of this lest my father should know about my supposed infractions. The following day I picked up Julien again, this time from his relative's home where I was cordially received, and drove him back after we had spent the day at an Amusement Park. We planned to meet at a soccer game the following day, which was Sunday and spend the afternoon together before his flight back to Montreal. I still lived in my parents' house and had never lied to them. Even though I was twenty years old, a Registered Nurse, gainfully employed, paying my own bills, including my college fees, I was still a Haitian girl from a "good family". Maman pulled all the stops: I could not invite Julien to meet my family. She had even heard something negative about one of his distant relatives a long time ago back in Haiti. Ironically, Julien whom my mother never met was exactly the type of young man my parents would have liked. I could tell from his speech, letters, and manners that he was a most traditional of Haitian suitors. We had spent an entire day alone and he had never attempted to kiss me.

"I don't want to shock you." He said at one point. I understood that his restraint came from a desire to build our relationship on a proper foundation. I went to the soccer game in spite of my mother's objections but was bombarded by conflicting thoughts. What would happen if I allowed myself to fall deeply in love with this young man? There was no one I could discuss this with. Having decided to major in the pre-Law program in College I had only just recently charted a course for my life. In our talks, Julien had made clear that he would never move to the United States, or even learn English. He was uncertain about what course of study he would pursue at the University in Montreal. Worse, I got the impression that he disapproved of my plan to go to law School. Although I loved to visit Canada in the summer and had several friends and relatives in Montreal, I knew that I would never adjust to the winters there. Neither he nor I planned to return to Haiti, at least for a while. It seemed to me that we were headed for more complications besides having to deal with my parents' rules. Confused and afraid, I took the coward's path and withdrew from our budding relationship without discussing any of my fears with him.

By American standards, single women my age were already living in their own apartments. I was comfortable in my parents' house until the little irritations brought about by our growing cultural differences soured our relationship. In the typical Haitian home, the father is king. The older I became, the more annoyed I got with having to subject my personal preferences to the whims of my father. He was surprised to find out that I expected to be consulted before he disposed of something that belonged to me or made a decision that affected our household. I gave orders at work to the people I supervised but at home I felt that my opinion was discounted. My budding feminist ideas and the traditions of the Haitian home were on a collision course. I respected my father, but I could not fit in the role that, subconsciously since we never discussed it, he saw for me. Manman understood that I could no longer remain in our family home. My mother was fiercely loyal to the memory of her father and submitted herself to her husband, but she felt betrayed. My generation did not have to "*bouche Nin bwe dlo santi*" as hers did. That phrase that she had used so often to justify her acceptance of things she did not like did not apply to me. Her actions, if not her exact words implied this. My father and I had already had some very unpleasant confrontations. Clearly, I did not have a conciliatory temperament.

"If I had run away from my father's house and gone to New York City, I would be far today!"

Manman said. She set up a standard of success that she could not attain. The possibilities in this country captivated my imagination and I soared high on the crest of a new found optimism so I was surprised to find that I could not rent an apartment in New York City. My difficulty had to do with my race. I had the idea that this sort of thing was confined to the Southern states. It annoyed me when an advertised vacancy would suddenly become filled as soon as the same individual with whom I had had a cordial telephone conversation would see me in person. My clothes and hairstyle were conservative for those days. I was gainfully employed as a Registered Nurse and a serious college student. Nothing in my five feet two and one half, one hundred and ten pounds appeared fearful to me. Between my Haitian middle class upbringing and English Boarding School experience, there could not be anything objectionable in my manners either. Still I had to go on with my life.

For three years, I worked with a Medical Director who made it clear that he thought that a High School drop out Assistant should be in charge of my department instead of me the College Student Registered Nurse. In Haitian circles, poor table manners are criticized as a lack of savoir-faire of the uneducated. So, for me racist behavior ranked, for the time being, with someone chewing at the dinner table with an open mouth. I made sure that this doctor could hear my voice when I gave his favorite assistant a vicious tongue lashing and dared her to try out any more of her insolent behavior on me. She, as the Union Shop Stewart, was effectively running the Medical Center that I found out, after being hired, I was responsible for.

"You do not have a High School Diploma."

I growled, at this woman. " I am Registered Nurse. Which one of us do you think the Administration needs the most?"

Eventually a young Orthodox Jewish couple rented me an efficiency apartment in the basement of their home close to the College I attended. I had my own car and paid my own bills, came and left as I pleased and relished the sense of power it gave me. Although I had grown to be very assertive in any one on one interaction, I could not speak in public. To correct this problem I took two communication courses at the College. My first public speech for a class assignment started badly: I fainted and the heavy wooden podium I had placed my notes on fell on my head. Although X-rays revealed no damage, my ego was bruised and only the fear of failing out of the course sent me back to the class

My social circle was broadening to include anyone in New York City's melting pot who defended the rights of Women, Blacks, and the downtrodden. Frequently the International Club at Queens college, that I became a member of held meetings hosted in the home of a widow, in her eighties who had emigrated from Germany to escape Adolf Hitler's Nazis. There were some similarities in both our pasts. In her youth, before she married, she had thought about becoming an attorney and was involved for a brief moment in local politics. Her family had had to abandon their comfortable home in Hanover simply because they were Jews. At first she, her husband, and four children tried to settle in Israel. Her husband, however, could not adjust to the climate there so the family immigrated to New York City. My friend, after having employed servants in her former European home, then learned to be a maid. In time, she had obtained the necessary higher education degrees to improve her employment status. She retired after a long career as a social worker in New York City. These and other life experiences had left her with an empathetic heart towards anyone who aspired to overcome adversity. She invited Jews, Gentiles, Arabs, White, and Black, of all ages, everyone who wanted to come to her home. Our lively discussions over the years spreading beyond our club meetings included Politics, the United Nations, Human Rights, and Women Rights. We disagreed amiably on the latter issue because my friend had more conservative views than mine. Since she lived close to the college, on occasion, I would stop by her house for breakfast or pick her up for a classical music concert. I felt free to share my views with her without the threat of condemnation. Her down to earth common sense manner appealed to me. For one, she was frank about the limitations of her age.

"I am going to take a five minutes nap right here."

She would announce in the middle of a conversation, close her eyes for a while, and awaken with a new spurt of energy to pick up where we had left off. I did not foist Nursing advice on her and she did not force feed any of the wisdom older people tend to saddle the young with. We simply looked at things in the light of the possibilities and within the bounds of civil debate. Her parties gathered more than just college students since she had friends from the choir she sang in and the community orchestra she played the violin with amongst others. She managed her affairs (she rented part of her house) in order to finance her visits to her children, grandchildren, relatives, and friends and to maintain her independence. I admired her.

At about this period a new organization attracted my attention. I bought the first issue of the magazine they launched and subscribed as a member of the National Organization for Women: N.O.W. Their rhetoric touched off a chord deep within me. Feminist ideology articulated how I felt about the injustices I had seen women subjected to. I also joined the American Civil Liberties Union. I was still exploring my options for the future and felt an intense need to guard my new-found freedom, keeping a suspicious eye on the alert for attempts to set limits on my life.

By the mid-seventies both Tikite and Pepe attended Colleges in upstate New York five hours drive away from home and for the first time in their lives, five hours away from each other. The first few weeks of this change were rough on the twins. At eighteen years old, neither had spent much time away from their family and they were, severely homesick. My parents' phone bill exploded with "collect" telephone charges. When they came home on visits the girls did not want to go back to school. Papa was sympathetic and the twins' sobs caused conflict with his wish to see them educated. Manman was adamant: neither girl had better come home without finishing what they had started.

"I don't care what kind of paper you bring home!"

She told them. We were all welcome to come back to the nest if we had a College degree. Manman confided once to me that she herself, as a young woman, had plotted to run away from her father's house to go to New York City to become a nurse. Her sisters had to attend Secretarial School in Port-au-Prince in secret. The younger of my aunts and another woman friend gave up their plans to attend the Engineering School in Port-au-Prince when the men of the University publicized their threats. Any woman who tried to study there would be tossed naked into a pond. Papa Gus, my grandfather, forbade his daughters to go to school and pursue careers outside of their home. His reason was that

"People will think that I am unable to support my daughters". Meanwhile he failed to amass the fortune that his daughters would need to live on after his death, since he did not see the need either, for them to marry a husband for support. Yet, he admired women. In later years, his most trusted physician was a woman doctor.

Manman did not fight her father to get an education. She did not like to have her father or her husband fuss at her because, she told me, she was afraid of what she would do if she lost her own temper. Now in her fifties Manman had to leave her home to work in the cramped and sometimes unsanitary conditions of the garment factories in New York City. She ate her lunch out of a brown paper bag set on her lap in the company of people she could not communicate with. She was not always treated well. Characteristically she did not rail against fate; she marched on. Whatever problem faced her, Manman found solutions. I was in awe of my mother's indomitable spirit. Once she carted out an old couch unto the curb of our home in residential Queens attaching a note that she had one of us write for the sanitation department to take it away. Manman said nothing when the couch was left with a response from the New York City Sanitation Department that they did not pick up furniture with the garbage. She dragged the couch back to the basement of her house.

"Do you know where the old couch is?"

She asked me one day with an air of satisfaction that told me she had gotten the better of the New York City Sanitation Department.

"*Mouin réglé yo*" she said meaning that she "got them".

Then she told me that she had dismantled the couch with a hacksaw and "fed them", the Sanitation people, pieces of the furniture in every garbage can they picked up from her curb until they had taken the whole couch away. As we were growing up my sisters and I would shudder at our mother's pronouncements that any man, meaning her husband our father, who left her would "go feet first". Later I concluded that she really saved Papa's life. He lived long after most of his friends had succumbed to the life of debauchery that Haitian society condones for its males. As a newly wed in tradition laden Haiti Manman had drawn the line in the sand and Papa's friends, after sizing up their opposition, quickly realized that they preferred her loyalty to her wrath. Even as she pinched her nose to ward off the stench of things she did not like, she had her limits as to what she would accept. She expressed disdain for any woman who was beaten by her husband, as was the custom in many a Haitian home. According to Manman, it was better for a wife to die machete in hand. From my earliest recollections, Manman consistently trumpeted her opinion on wife beating. She suspected that her father had abandoned his family because in addition to his philandering her mother would not accept his attempts at physical abuse. Manman remembered her parents fighting. Man Lillie, petite and less than five feet tall was no match against Papa Gus's six foot frame. He, however never succeeded against her determination to maintain, as Manman saw it, her dignity. In one memorable scene, Amélie jumped atop their dining table, heaved a cast iron hand sewing machine, and attempted to brain *Monsieur* Toulmé.

A Haitian woman, even in more modern times had no recourse with the law. Many of my mother's contemporaries endured years of abuse. The woman stood alone. Our society condoned it. Not Manman, she never passed up an opportunity to reprimand a suspected wife beater. Her status as Papa's wife and ironically Auguste Toulmé's daughter protected her. One relative with two brothers-in-law, who were notorious for physically abusing their wives and mistresses, set the boundaries very early in her own marriage. Manman told me the story several times: the woman picked up a very valuable vase and smashed it to smithereens on a wall, inches away from her husband's head. That man never beat his wife.

I sensed that my parents' marriage was in trouble but both kept up the appearance of a harmonious home. We could not discuss that sort of topic. It was also better for me not to divulge the details of my own life to them. They would be severely disturbed if they really knew me. There was a rift between their ideas of right and wrong and mine. Haitian parents do not admit, even if they think it, that their children have the right to disagree with their elders. When my father passed the New York State Dentistry Boards and obtained his license to practice in New York, Manman stepped in to help him with his private dental office while she continued to do all the chores in their home. For my generation, especially In the United State of America, there were other options: education was easily accessible to women as well as men and as I saw it, paved the way to power and independence. I was not looking for a fight, I simply did not care to have anyone whether Black, White, Purple, Male or Female running my life.

Living in New York City in the nineteen-seventies, I did not deny my Haitian roots but could not embrace the entire Haitian community and its culture either. Resentment for past wrongs or present ills ran deep as did class, religious, and color prejudices. For one, Duvalierism and its legacy of fear and suspicion exacerbated the traditional tendencies of a people that had never learned to live well together. Recently while watching a video, I thought about the perversity of the human mind. In the American made movie Rosewood, the white population of a small Florida town seize on the excuse of the barely credible tale of a young White woman, known for her promiscuity, to accuse and then lynch her supposed rapist. Rosewood was an all Black town where Blacks prospered by being economically free of Whites. This true story from the Jim Crow American South ends with the torture, maiming, murdering of several of the Black citizens of the town and the burning down of the entire town of Rosewood, Florida. As I watched the movie characters portraying the white lynch mob, I was reminded of the people, blurred faces really, from my own hometown of so long before. The similarities in the stories were striking in that the behavior of both sets of people had at least one identifiable root cause: envy!

In Les Cayes Haiti, neighbor too envied neighbor. My father once collared a man who was part of a mob that had invaded his office, on some flimsy politically motivated excuse. The man, who was wearing a shirt that my father recognized as one that he had given to him, was busy smashing up Papa's furniture. Ordinary men joined Duvalier's "*Tontons Macoutes*" in order to steal and exert power over others. Every family in Haiti that was not connected to the Duvalierist regime had similar or worse stories to tell. For my godmother and her family, trapped in the country the persecution lasted a lifetime. Hers was a prosperous, well-known family whose men had been distinguished leaders of the country. Three of her older brothers openly defied the newly empowered Duvalier who quickly forgot that the same family had fed him, his wife, and children when he himself had been on the run as a political dissident. Over a period of thirty years, Duvalier and his henchmen beat, imprisoned, assassinated, and harassed, members of the family, appropriating their lands, houses, and property. The remaining family members, terrorized over the years, hauled off to jail on a whim repeatedly found themselves unable to collect even the most intimate of their personal belongings. They warned friends not to come to see them since visitors and once even the student of one sister who gave piano lessons were picked up in the unpredictable raids. My mother's two sisters living in Port-au-Prince disregarding the warnings always tried to find the family to offer some words of comfort. The Toulme sisters were true friends my godmother told me later. Something snapped in her polite world of Haitian society:

ordinary people would take advantage of the government raids on her family to pick up their own loot. After one such episode, the family home was simply turned over to a government department and eventually housed a section of the government Nursing School.

Many years later while living in the United States, one of my Nursing colleagues casually mentioned in the course of a conversation, that she had been a student in Port-au-Prince at this government Nursing School at the time and that she and her classmates had been quartered in that same family home. This woman went on to describe the scene she witnessed. There were signs, she said, that the dispossessed family had obviously not had the time to pack any of their personal effects. Her fellow students and her had sifted through the items that had been left behind and, she continued unaware of my connection to the people of whom she spoke, helped themselves to anything that caught their fancy.

" I myself took a beautiful powder box"

My colleague added matter of fact. I was speechless. A silent scream surged up within me. Just as with the people who witnessed the carnage in the American tragedy of Rosewood, these Nursing students were able to distance themselves from the evil, blotting out the stirrings of their own consciences. I did not tell this woman about my relationship with the family in her story. As a child, I had spent hours in that elegant gingerbread house once filled with the bustle of a large family and numerous friends. I remembered so well the stout, very black-skinned woman with the cotton white hair who sat impassive amidst all the activity, in a large tall-backed wooden rocking chair, her nimble fingers working a crochet hook into the folds of the large white bed spread draped over her long immobile legs. In a day when the elderly held a place of respect in Haitian society, the matriarch of this as in other families maintained order in the household with a simple look, a tilt of the head or a barely perceptible move of a hand held up in quiet reproof.

One gentle soul who had lived in that home with her family and aged mother was the same sweet friend of my mother's childhood, the one who had carefully selected the white lace-trimmed dress, booties and bonnet for my infant christening that I still keep in the small suit case that she, my godmother had presented it in. My godmother always sent me gifts, distinctively unusual and elegant souvenirs. I keep one of these today on the kitchen wall of my home. It is a slim ceramic plaque painting of a colorful gingerbread house of old Port-au-Prince, which reminds me of her own lost family dwelling. Her presents mirrored her own taste for beautiful things. That is why I think the powder box in that pillaged home must have belonged to her.

In 1971, Francois Duvalier died after installing his nineteen years old son Jean-Claude Duvalier to succeed him as president of Haiti for life. As pictures of the benign looking, overweight younger Duvalier made the news; people remarked that he could not possibly hold on to the Duvalierist power. Hope soared in the Haitian exile community in New York City that the country was now soon to be free. Many exiles packed up bags and lucrative careers to fly back to the homeland. Others thought that it would at least be safe to visit and even vacation there.

The common story from these vacations was the attempts by government officials to extort money from anyone who still held a Haitian passport. Traveling Haitians would incur more expenses to get back to family, home, and job in Canada, the United States, and elsewhere. Young men and women who could have replaced the professionals in exile continued to leave the country in a steady stream. Occasionally I would look into the eyes of a young man newly arrived from the old country. He would look much older than his twenty some years of age. His eyes would remind me of those of the Israeli couple I had known in Suakoko; like them there was something unsettled about him as if he searched his surroundings expecting someone to come looking for him at any moment.

I remember the arguing of two friends, both young Haitian men in their early twenties, whom I had met through the Queens College International Students club. Both had secured good jobs at a reputable brokerage firm in Manhattan after graduation. One was planning to return to Haiti to help rebuild the country. The other argued that it was more prudent to remain in New York City. The irony was that gentle, bespectacled, courtly Jean-Luc; the one who entertained such altruistic dreams for his native country was the cautious one. He never drove over the speed limit and chided his friend for his, at times, reckless behavior. Jean-Luc, with an unknown number of other young educated professionals did go to Haiti and worked in a project to help *paysans* farmers improve their crops. It was dangerous work because of the all-powerful interests controlling Haitian economic ventures. He died in Haiti within two or three years of his arrival when the car he drove went off the side of a mountain road in an unexplained car accident. The awful truth became apparent soon enough. Having survived nine attempts to overthrow him through various invasions and insurrections the older Duvalier had left a solid network of well-armed thugs to carry on his legacy of terror. The *Volontaires De La Sécurité Nationale* or *VSN* as the *Tonton Macoutes* were now known were still masters of the country. Even the most patriotic among the exiles sank into a deep depression.

In 1976, the year I graduated from Queens College, was admitted to Law School and turned twenty-five; I abandoned the citizenship, which I received at birth. In this land of the United States of America my case is not special, yet I thought of the words of the Russian poet Anna Akhmatova: " I am not one of those who left the land." True I did not consent to leaving my birthplace those fourteen years earlier. I had spent more years outside of Haiti than in the country. Even then my memories spanned a period of just three to four years, since I could not recall very much as a very young child. Years and years, I chanted the words of the Haitian National Anthem: "*For the Homeland!*" treasuring the lyrics, remembering the sun, the schoolyard where my voice echoed. I had had seven years of schooling and indoctrination to patriotism. My teachers are exempted from all blame. Their enthusiasm for the history, culture, and passionate defense of the cause of civic duty made a lasting impression on me. At age ten I was, as most Haitian schoolgirls of that time, patriotic. This was the one link between my compatriots and me. It transcended the fear, the confusion, and hysteria of the Duvalier Regime. Cultural and political rituals merged. I did not question my role then. As for my mother, and for generations before, the path of my life was traced. Even my dreams were tailored to fit that ancestral pattern.

If the brutal events that no one could explain changed my perceptions, I did not understand it then. I remember only the chaos that life had become in Haiti at the end of 1962 when my family and I fled. For years, I roamed Africa, Europe, explaining everywhere, apologizing for my presence. I was always out of place. When I came to New York City with its substantial population of Haitians and proximity to the Caribbean, I renewed old ties. I talked, danced, and sang with those who celebrated the memory and the traditions of my old country. Still, I felt out of place.

New exiles cast a critical eye on my lack of passion, fervor, and (what many thought) authenticity as a Haitian. Even as I fought to prove to my critics that I was a true Haitian, I became less and less convinced. I wondered how many more of the young men would return home to die an inglorious death, in a ditch, in a ravine, or in a foul dungeon cell just to say that they had returned to the homeland! Did that insatiable soil need more death sowed in its sterile furrows? My grandfather Auguste Toulme, who had in his youth refused to be drafted in the French army to fight for a country that he did not know, chose instead to offer his life in the service of his adopted country. Even he, at the end of his life, expressed his deep disappointment as he witnessed what Haiti had become. He advised his grandsons not to return to the homeland. He and I never had he opportunity to discuss what his advice was for his granddaughters. I wondered at times, how he would counsel my female cousins and I. After all, he had barred the way for his own daughters to obtain a university education in their day.

The tragedy of Haiti weighed for so long on my heart that I wearied of mourning. A point in time came when I could no longer ascribe a shape to my sadness. The world of Haiti became increasingly distant. In the United States, I found avenues to fulfill dreams that I would not even allow my mind to think of if I were to settle in Haiti. Slowly I reevaluated my conceptions of a "homeland" and made my choice.

15

My sister Tikite came home from Ithaca College the summer of 1977 to Queens, New York, with a degree in Physical Therapy. She had also been searching for the deeper meaning of life. An instructor at one of her last clinical affiliations at a training hospital on the last day of their tour of duty told her about her own beliefs in God. Tikite wanted to know more. Back at home in New York City she sought out the neighborhood Catholic priest for answers, next she and her boyfriend started to attend a Protestant Church that was different from anything that she had ever seen.

At first, I thought that my sister's newfound interest in things religious would pass just like the fads she pursued in College, like eating sunflower seeds. I did not want anything to do with religion. In fact when I heard anyone discuss religion or God around me I immediately felt anger rising up inside me as well as mistrust. When I tried to dismiss everyone who spoke about God or who attended church as hypocrites however, I remembered *Mère Saint Gregroire* the devoted Catholic Canadian nun who had founded the kindergarten school I had attended in Les Cayes. I also thought of *Soeur Jeanne d'Amboise* a Haitian nun/teacher who told me about God's miracles at the Red sea. These women had inspired me to find out more about God. I also remembered the kindness of the English Christians in Yeovil England at the Park School and its affiliated Brethren congregation. I remembered the hospitality at the Christian home of Priscilla one of my roommates. The genuine compassion of Gabrielle, Margie, and Jeannette, my Suakoko Elementary School classmates also came to mind. These memories tempered the cynicism I had cultivated after my disastrous year at the Catholic Boarding-school in England. Then there was Manman. She taught me quite early that God existed; that He was all-powerful and all knowing. God had rules, I knew. I did not want to find out about these rules. I, however, wanted to be free: free of the dictates of God. Man made rules were enough to contend with.

As a card carrying member of N.O.W., the National Organization for Women I had attended a conference in Washington D.C. and spent a week in Mexico City at a World conference on the rights of women. My newfound heroes: women political leaders, writers, professionals from all occupations were also there. Tales of survival and the breaking down of discrimination barriers thrilled me. I spent hours listening to the records of Billie Holliday singing the blues and those of French singer Edith Piaf. Both women had struggled to succeed in a male dominated world. The works of feminist authors dead and alive inspired me to fight on for my own success in a male dominated world. I felt a sense of belonging as I looked around at the members of the female gender at the Mexico City conference. Strangers of divers socio-economic and racial background were acquainted. As *"women libbers"*, we were all sisters. This was at least within feminist circles. I always gave people the benefit of the doubt as to the race issue. Even so I was disappointed when during my first year in law school I met White as well as Black racists.

As I explained to a classmate in Law School who would ignore someone, I tried to introduce to her because that individual was White; Blacks had been the first to hurt me. Black Haitians had stolen my childhood, my home, and my country. I was suspicious that Black males were now trying to steal my independence. They and the dominant White male power structure in this country blocked my path to opportunities. One of the chief architects of this state of affairs, I believed were the Church fathers. I had never read the writings of Saint Paul but agreed with the feminists who wrote about him that he had to have been a misogynist. The world seemed to me to be filled with women haters. There were times when I resented being a woman, having to prove myself repeatedly to the world. In fact, I resented not being a White Male. As I told my sister Tikite when she tried to talk to me about her faith, I did not ask to be born and did not care to know anything about God.

Sometime during my first year at Queens College, I enrolled in a class on Constitutional Law taught by a matronly Orthodox Jewish lawyer whose lectures stirred up a new passion in me. I fell in love with the American system of Law and Government as I was now discovering it. It shone in comparison to the seemingly flawed, capricious and at times arbitrary nature of what I had seen govern the countries of Haiti and Liberia. I was captivated by the Civil Rights movement's court battles. I knew of my teacher's religious affiliation because of her last name, and the fact that she always wore a wig as the head covering required by Orthodox Jewish law for married women. This woman also had a Ph.D. in Political Science. Although she never told us this directly, I realized that my professor's sense of ethics, were grounded in her religious convictions. I admired her quiet strength.

In the United States, the law had power. Lawyers, I also noticed in this society wielded that power. Here was a profession that also allowed women, and Blacks to compete with their White male counter part, so it seemed to me, on equal footing. I also noticed that lawyers made a good income. I realized that it was important to have a lot of money in this country. Money meant choices as to where and how I lived and I did not have to continue to be a nurse. I would rather work with my brain than my brawn I decided, and have more money. I would become a lawyer.

My Creative Writing teacher at Queens College offered me a seat in her coveted Tutorial course. I had improved steadily each semester with her coaching. I loved to write. Before leaving Haiti, I had been the self appointed scribe for many of the adults in our household. Since arriving at Queens College, I had penned volumes, now that I had my class work as an excuse. I had my eyes set, however, on doctoring up my grade point average to be admitted to law School. My major was Political Science, which required at least one major Term paper in each course. I had a full-time job. Since the Tutorial would require a large amount of writing, I doubted that I could keep up with my professor's expectations. I declined her offer, knowing that I was passing up on a once in a lifetime opportunity. The choice was admission to Law School or becoming a writer. In my thinking twenty-five years old was too old to be a struggling writer, especially since I wanted to leave my nursing career behind.

In 1976, I resigned from my day nursing job, to take a part time night position in a Hospital while I attended Law school full time during the day. I had saved up for the tuition for my first year, planning to continue to live on and finance the rest of my schooling with my income as a nurse. I had crammed four years of College in night school while I supervised a Medical Center fulltime. The volume of work, however in Law School was different. My new job was also taxing; I had not worked in a hospital setting in three years and there was no transition period offered to part time workers. I was expected to give Nursing care to 23 patients with minimal auxiliary help on the 3-11 shift of a Medical Surgical unit. Keeping up with the pace of the Nursing work was exhausting and my school grades started to slip. The school put me on academic probation. It was rumored that the school administration expected at least half of the Freshman Class to fail. The physical facilities were inadequate to accommodate as large a body of students as had been admitted on through to the remaining two years of the program.

The atmosphere at the Law school, situated in the downtown section of Manhattan was very different from that of Queens College where I had mingled with a much more ethnically mixed student body and instructors who for the most part were at least cordial. I chalked off the tension I felt at my new school to a need to toughen up the law students for the profession, to get us ready for the Court Room battles to come. Predictably, the women law students in our number were selected for intensive grilling during classroom recitations. There were two other nurses in my Freshman Class: a Black woman and a White one who was married to a Hispanic. We quickly became friends and enjoyed comparing the behavior of some of our Law professors to a chauvinist male doctor or two we had worked with.

The one woman Law Professor on my schedule was a personal disappointment. Did I notice, someone said to me, that this professor never responded to any of the Black students greetings, even in the elevator? She was very tall and wore very thick eyeglasses. Maybe she just does not see me I explained and my voice could be too soft. I found it difficult, however, to excuse her when this educated woman allowed a door to swing back in my face as I walked behind her in the school lobby. I flunked her class.

In an attempt to boost my grade point average at school during the second semester, I stopped working, and tried to stretch my savings long enough for *something* to come through. I had not yet been able to secure a Graduate School loan. My father was not doing well with managing the business end of his Dental practice, so I could not ask my parents for help. With both my sisters in colleges away from home and no more visiting cousins, they were alone in the Cambria Heights house and I could move back with them. I was afraid of the tension that had built up between my father and I when I returned to their home after Nursing School. In the way of Haitian parents, nothing I had to do was ever more important that their own wants. My twenty-one years old sisters had spent four years away from home and I was still being called into account for their deeds, even after I had moved into my own apartment.

One five am telephone call did not awaken me. I had been jolted out of a deep sleep thirty minutes or so earlier by a nightmare so vivid that I was drenched in perspiration. Nevertheless, the timing of the call alarmed me. It was my father: did I know what my sister was up to? He demanded. I had just stepped out of the shower thinking that it was best not to try to return to sleep since I was to meet with a study group of fellow students an hour drive away early that morning. The thought that crossed my mind was: *these are your children not mine and I have final exams to study for and am worried about finding money and staying in Law School.* To voice this would have been disrespectful. I could tell that my father was already in a rage.

"What sister, Papa?"

It was the sister with the college boyfriend. The boyfriend, that the twins and I had conspired to keep hidden from our parents, had out of revenge for my sister breaking off their relationship, telephoned to introduce himself to my father in the middle of the night. I kept my end of the conversation to a minimum. There was no point to my saying anything. I certainly no longer saw a need to defend myself or even explain my actions to my parents. Thankfully, my father did not ask me if *I* had a boyfriend. Papa announced that he was canceling all of his appointments for the day, closing his office. He and Manman were driving to my sister's College that same morning. The American way of life still baffled them.

By the summer of 1977 my world crashed. I had been thrown out of Law School. The Black and Hispanic students were saying that white male students, with lower Grade Point Average or GPA than me were removed from Academic probation and retained in the school. During the final months at the school, I had a study partner who was white and whom I knew had a much lower GPA than I did. He was allowed to come off academic probation. My own application to the Academic Probation Committee was denied. One of my professors offered to change the grade I had received for his class after he actually read the final exam paper I had submitted: a graduate student had corrected the papers. The instructor, a visiting professor from Harvard University who had very poor eyesight relied on his Harvard graduate Law students to read and grade his New York students' work. This man told me that I did not deserve the "D" grade that I had received after he read my paper at my request and offered to raise my grade.

" You should not flunk out of Law School on the basis of this paper" he said to me.

He requested that the Dean of the Law school review my case. She, a White woman refused. I felt betrayed. Particularly galling to me and several other students in the same situation as mine was the change in curriculum that had occurred in our second semester at the school. Several people I discussed this with had done poorly in the International Law course, taught by the Harvard professor I mentioned earlier, that had been inserted in our mandatory program. A course at this level was usually reserved for third year students. This professor was a gentle courtly scholar whose lectures and textbook, a compilation of his own writings, sailed over most of our heads. The Dean at our school considered that having this famous individual as a teacher in our school to be quite a catch and extensively advertised his class. When this man first arrived from his Ivy League school, access to his class was reserved for senior students, the "cream of the crop" that had recommendations from other professors for scholarly achievements and as worthy, to be taught by this revered man. Within one week of the start of classes, the chosen seniors dropped out of this class in droves. Juniors were hastily recruited to fill the empty seats. Again, to the embarrassment of the Dean, only a very small number of students could be coaxed into finishing out the Course. At the start of the following semester, my classmates and I became the sacrificial lambs. The famous professor was added to our slate of mandatory courses. It was, the *"coup de grace"*, which finished off my ailing grade point average.

I had planned for a law career for close to four years, holding on to a very tough nursing job in order to save money for the tuition fees. Some of my former classmates spoke of suing the Law School because the administration had enrolled an excessive number of students and then created circumstances that ensured the fall out of a certain percentage of us. The school did not have the physical facilities to keep such a large body of people for the entire three years of the program. I was contacted once or twice about joining in a Class Action lawsuit against the school. Several other Black students and I felt discriminated against but that the fight was not worth the sacrifices at the time and moved on with our lives.

At first, I tried to make a new career in Insurance Sales. I had actually answered an advertisement for *Executive Trainees*. The projected income was promised to be much more than what I could make in Nursing. If only I could earn a lot of money quickly, I would feel successful in life. Money would keep me in control of my life. *Instead of becoming a lawyer, perhaps I could make it as a successful Business Executive*; I thought, pouring myself into the work. Within a few months, however, I had to supplement my earnings with a nursing job. I worked ten, twelve hours a day six to seven days a week, driving around the, Bronx, Manhattan, Brooklyn, Queens and Suffolk County. The more I worked, the less time I had to think about my loss. It soon became obvious, however, that I had no aptitude for Insurance sales. The commissions I earned at the insurance company job amounted to a negligible portion of my income and I had spent the remainder of my savings on business clothes. Winter was approaching. In the ten years that I had lived in New York City, I really had never adjusted to the winters. I realized that I could not do as much driving around the five Boroughs of the City and would need a better paying job.

My sister Pepe was also looking for a change in scenery. She had spent months after her graduation from Philadelphia's Temple University looking for a job as a Recreational Therapist settling eventually for a low paying clerical position at the same company I worked for. I had by then moved to a one bedroom walk-up apartment which, in addition to having some major concealed plumbing and other flaws, was in a neighborhood that had a benign appearance in the daytime but turned out to be a night and weekends hangout for white drunken teenagers, with a surly attitude towards anyone of color. One day, late in 1978, someone I met on a sales call introduced me to one of her cousins who in turn invited me to visit Brunswick a small town on the coast of Georgia. I had been across the United States and spent a month in California but I had never gone further south than Washington D.C. At first, I hesitated. Alabama, Mississippi, and Georgia ranked high in my mind as places that were unhealthy for a black woman to be in.

16

Eventually, it seemed to me that I could nurse my disappointments with life better in a warm climate. I detested the cold in New York City and found that I suddenly could not face another winter of drudging through snow and sleet and icy mud slush. My new friend assured me that the South had "changed". Brunswick is a resort area that also has the Federal Law Enforcement Training Center (FLETC) as one of its main employers. People from all over the United States worked at the F.L.E.T.C. that trained Federal agents for all the federal law enforcement agencies.

Sometime before my visit to Brunswick, a group of Federal Law Enforcement training officers had arranged for an Atlanta based law School to establish a branch in town for them to attend. Tuition was much lower than the Law schools in New York. My failure at the law school rankled still, I had not found a comfortable pattern for my immediate future. The cost of living in Georgia was lower, the climate warmer than in New York City and there was a local hospital to work in. I ventured south for a week to check on my prospects in Georgia. The tranquility of the area and its sunlit marshes immediately appealed to me. Since I did not encounter any Klansmen (this would happen later) and I had tired of fighting with my New York City property owner over the broken fixtures, the plumbing and the heating, I packed up my belongings and moved down to Brunswick. My sister

Pepe, who had been unable to find a job in Recreational Therapy, came with me but had to return to New York City since the job market for her field turned out to be worse in Brunswick.

In New York City, I was on a thread mill of work, school, work; every aspect of my life had to be carefully scheduled. There was always an abundance of parties and other social events to choose from. Once I flew out to and spent a week alone on a beach in Puerto Rico just so I could relax. Now I had hours all to myself. In Brunswick aside from one or two couples, no one knew me. There was, however, a clear demarcation among the inhabitants of Brunswick Georgia along racial lines. I immediately became aware of it when I started to work in the Emergency Room at the one local hospital. Although the painted signs had been removed from bathroom doors and water coolers, an invisible force maintained segregation. Blacks and Whites did not mix socially. Luann, one of my white co-workers who was a few years older and married to a "Northerner" and I were the only exceptions that I could see. Mainly we played tennis on our days off and chatted on the phone. In my apartment complex, I was the only Black living there at the time and people looked the other way when they saw me at the Laundromat or in the parking area. Some store clerks did call out from the safe distance of their selling counter or a drive up window of a fast food restaurant:

"You' all come back and see us."

But there was no mistaking the general lack of civility of total strangers towards me in particular. This would not have bothered me as a recently transplanted New Yorker used to the impersonal nature of street encounters in a crowded city, were it not that I noticed that whites in Brunswick were very friendly and often elaborately courteous towards each other in this small community. Black inhabitants I met looked puzzled as if they wondered about what I was doing in their area.

Even with the stories I had heard of the difficulties that Blacks experienced in the South of the United States I decided to move to Georgia because I was tired of the weather and of the fast pace of life in New York City. In fact, my standard of life immediately went up because of the lower cost of living. Yet at the Emergency Department of the Brunswick Hospital in 1978 as the Head Nurse who hired me told me frankly: there had never been a Black Registered Nurse in her department and she worried about the reaction that my presence would cause particularly, among the physicians there. Since I was waiting for the state of Georgia to issue me a Nursing license (based on a reciprocity agreement between states to which Georgia and New York subscribed) we both agreed that I would start working in the Emergency Department at the lower rank of Nursing Assistant. Everyone on Staff wore "scrubs" uniforms and I did not attract any attention as I went about the unit cleaning, fetching and doing other menial tasks, until my status was changed to that of Registered Nurse when my license to practice in Georgia came in. There was a definite shift in the attitude of at least two of the physicians there towards me. One of them an "old timer" mostly referred to Blacks as "niggers".

"Is that nigger ready for me to examine him?"

He would ask me. In the two years that I worked there, I managed to avoid any confrontations. My co-workers were friendly enough. There were several non Segregationist-bred employees mostly from Northern States and I was generally included in the extracurricular activities among the ER Staff. We ate together. Often on the way home from the night shift we would stop as a group at a local eatery. Once, I remember, the doctor who was fond of using the "N" word paid for the whole group's tab. I quietly pulled out and settled my own check. He and I at times looked each other in the eye but never exchanged any word outside of our work context. He was a small man, short with sagging cheeks, loose fitting dentures and badly dyed hair that he swept to one side to hide his bald scalp. The grating thinness of his voice irritated me especially when he gave me an order. There was only one Black physician, who had admitting privileges at the hospital. Once I noticed a drunken White surgeon verbally and physically, abuse a Black man who came in to the Emergency Room for treatment so even though I had not needed any medical care I remember thinking that this was not a safe town to stay in. Yet, I wondered where on this earth I was to live, and call home.

Brunswick catered to out of town tourists who traveled along Interstate 95 on their way from the north to Florida. Other than one encounter with a Sheriff's deputy from nearby Darien who shouted at me to "shut up " when he gave me a ticket, or having my apartment door "egged" once or driving through a KKK midday march (replete with white robes) my life there was peaceful. I had not heard anyone talk of the Klan as being active in this area so I assumed that they operated in a more remote, inland location. "This is a charming place", I told people back in New York. A stone throw away on the interstate north of Brunswick was Darien, Georgia. My friend Elnora, a Black woman from the Dominican Republic I had met in Law School in New York City came down to visit me in Brunswick. She raved about my clean, modern apartment, the baskets of tomatoes and peaches that we bought for so little on the side of the road close to my home, the generous portions and good food of the restaurants. I decided to show her a pottery store I had discovered up the road on the other side of Darien.

We drove out in my small Datsun. The car had no air conditioning and we had the windows rolled down. It was around two in the afternoon under a clear, bright, cloudless sky. The side road through Darien was on a slight incline.

We did not realize, deep as we were into a conversation that there was a crowd in the street until we had driven in the midst of a gathering of white robbed, with the unmistakably pointed shape, hooded Klansmen. Elnora let out an expletive under her breath. My hands froze on the wheels of the car. I had never seen the Ku Klux Klan other than in pictures or in movies and certainly not this close to me. So many years had passed since my face-to-face encounter with the evil *moh* on a dark street of my hometown in Haiti. Here under the brilliant sun of the South Georgia sky was another type of evil. I was taken by surprise, a sickening feeling slowed down my reflexes so I didn't notice that the white robes were moving aside to let us through and that there were no hands holding on to the car. My left foot slipped off the clutch pedal and the lurch of the engine startled me into regaining enough control of myself to push down on the accelerator without switching gears. We sped off.

"Yeah the South has changed!" My passenger said sarcastically.

After this experience I would wonder at times when I looked in the eyes of a white man in town or worked next to one at the Hospital: "Is he *one*?" One thing I noticed Klansmen and the Duvaliers' *Tonton Macoutes* and other bullies have in common: cowardice. Both in Haiti and in the United states such men hid behind anonymity and their communities' willingness to tolerate them. When American officials complained out loud about what was happening in Haiti during the nineteen-sixties and suggested that troops should be sent in to rescue people, Francois Duvalier countered that the American Government should send soldiers instead to Alabama, Mississippi, Georgia and other places in the South and rescue its Black citizens from racist Sheriffs and other murderous government officials. Luann shook her head sadly when I told her about the KKK march:

"This is such a pretty area. I have lived here all my life. These people are messing up my home!"

She and I just enjoyed our friendship without agonizing over the misdeeds of others.

"Sugar," Luann would say, "don't you pay that ol' heifer no mind!'

Generally, we did not dig into the history of Luann's hometown. I wondered about the secrets that the inhabitants of this town kept hidden. The subject of race relations never appeared in the local news or any in any other forum. In the present, my friend and her husband thought that segregation was wrong. I relied on her to translate some of the more obscure local sayings as well as bringing me up to speed on pertinent customs. It took me weeks to decipher the South Georgia accent. People came to the emergency room complaining of such things as a *"rising"* they noticed somewhere on their body when I had grown accustomed to referring to such things as "lumps". Even my fellow nurses confused me when they referred to a broken piece of electrical equipment as being *"tore up"*.

There were no opportunities to socialize when I enrolled in the Brunswick branch of the Atlanta based Law School. Our group met in a conference room with an instructor in town on two to three evenings every week. Some of us did our research at the Courthouse library. Those who worked at FLETC had access to a full-fledged Law Library. A few students drove in from outlying rural areas and were anxious to get home after the late night lectures. In addition, I worked twelve- hour shifts at the hospital. My other friends were a black couple from Washington DC. The husband worked at the FLETC. Since I did not attend any church, I did not get to meet any other blacks in the area and I could not observe whether there were any mixed church congregations. I had moved out of New York City for a slower pace of life so I welcomed the partial isolation. I had more time to myself to think.

In April 1979, I went back to New York City to attend my sister Tikite's wedding. Apparently, my future brother in law had fulfilled the prescribed courtship rules, to my parents' satisfaction. My sisters had shed their adolescent pudginess and matured into two beautiful young women about five feet tall. Tikite's large, deep brown eyes, framed by long black lashes still lit up her soft caramel toned face. She wore her black hair shoulder length while Pepe cut hers short. Pepe's own lighter brown eyes had lost the timidity of childhood and sparkled easily with laughter. Old friends inspected their faces and mine in order to detect any resemblance to our parents' families. New acquaintances paired Pepe and I as the twins in the family because we shared the same light complexion. This was when the three of us caused heads to turn by entering a room.

Papa, handsome and distinguished in his black tuxedo, walked each one of the twins down the aisle at their respective weddings a year apart in the same church. The remainder of Papa's hair had turned silver gray just like Manman's own curls and their matching metal-framed eyeglasses added a soft touch to their sturdy features. *Tante Féfée* and her sister *Tante Foufou* two faithful family friends, sewed the twins' wedding gowns and made the two richly decorated wedding cakes. Manman tailored each of the girls' wedding veils putting to use the experience she had gained at the factories she had worked in while living in New York City. For Tikite's veil, the whole family including Papa worked at the dining table on the night before the ceremony to glue the small decorative pearls Manman had included in her design. Pepe made the bridal bouquets for herself and Tikite. She was the craft artist among us having inherited Manman's flair for creating pretty things. Our family home in Queens, New York was too small for the receptions, so Tikite and her fiancé Jim Cartright rented a Haitian-owned catering hall for theirs while Pepe and Reynald Holly, her groom received their own wedding guests, a year later in the large fellowship hall of the church they all attended.

Both my brothers in law had been born in Haiti and left the country like us when they were very young. Reynald Holly's great-great-grandfather James Theodore Holly had emigrated from the United States in the mid 1800's and recruited our own great-grand father Charles Emmanuel Benedict to set up a branch of the Episcopalian church in Les Cayes Haiti. Family history is unclear about our own ancestor's origins. It was widely known that the Holly patriarch had left the racially hostile, environment of the United States for that of the independent Black Republic of Haiti. Now his descendants fleeing tyranny of another kind had returned to the United States. This was the second time, in the course of the families long association, that a Benedict was marrying a Holly. The melting pot which characterized our family gained more variety with James Cartright whose maternal grand-father was Syrian. At my sisters' wedding receptions in nineteen seventy-nine and nineteen- eighty, cousins came from Montreal Canada, as well as from various parts of the United States. These two reunions illustrated the extent of the brain drain from Haiti: physicians, engineers, architects, teachers, nurses, dentists, electricians and business men and women from our family alone, all working either in the United States or in Canada.

While visiting my family in New York, I realized that Tikite and her husband Jim were serious about their religious faith. The people were friendly at the large church they attended in the Jamaica neighborhood of Queens and behaved as if everyone was related to each other. I privately thought the noise the whole group made during a church service was irreverent. There was no denying however that this was a happy crowd. My sister and brother in law gave me a Bible, encouraging me to read it. In all sincerity, I told Tikite and Jim that I believed in God's existence but would never join a religion. Then they both came to visit me in Brunswick some months after their wedding. Jim especially wanted me to "get saved" and again urged me to read the Bible.

"Tell your husband to stop preaching to me!"

I was angry but I knew that my sister and her husband wanted to share something with me that they obviously felt I needed and which they believed would benefit me greatly. Again, I told them that I did not need to read the Bible to know what a killjoy God is. For one I said, I had not asked to be born. Why would God expect me to follow His rules? Church fathers were notorious for setting up special restrictions that applied to women alone. I on the other hand intended to remain a liberated woman and make my mark in the world. Besides, I also found Elizabethan English, since I was not taking a literature class, tedious reading. Jim and Tikite were not easily dissuaded; they bought me a Bible written in modern English. One major thing that I noticed about my sister and brother-in-law was that their life style had changed. They no longer were preoccupied with the New York disco parties scene. Something had happened to change their priorities. Had they found the real meaning of life?

VII. A Branch connected to the True Vine

"Yet I will rejoice in the Lord, I will joy in the God of my salvation" Habakkuk 3:18(KJV)

17

Sometime in May of 1980, I began to read the Bible. My sister Tikite had suggested that I started with the book that John, one of the close friends of Jesus while He lived on earth, wrote. Therefore, I started to read the Gospel according to John. Even though, at times I checked some of the references to other parts of the Bible, I read straight through. Some things were already familiar to me. I already believed that Jesus is God's son, and that He had been born to a young woman named Mary who was a virgin at the time of His birth and that His cousin another man named John started to tell people to get ready to receive the Messiah or savior of the world. What surprised me was that John's book was all about Jesus. There was barely any mention of his mother Mary. I began to search for the reason why Mary had been such a central part of my life as a child. All those Rosary beads I fumbled with when I recited *"Hail Mary full of grace..."* thousands of times.

I remembered when I was a young child in Les Cayes, all the feast days that were reserved for the worship of Mary the mother of Jesus. The devout I am sure believed that Jesus the Messiah died on the cross for his or her sins. I do not think he or she realized however, as Isaiah the prophet stated nine hundred years before the birth of Jesus Christ, that just as "He was wounded for our transgressions, He was bruised for our iniquities: The chastisement of our peace was upon Him, and with His stripes we are healed" Isaiah 53:5. Any believer has access to supernatural healing. There was no need to make a bargain with Mary, a dead woman, however exemplary her life had been. In Les Cayes, the scriptural record in which God forbids worship to anyone but Him was disregarded as well as the mention of the other children whom Mary and her husband Joseph had after the birth of Jesus. The church continued to refer to her as a virgin. I read long histories of how an individual qualified for sainthood but never heard, since we did not have a Bible in our home in Haiti, about the Apostles Paul, John, and Jude's teachings that every born again believer becomes a saint of God. In fact, I had not heard that anyone needed to be born again just as Jesus told Nicodemus in the gospel account.

What about all that penance I did? Did not a *"Hail Mary"* do anything for all those sins the priests of my childhood told me I paid for by repeating those words? Now I was discovering that there was nothing said in the gospel narrative about going to a confessional to receive absolution for one's sins or of burning candles to help dead people who had sinned go to heaven.

I knew that Church authorities had created all the rituals I had lived by during the early part of my life. What I was observing now about these rules, ceremonies, and doctrines was how contradictory they were to what I was now reading in the Bible. I had been a good student of the Women Rights movement, spent a year in Law School, and had been questioning my own reason for being in the human race. There were so many prescriptions for living in the Haitian culture that did not make sense to me personally that I avoided them as rules that might restrict my life whatever their source. As a child my actions had been hedged in by pronouncements of *"Ca pa bon!"* (*It is no good*). This did not even try to differentiate between superstition and the nebulous whims of my elders.

My experience in 1964 at the Convent School in England had scarred me and left me determined to avoid any personal involvement in religion. I met several African Americans during my college years in New York City who had converted to Islam because they felt that Christianity was the religion of the White race. Nothing was said of course about Islam's role in the Atlantic Slave Trade. To me the Black American Muslim women's clothing resembled those of a Catholic nun. I was wary of what I would discover about God through the Bible. At first, I thought, this book must be dangerous to me. There was no question in my mind that the Bible contained the truth about God. I was afraid that I would find out that He was not on my side.

Of all the books I had been forbidden to read, the Bible was the only one I had stayed away from. By age twelve when I lived in Liberia I had read the entire collection of the French Classics which adults had told me were inappropriate for my age. Later, I had meditated on the somber writings of people like Sylvia Plath, Anne Sexton, and others who eventually killed themselves. Anything labeled as provocative had instantly attracted me. Here was the most provocative book I had kept on the shelf for years untouched! I started to read the New Testament first, because it explains the Old Testament. The voice of Jesus, as reported by John the Gospel writer was unlike any other I had heard so far. Jesus was talking to me, through the things he said to others before me, about himself. I could not put the book down.

Chapter after chapter amazed me. My first thoughts were that someone had tricked me about Jesus, I really did not know who He is. Here was the most important information of my life hidden in plain sight! Jesus is real! Hell is real! I have an immortal soul that will live on forever after my earthly body dies. I had always known this. When I was a child, I had been taught what God required of me. I knew that He had made Heaven for anyone who repented of his or her sins and that anyone who did not repent would go to Hell. From the time I became aware of all this I had tried to do all the things I had been taught to do in order to avoid having my soul live in hell forever. I had obeyed my teachers in matters of religion. I had obeyed up until I had declared my independence from God at the age of thirteen. At thirteen years old, I had made the personal decision that even when I was forced to attend a religious ceremony I would insulate my mind with other thoughts. I maintained my personal independence thus, never sharing this information with anyone. Did I at twenty-eight years old have even more freedom of choice? The answer to my question thundered in my mind: I did not have the option of ignoring God!

While living in New York City I had dabbled with the Occult, without even admitting to myself what I was doing. I do not remember how it started. Some of my friends "read" cards to foretell the future and I became intrigued and soon was seeking to know the future on a regular basis. At the same time, I started to read, the *Horoscopes* published in daily newspapers and in books. It then became an obsession. I *had* to know the future. That information guided my actions; it gave me the power, I thought, to change things to my advantage. I drove quite a distance to one of my *readers* regularly once per week. On her advice, I paid an "expert" to draft up an Astrology chart for me that I studied carefully. For quite a while, I patterned my life on the advice of my Astrology chart. Yet, I would have argued with anyone that I was not superstitious. I was simply obtaining information. Information was power. I do not remember thinking too deeply about the *source* of that information. *Where* did information about the future come from? The Holy Spirit of God is the Spirit of truth. God is all knowing. Consulting mediums, card readers, or otherwise calling up demons that only have partial knowledge is a poor and dangerous alternative. Demons reveal the information they have only as part of their overall scheme to entrap humans into sin and destruction.

Even though the Ten Commandments God gave to an ancient character named Moses had been drilled into me from my earliest childhood, I noticed that no one was really expected to obey them. That was the impression I had from my very first teachers. I had been told stories about certain men who told the future to certain others and at times to a whole group of people. These announcers of the future were known as *Prophets*. They readily proclaimed *where* they had received their information: *God told it to them*. The accounts I had heard of these prophets' stories had always fascinated me. My own conscience had been shaped by the principles in these accounts sensing the truth in them: " Thou shalt have none other gods before me." Deuteronomy: 5; 7 (KJV). I had always felt uneasy about praying to *Saint Joseph, Saint Antoine, Sainte Therese,* and a host of other statues and reciting countless "*Hail Marys*" and could never shake the feeling that they were my "*other gods*". Now my suspicions were confirmed: I had other gods. Yet, I had stopped praying to Saints for years. Why then was I feeling guilty?

As I read the Bible, I became aware of the major source of discomfort the text caused me: my guilt stemmed from my declaration of independence. I had ignored God and His commandments. If I thought that I did not have other gods, I did not have God himself either. Leaving Him out of my life was not an option. Ignoring God's command to worship Him entailed deliberate acts of disobedience as well as omissions. My own wishes, desires, and ambitions had precedence over the will of my Creator. In fact I had made up my own rules about what I thought was right and wrong. In wanting to be the *captain of my own ship and master of my fate*, I had made myself my own god! Because I had never read the Bible, I was misinformed about God's requirements, and His expectations of me. I had disobeyed every one of His commandments many times over, by even committing murder. Many times, I had nurtured hatred in my heart and my tongue had murdered with impunity. Jesus talks about that type of murderous act in Matthew 5:21,22.

When I reached Chapter 15 in the book of John, verse number five leaped at me. I felt that Jesus, the Son of God was addressing me directly: *"I am the Vine, ye are the branches: He that abideth in me, and I in him, the same bringeth forth much fruit: for without me ye can do nothing"*. (KJV) The Bible verse sank deep in my soul. My sense of independence was the most treasured of anything I possessed. Self-reliance had become my personal creed.

From the day I had received my first wages at age nineteen, I had worked to be successful, to be *"something"!* Money was evidence of success. I had attended school, studied, fought racists, sexists, friends and foe, denied myself some of the perks in life, such as a silver blue Datsun 280Z, and avoided romantic entanglements in order to retain the money I had earned and invest it in obtaining more of it and thereby become a success. The idea of being successful consumed me. I firmly believed that in this country of the United States of America, education is a major factor in achieving success. A woman, especially a Black one, could not depend on anyone to help her in life. I had reached the conclusion that my success depended solely on my own abilities. At this point in my life, there was no one that I could depend on for help with anything of importance. Mostly I had to fight off feelings of bitterness. I could not remember when I had last asked God for anything. Now I was hearing Him say that I needed Him! Both my grandmothers, the long-suffering pastor's wife that I had never met and poor gentle, broken Man Lillie needed God. Haitian women needed God. I was a self-sufficient liberated American woman! I could not need God.

"I am the true Vine..." Jesus said according to the record in John Chapter 15, verse one. I knew instantly that I had

discovered a very deep secret. I sensed the profound importance of this information that was about to radically change my life. I felt spoken to directly, intimately although I was alone in the living room of my apartment in Brunswick, Georgia.

The moment I read this passage I became aware of a truth I had tried to suppress to myself: my reason for being, the purpose for which I had been created was to have fellowship with my creator. My attempts at living life on my own terms had left me with a feeling of dissatisfaction. I had avoided facing one simple fact. Inside of me for more years than I could recall was a hole, an empty space that had gotten bigger over time. It created in me an indescribable longing that permeated my thoughts. Angry outbursts temporarily soothed this craving and I had the good sense not to try to fill it with alcohol, drugs, or even sex because more than anything I hated the idea of loosing control of myself. I did not allow myself to feel sad for long. Thoughts of vengeance were more satisfying.

Periodically I rehashed the list of people whom I hated: my math tutor who had hit me with a horsewhip and *Clothilde*, our maid in Les Cayes, over the years, whenever I thought of these particular women I would feel my blood boil even though I had not heard whether they were still alive. There was also the ten years old girl I had fought with everyday for two weeks while we were students in the Port-au-Prince Primary School my sisters and I had attended while we were waiting for our exit visas out of Haiti in 1962; I hated her for years after. I also hated the two boys who teased me in the school in Africa before I had learned English, dreaming of the day when we would meet again and I would castigate them with the English words I now had mastered. One summer when I was on vacation from school in Europe and returned to Africa, I did run into one of the boys. We stood several feet from each other and I noticed by the expression on his face that he had recognized me and was about to approach me. There was a gleam of anticipation in his eyes. He froze in his tracks, however, as I purposefully directed a blank stare beyond him. I relished seeing his obvious embarrassment as I strode off.

The worse feelings of resentment I nurtured were for the nuns in the English Boarding School I had attended in 1965. In fact, from that year, I avoided speaking to any nuns and priests I encountered, turning from my path and moving away whenever I spotted the familiar cloth habits they wore. Evil thoughts filled my mind whenever I remembered one particular Nursing instructor who had tried to prevent my obtaining a Nursing diploma, the Law School professor who allowed a door to swing back in my face and gave me a failing grade in her class, a Nursing supervisor who was unfair to me. The Duvalierists, who stole my home and country, rounded out the long inventory of those who had wronged me. I spent hours conjuring up scenarios in which I had been vindicated through the downfall of my enemies. Reading and studying helped me prepare to do battle with circumstances, to protect myself, control my life as much as possible, to gain power; until the opportunity came to hit back at my enemies. Although I loved my parents and did not wish to harm them, there were many times when I seethed with anger at the memory of some of their decisions. Several times in my life, I had felt betrayed by them. I could not place my trust in anyone I had known so far.

I never doubted however, that God was all-powerful. I had known people and had read about many others who had power. Hitler, Stalin, Duvalier, the *Hougans*, and Satanists of my childhood in Haiti and Satan himself had power, but were not all-powerful. In College and in Law School I had Buddhists, Muslims, among others try to indoctrinate me into their beliefs. None could ever convince me. Somewhere in my childhood, my mother and the Catholic nuns had somehow explained to my satisfaction that only the God of Abraham, Isaac, and Jacob, and of the Jews, was all-powerful. Yet, I had a fatalistic attitude about this belief. It was not supposed to be something that could be relevant to me personally for the time that I lived on planet earth.

Now I was discovering a sense that God, all-powerful God himself was telling me that He was the one missing in my life. Why would He be interested in one individual life? How did I matter to Him? I had wished, just like Job a character in the Old Testament, many times that I had never been born. Why would God be interested in me? I flipped back to the previous chapters I had read in the book of John. There was no doubt in my mind that what I was reading was the truth. This revelation tapped into a longing deep inside of me. I went over John's explanations, re-read Jesus' own words. Why? Why? Why is all-powerful God the creator of everything interested in me?

For all of my life I had assumed that there was too big a distance between a Holy God and a hate filled vengeful self-centered sinner like me. I had also assumed that I needed to go to God through a human priest or a "saint". I had heard that God is holy First Samuel 2:2. However, I did not know the story behind the inner sanctum in the Jewish Tabernacle and Temple that, under penalty of instant death, only the Jewish High Priest was allowed to enter and that even he had to be worthy to offer the sacrifice to God. The Old Testament also reports the story of Nadab and Abihu the two sons of Aaron, the priest whom God struck down with fire for daring to "offer strange fire" to Him or an unacceptable, substandard offering. Leviticus 10: 1,2. A chasm lay between a holy God and impure human beings. Yet, this book said that Jesus has given the Born Again Believer direct access to God, without any human intermediary. Up until my thirteenth year and experience at the English Convent boarding school, I recited hundreds of *"Hail Mary"* incantations since I believed that they would magically pay for my sins. Now I was finding out from the Bible that even the Jewish High Priest in the Old Testament account with his life of dedication and the elaborate rituals of his service did not have the power to forgive sin. Only God does and He does not delegate that power to a human being.

As a child in Haiti, I witnessed that people appeared to fear God. Everyone genuflected upon entering the sanctuary of the church and made the sign of a cross with their right hand touching their forehead, chest, left shoulder and right shoulder in a show of respect. However, I also witnessed that this show of reverence did not keep people from openly telling lies, cultivating hate, cheating etc. There was of course the false assurance of the confessional. There was a period in my life when I routinely went to the confessional every week to confess my sins and ask a priest for absolution or forgiveness and did the penance he prescribed. I did not have the power to stop sinning. The thought had not occurred to me that it was the role of the Holy Spirit of God to infuse the believer with strength so that he or she can have the power to obey God. The Holy Spirit was just that mysterious third person of the triune God. Even with all the good intentions I could muster as a child, I never felt forgiven. I never felt approved. When I saw the self-serving hypocrisy of some of the religious people I had known in my youth, I did not feel that I could trust anyone to tell me the truth. When I enrolled myself at Queens College in 1972 and first began thinking of myself as an adult, I also made the decision that I did not need anyone's approval. Thereafter, I began to give myself permission to excuse my own sins.

"The little baby Jesus loves you". I had heard this and seen countless nativity scenes re-enacted. Since the baby Jesus grew up and died to pay for all of my sins, why then did I have to do penance? The truth about God the Father, Jesus, the Holy Spirit was hidden from me because I did not think I should read the Bible. For most of the times that I attended church, I believed that it was the privilege of the priests alone to read the word of God and then to tell me about selected passages. That is why that even as an adult I resisted all invitations to read the Bible directly.

In Haiti, my teachers read to my classmates and I from a book entitled *"Histoire Sainte"*. This book retold Biblical stories. I was fascinated by the account of how God opened up the Red sea to save the Israelites from the pursuing army of Egyptians and then fed them manna in the desert. Left out in this history book narrative was God's expectations that every human being would treasure and read the whole record of His message to the human race. This was news to me. God created man not to live on food only but *"by every word that proceedeth out of the mouth of the Lord doth man live"*: Deuteronomy: 8; 3. (KJV) Those same Israelites were expected to know this book of the law written by their leader Moses under the inspiration of the Holy Spirit and to teach it to their children. How can anyone teach something unless they first understand it? The Biblical account relates how Moses grew up and was educated at the court of the Pharaoh of Egypt. His readers, the Israelites that he addressed however, the same parents whom God expected to teach their own children His word were former slaves and possibly illiterate. *"And these words, which I command thee this day, shall be in thine heart: And thou shalt teach them diligently unto thy children, and shalt talk of them when thou sitteth in thine house, and when thou walketh by the way, and when thou lieth down, and when thou risest up"*: Deuteronomy 6:6,7. (KJV) The word of God although some parts are more difficult than others to understand is clear enough to all who read it.

Adults in my family recited portions of the Psalms like a mantra without pausing to meditate on the implications of the words, to their own life. From my own observations, reading the word of God did not seem to have much impact on the behavior of the readers. For all of the intensity with which the people of Les Cayes and throughout Haiti pursued religious activities, they had missed it! In Haiti, stories of the ancient Israelites' relationship with God only served as entertainment yet the Psalmist David said: *"Thy word have I hid in mine heart, that I might not sin against Thee"*: Psalm 119:11. (KJV) The text that king David read and studied, now collected in the Bible, gave instructions on how to live life on earth and not sin. Now, that was an answer to my recidivism and repeated trips to the confessional!

I knew right from wrong. Somewhere between the classrooms of the *Ecole Maternelle* and my mother's lap, I was taught the concept of sin. Swift retribution came at the end of Mère Saint Gregroire's thin bamboo cane when I disobeyed the class rule and turned to speak with the child seated behind me. That was all that I expected disobedience to cost me. I had drafted a loose list of behavior that I calculated would send me to Hell and those I thought it was safe to engage in. What I had classified as the big sins like murder, adultery would send me to Hell. I did not realize in those days how much God hates all disobedience. Jesus himself said: *"But I say unto you that whosoever is angry with his brother without a cause shall be in danger of the judgment: and whosoever shall say to his brother, Ra-ca, shall be in danger of the council: but whosoever shall say, Thou fool, shall be in danger of hell fire"*: Mathew 5: 22 (KJV). I had said worse directly to people and in my mental flagellations of those on my hidden hate list.

When I read the Bible text, not an abbreviation, or segments taken out of context, I found the truth. The book written by the Apostle John so many years ago about what he had seen and heard Jesus do and say, gave me a new depth of understanding about God. I not only found out the truth about God, I also found out that I was a guilty sinner on my way to an eternal hell without reprieve. There was no stopover in Purgatory. Purgatory does not exist. Eternal life is found in Heaven alone and then there is Hell. On my own, without a doubt, I was headed for Hell. I needed a way out; I needed to be rescued. I needed a savior.

"*In Him was life.*" John the Apostle wrote. John1: 5. He spoke of his hero, *Jesus of Nazareth*. I thought about my personal heroes. There was Papa who swam in the river at *Gelée* a long time ago, with both my small sisters sitting on his broad back and could pull out a tough molar with a twist of his strong left hand, he was my first hero. Papa had rescued me from a drowning death in the river at *Gelée* when I was a small child in Haiti. Nothing stopped him from going to work everyday to provide for his family and doing whatever job, he had to do. In five years, he had worked as a dental lab technician, become a Respiratory Therapist, often holding two jobs, studied for and passed the New York State Board of Dentistry exam, when he was close to sixty years old, and opened a private practice. My father fulfilled his role of protector and provider. The bureaucracy in the United States, however, frightened him. Several times, he had been victimized by human treachery. His integrity and diligence were not enough in this world to protect our family.

My mother was on par with my father as a hero because of her bravery. Growing up in Haiti I knew that the mention of her name protected my sisters and I from abusive schoolteachers. People knew that anyone seeking to harm us would have to go through our Manman. Once I saw her position herself between my sisters and I and a drunken man who was leaning towards us in a New York City subway train. When the drunk took note of Manman's strategically held umbrella and her combat stance, the man backed off. As the need arose, Maman too had taken the bus, and subway train to a hostile world working in garment factories for people who tried to demean her. She faithfully stayed at her husband's side, worked with him as his assistant, and managed his practice, saw her three children graduate from College. Now, however, she was growing bitter at the never-ending struggle.

In Haiti, and the United States I honored the memory of those men and women who had died in the Haitian Revolution to end Slavery and create a new nation, and those who sacrificed their lives for the American Civil Rights Cause. So many people had given up so much for me to live the life I now lived and have the options I now had. The pioneers of the Women's Rights movements were also my heroes up to a point. I admired some contemporary leaders from time to time even as I deplored some of their shortcomings. What I needed in this lifetime and beyond was a living, invincible hero. A living invincible hero would answer the nagging question I had about my life on earth. He would also know the answers to my questions I felt certain. Who was I, why was I here on this planet and where was I going? I instinctively knew that the answers to the questions I had about my identity, my purpose in life and my destiny lay outside of me. Some things I was powerless to change. Just as I had not selected the conditions of my birth, I knew that the length of my life and the circumstances of my death are beyond my control. Jesus of Nazareth, the hero of John the Apostle's narrative, who with the Holy Spirit shared the godhead with God the father, All-powerful God the creator, the giver of life, knew the answers. The answers to the dilemma in my own life were to be found in the one who has life; they were in Him! Just as John, the first century writer recorded.

One of my sisters loaned me a thirteen-inch black and white television set she had used in college. My apartment came with a free television cable connection so I started to tune in to the broadcast of some of the religious programs. I listened to many discussions about the same Bible text that I was reading. At first, the speakers seemed to be too emotional and I criticized their behavior and doubted their sincerity. When the Television program preachers asked money to be mailed in to them my old cynicism would rise up and I would switch the television channel. I continued, however to read the Bible. I now understood that as a human being I was unable to stop disobeying God because I was born with the nature of a sinner and therefore sins. I, am born just as every man, woman, boy or girl on planet earth, in the image of God as it states in Genesis chapter one verse twenty-six and twenty-seven, with however a sin nature which I inherited from Adam and Eve; mankind's and therefore my ancestors. That sinner's nature has to be voluntarily exchanged for the nature that does not sin.

Philosophers of all of the cultures of the world who have observed the sin problem throughout the ages have spoken and written volumes of prescriptions and instructions on how to cure it. Some, like the ancient Greeks understood that the root cause of this problem lay in the nature of man. What was also understood through the ages was that man needed a supernatural being to help him overcome his weaknesses. The imagination of man has always created supernatural beings from which they claimed to receive instructions. A man named Abraham centuries ago was reported to have talked with the ultimate in supernatural being: God. Abraham started a whole new way of thinking that this God of his had created everything, even created man in his own image and demanded allegiance and obedience to Him alone. The descendants of Abraham became a new race of people who professed allegiance to the God of Abraham.

The God of Abraham is all power, He knows everything, and is everywhere yet he wants direct contact with mortals. There is just one problem: God the almighty, all power, everywhere present has no sin and is all goodness. God is pure. The ones God seeks a relationship with are impure, sinners who cannot stop doing bad things. In the Bible, the separation between a sinner and the sinless God is viewed as a chasm. Since God by his very nature cannot sin, the only way for sinful man to approach him is for the latter to remove his sins. Disobedience, or sin against God had to be paid for. Abraham, his son Isaac and grandson Jacob, later known as Israel, his own children, children's children offered sacrifices to this God in payment for sin. The Old Testament account of the Bible shows that payments for the sins of the human race, was never ending and inadequate because the sacrifice did not measure up to the requirements of a perfect God. The sacrifice has to be pure and only God is pure. The sacrifice has to be God himself.

Why does God, the all powerful, not annihilate the entire human race just as he almost did when he allowed just one man named Noah and his family to remain on earth? The answer has to do with something that I will never understand in this life: God's unconditional love. " For God so loved the world": Book of John chapter three, verse sixteen says. He knows that the immortal soul with which he created man will go to Hell for eternity unless a transformation occurs. Man has to change the sinful nature of his immortal, Hell bound soul. Hell is a place of eternal torment created to punish God's enemy, the Devil, his demons, and every sinner who remains a sinner when he or she dies. God so loves the men, women, boys and girls that He created that He does not want any, not even one to go to Hell, so He holds back destroying the human race no matter how sinful it becomes for a while longer. Man is given time to get rid of his transgressions before passing into eternity: his sins need to be cancelled out. I was rescued from drowning in the river at *Gelee* when I was about eight or nine years old, escaped from the Duvalierists, did not jump off the window ledge at the Convent school in England. God had allowed me more time on earth to avoid going into Hell for eternity.

This God of Abraham Isaac and Jacob, who loves the people whom he created unconditionally, decided to provide the unadulterated sacrifice needed to pay once and for all for the sins of the whole human race. Only God is pure. God is the only sacrifice pure enough to pay for the sins of man. God through His Holy Spirit placed His son in the womb of a virgin girl named Mary who gave birth to a child in a stable in a small town called Bethlehem. For centuries, God gave the scenario of His dramatic solution to the sin problem. Through the messages He gave to several prophets whose writings were carefully preserved by Abraham's descendants, the people of Israel in the Bible, God described how He would enter the human race in the form of a human baby who would, as a full grown man, pay for the sins of the world through His death on a cross. For centuries, the Israelites preserved the sacred scrolls that spoke of this event. One writer Isaiah mentioned it fifty-two times. Enter Jesus, of Nazareth Son of God the Messiah of the Jews: Savior of the world. This same giver of life chose to manifest Himself in the form of a human being.

Jesus the carpenter of Nazareth is the only human being who walked the earth for thirty-three years and never sinned. His mother Mary, sinned, his step father, Joseph sinned, as did his brother Jude, his brother James, both authors in the New Testament, and his other brothers and sisters. Jesus refused to give his mother, and brothers special privileges: In Luke chapter eight verse twenty-one when people told him that his family was waiting outside of the crowded room where he was preaching He replied that *"My mother and my brethren are these which hear the word of God and do it."* (KJV) All sinned just as the Scriptures say: *" all have sinned and fallen short of the glory of God"*. *Romans*: 3; 23. This carpenter, born into a family whom scores of people in Nazareth knew: in Luke chapter four verse twenty-two: *"Is not this Joseph's son?* (His stepfather)". In Mathew chapter thirteen verses fifty-five and fifty-six: "*Is not this the carpenter's son? Is not His mother called Mary? And His brethren James, and Joses, and Simon, and Judas? And His sisters, are they not all with us*". The same man Jesus lived, worked, ate, slept, was tempted just as everyone is who walks, talks, even thinks. The scripture says sin starts in the mind: Mathew chapter five verse twenty-eight " *But I say unto you, that whosoever looketh on a woman to lust after her hath committed adultery with her already in his heart*." (KJV) Unlike everyone else who lived on earth, this man Jesus never sinned: Hebrews 4:15. First John: 3:5.

Jesus, unlike the rest of humanity was born sinless: Second Corinthians: 5: 21. Hebrews: 4: 15, 7; 26. First John: 3:5. To refuse to do what God says, not rules fabricated by man, is sin. Jesus always did what God says. He lived in complete obedience to God therefore demonstrating his sinless nature. Jesus never sinned. Only God is without sin. Jesus is God. God, who is spirit, came to live on the earth in the flesh as Jesus the carpenter of Nazareth.

"*I and my Father are one*" John: 10: 30. We know God the father, God the son, and God the Holy Spirit by looking at Jesus, the carpenter of Nazareth. All three persons operate in perfect harmony. Jesus never contradicted the Father or the Holy Spirit and vice versa.

One topic of discussion on the religious television programs I was watching revolved around being "*born again*". I related that to the discussion Jesus had with a Jewish leader named Nicodemus in the third chapter of John's Gospel. Essentially Jesus told this very learned leader of the Jews that he was not fit to go into Heaven for eternity unless he was "*born again*". At first Nicodemus was puzzled by the term "*born again*". Jesus broke it down further: Nicodemus had to change his nature. He had to become as a newborn baby. A spiritual transformation had to occur of such magnitude that the old man would no longer exist but be replaced by a brand new creature. By then, I had heard several of the television preachers say to their listeners: "give your heart to the Lord Jesus! Be born again! Be saved! " I then understood the formula needed for a sinner to be delivered from sin. Jesus, the son of God died on a cross in payment for my own personal sins but I had to voluntarily accept that payment by exchanging my sinful nature for His own sinless one and inviting Him to live in me. I had to become a new creature. Through the process of a new birth the nature of the lord Jesus Christ living in me would make me a new creature!

18

The message was personal: *"without me you are nothing!"* I had reached chapter fifteen of John's narrative. A bolt of recognition pierced my mind, nailing down an undeniable truth. Suddenly I saw myself as I really was. I was a living being. Yet, eventually I would turn back into the dirt my body was made of. For an all too brief time, I could breathe, and feel and think and act because the One who created me out of the dirt of the earth allowed me to. God, my creator, had a claim on my life not only because he made me but also because He paid a dear price for me on a cross at a place called Calvary. I felt treasured.

Suddenly It was important to me to feel treasured, to feel loved. After living alone in Brunswick for a year and one half, with occasional telephone conversations with family and friends, I had given way to loneliness and was about to be married. Yet, I did not feel loved by my fiancé. Even at twenty-seven and one half years old, I did not think that I needed to marry before I had at least finished Law School but after a few months of dating a fellow student I had met at the school's Savannah branch, I had agreed to change my plans. We lived two hours apart, held full time jobs each in addition to attending law School and corresponded mainly by telephone and letters. Three months earlier, on Valentine Day I had agreed to his proposal of marriage. Now, the quiet reserve that had first attracted me seemed to me, a sign that my fiancé did not feel as deeply in love with me as I wished.

In New York, I had avoided relationships with men who drank, smoked, womanized, got into fights, or could not hold their temper. I was also on the look out for an educated man who was gainfully employed. This man fit the bill. We met when I transferred from Brunswick to attend the Savannah branch of the school. The student body had been recently told, that the Brunswick and Savannah branches were both about to be closed. My fiancé who was a year ahead of me, would graduate before these closures, I would have to eventually move to Atlanta to complete my degree. Meanwhile, all the students attended the same lectures in one large room of the Savannah facility. One evening when I returned to my seat in the classroom after one of our breaks I noticed a folded piece of paper on my open textbook.

"If you are not married", the boyish script read. " I would like to invite you to go out with me". It was signed "Lloyd Johnson Jr." With the postscript: "person in green".

Intrigued, I thought: *that was a new approach!* I scanned the rows in front of me as the other students were settling into the lecture chairs, and our professor returned to the dais. There was a green sweater, two or three rows ahead on one side whose wearer had his head bent intently over his class material. Among the group of mostly men of varying ages, I had noticed one African American with a reddish brown complexion, in his late twenties who once asked me a simple question about a class assignment, while we stood next to each other in the school lobby, that I felt was odd. That particular fellow looked intelligent, and I had wondered then about the necessity of the explanation he sought. Was he now wearing the green sweater? The Savannah branch of the school was held in a large Victorian era house, with an elaborate centrally located staircase that could only accommodate two people at a time. There was always a queue of students at the bottom of the stairs trying to reach the library on the second floor. I usually set out for my two hours drive to Brunswick, often to start my shift in the Hospital Emergency Department, immediately after our last lecture for the night. This meant that I would use the breaks in between classes to run up to the Library. That night I could not tell whether the "*person in green*" was at the top of the stairs or somewhere in the crowd milling about the lobby of the house. I made it to the library. The interior doors of the house had been removed to allow for uninterrupted access to rows of bookcases in ceiling high wall units shelved in a maze of multi-colored volumes. As I started to scan one of the rows for a particular book, my attention was drawn to the far corner of the room. There he was, the young man wearing a green sweater over a pale collared shirt, looking up from the large book he held in his hands. He stood about 5 feet 7 or 9 inches tall with a military haircut in an elegant athletic stance. I noticed his neatly creased trousers, clean hands, and polished shoes. There was an obvious shyness in his hazel eyes. We were alone.

"Did you leave a note on my book downstairs?" I asked, wary of the possibility of this being the latest "pick up line". I had heard a good number while living and working in New York and in other places I had visited. The expression on Lloyd Johnson Jr.'s face was sincere.

"Yes", he answered smiling. *Healthy white teeth!* I thought trying to justify how the simple smile of a man I had barely met should stir up in me what I was feeling at that moment. Lloyd and I discussed our class material and I was impressed by his intelligence and unassuming manner. I liked the sound of his voice. At times, I did not understand his South Georgia accent and he too seemed puzzled by my New Yorker's faster speech, laughing softly when we both explained ourselves.

Over the course of the following weeks, we became better acquainted during classroom breaks and telephone conversations. He lived in Savannah with his divorced mother, he told me, who was a schoolteacher and semi retired. I got the impression that he was helpful to his mother and protective of her interests. He had some other family members in Savannah, he said, but after a quarrel some time ago, his mother kept her distance. " We have not been close to our family in years" he would reply when I pressed for more details. My father had been at odds with his siblings from time to time. I knew that there were long periods when uncle Miyou and Papa did not correspond with each other, so understood that a family quarrel could create division among relatives. That Lloyd honored his mother wishes was evidence that he possessed the trait of loyalty. He would understand some of my family's closeness, I thought. When we spoke, I told him my and my family's story in details. In between, I held one and one half Nursing jobs in Brunswick, and commuted three evenings a week to Savannah.

"You need to spend more time together with Lloyd."

My married friend Luanne told me. "Both of you need to know each other better." I was interpreting his silences she cautioned, to fit my own dreams. Those dreams were clouding my judgment. I wanted to believe that all was well. Then, the day after our engagement, my fiancé wrote the first of several letters to me whose tone worried me. Mostly he questioned my faithfulness. This disturbed me, since I knew that I had never given him cause to suspect me of any wrongdoing. We both knew that I would have to move to Atlanta to complete my Law degree. By this time, I was working full time at the Health Center of a Vocational school while working evening and night part time at the Brunswick hospital Emergency Room. My Jobs and Law School classes took up most of my time. Despite my reassurances to Lloyd that in view of my schedule I could not possibly squeeze in an affair with another man, he continued his unfounded accusations.

"You should try to spend more time with Lloyd".

My friend Luann repeated. I wondered if Lloyd was discussing our relationship with the two men in school who appeared to be his friends. We did not meet up with anyone outside of school. Although at times, I commuted with three other students who also lived in Brunswick, our schedules did not allow Lloyd and me to see these students socially.

Another source of contention between my fiancé and I were our differing views of a wedding ceremony itself. He wanted to "just go to the court House" for our wedding whereas I would never do something that important without at least my immediate family in attendance. There was a conservative streak in me that held me to the conventions of the traditions of my elders. I never entertained the thought of living with anyone outside of a marriage relationship. That situation, in my mind, took as much commitment as being married. Marriage was a serious commitment even to an avowed "woman Libber". Yet, even without any religious affiliations, I would not consider a civil ceremony adequate. I also needed to spend a year in Atlanta to finish Law School and then we could be married in Savannah or New York. We had discussed and I had voiced my willingness for us to share a home with his mother. Lloyd insisted, however, that once I left for Atlanta I would never return to him.

This was the first time in my life that I had contemplated marrying anyone. So often, I felt as if Lloyd and I were so close in our thinking. We were obviously physically attracted to each other. He was handsome, but I was enough of a realist to love what I thought was the inner man. Surely, we could become the best of friends. I was committed to our spending the rest of our lives together. Now that my younger sister was married, it was easier to announce to my parents, that I was engaged. In addition, since Lloyd was American, there was no concern of his being from the *right* Haitian family. My parents were sufficiently impressed by my report that my fiancé was a Law student who had a good job. Meanwhile, I made allowances for what I saw as Lloyd's inability to trust me and for his mother's, whom I had only met once, dislike of me. I had lived for so long with people who were continually suspicious of each other. Yet, I worried about my fiancé's feelings towards me.

"It's not that I don't love you." He would say.

I pointed out his attempts to manipulate me. Getting a Law degree was my route out of the Nursing profession and for achieving some degree of economic stability. If he truly loved me, why would he not support my dreams? I asked. Why did I want to leave him? He would counter.

Three months after my decision to marry Lloyd I started to read the Bible. He was raised in a Methodist Church, he told me, and knew all about the Scriptures. To me this book contained life-changing information. The most important news I had just received was that God loved me unconditionally. No one loved me unconditionally. I had never loved anyone that way. Yet God loved me enough to enter the human race, suffer the inconveniences of a human life, accept to be tortured and put to death on a cross to pay the price of my sins. I belonged to the God who made me and paid to have my sins cancelled out.

" *If my people which are called by my name*" Second Chronicles 7:14 (KJV) God told the ancient Hebrews and those who chose to be grafted into the family of God. For the first time in my life, I felt understood. Since God knows my every thought, it was comforting to me to know that there could not be any misunderstanding between Him and I. He still loved me, in spite of my many faults, and knowing who I am. My heart now craved for a relationship with Him. I had found the missing picce in my life. It gave me a sense of belonging to a larger scheme. Now I recognized my identity. So often in my life, I had been labeled Catholic, Protestant, Haitian, American, Black, and Woman that I hesitated to describe myself. *I am*, the thought now exploded in brilliant clarity, *a child of God!*

Alone in my living room, I knelt on the green shag carpet and talked to God. Time was past for meaningless babble and robotic recitations. The God who had created me knew me. I sensed the reality of His knowledge. His presence was real. Even as I felt loved, I became uncomfortable about the things I kept hidden in my heart, knowing that God could read my every thought. The word confession took on a new meaning. It was a matter of my acknowledging that I had disobeyed His laws. *"If my people which are called by my name would humble themselves and pray,"* God said in Second Chronicles 7:14 (KJV). I asked Him to forgive me. It was not enough just to say that I was sorry. Why would He forgive me? I had to decide not to do the act I had asked Him to forgive. God and I both knew what that meant. God and I were having a conversation: I had learned to humble myself and to pray!

I told God that I was giving up hating people. That was the major sin that I was aware of because it dominated my everyday life. This involved giving up my right to retaliate against those I felt had wronged me. I immediately felt the presence of God filling up the whole space of the room. The love of God the father, the gentleness of Jesus, and the soft guidance of the Holy Spirit surrounded me. Simple instructions came to my mind. I asked God to forgive me for all of my sins in the name of Jesus because I wanted to have Jesus live in my life. Because I repented of my sins, He had forgiven me. I acknowledged that without Him I am nothing and could do nothing. I was learning to *"seek"* the face o God as the Bible advised.

I had grown up as a child in Haiti in a society of seekers. People sought for someone who might help them. So many people repeated thousands of "prayers", lit candles, walked in endless processions, performed rituals, rubbed down the polish of countless church pews and fumbled with chains of Rosary beads endlessly; seeking. My Catholic grandfather Papa Gus who did not attend church and my Protestant grandfather Pasteur Benedict, recited the Psalms, I was told, religiously. Manman kept a handwritten copy of several Psalms in her Catholic prayer book. The devout seekers of Mary, Sainte Therese, Saint Antoine, and others spent innumerable hours in their quest. How many sought the face of God?

A physical weight of which I was not even aware lifted up through and out of my body. Tears rushed out and flooded my face but I was not sad. In fact, I was now aware that feelings of anger, anxiety, pessimism, cynicism among others had gone out with the hatred. Everything is new, I remember thinking, I am new, and I like it! I laid with my face down into the carpet feeling as if I were on a beach in the shade with a sweet sea breeze soothing every part of my being. In the silence that wrapped itself around me, I felt the presence of Jesus. I was no longer alone. It was as if I were a small child coming from a dark place whose groping hand found a reassuring one strong and warm and gentle to guide her along. When I stood up from the floor in my living room on that day in May of nineteen-eighty, I was changed.

I do not remember crying much as a child. At twenty-eight years old, I started to make up for lost time. Tears were needed to wash away the hardness of my old heart. One of my friends had told me once before I left New York that I needed to soften up, "People are afraid to go near you" she had said. I had over the years cultivated a vicious tongue and could cut someone's ego in pieces with just a few words. There had been no incentive for me to control my temper; I did not care what anyone thought. Now things were different.

"If my people which are called by my name would humble themselves and pray and seek my face and turn from their wicked ways" Second Chronicles 7:14. I instantly felt remorse when I spoke harshly to anyone and I would feel

prompted to apologize even when my pride held me back. My tongue was restrained. My vocabulary had changed: I could speak without cursing. There was a new determination in me not to be wicked. The Bible showed me how to turn away from wickedness. I read the Bible now with more intensity and grew less critical of the television preachers. There was a new hunger in me for God. Jesus Christ, I was learning, is my model on how to live in a body that has a sin nature and not sin. I sought out discussions about God and the Bible. For all of the spiritual activities I had seen in my native Haiti and the religious activities I observed, from a distance in the United States, there had not been a perceptible change in individual behavior. How many individuals does it take to stop stealing, murdering, lying and cheating to allow Haitians to live at peace with each other in their land. Can the incongruous sight of a segregated house of worship become obsolete, in the United States? Individual regeneration would give birth to a national sense of integrity. Tikite and Jim were very happy when I called them on the phone. "M S you are saved!" The television preachers on the Cable Network taught me about what being "saved" meant. I wanted to be around the people who were *saved* like me but did not know were to find them. Lloyd was surprised that I knew so little about the Bible and cautioned me about becoming what he termed a "religious fanatic". That was what I had called my sister Tikite and later my brother-in-law Jim. There was a new feeling in me: After over twelve years of avoiding it, I wanted to go to a church.

Since I had been partly brought up in the Episcopalian faith I searched for and found a church of that denomination. I was disappointed that no one there appeared to be excited about what had just happened to me. This was an all White congregation but the people were cordial before the church service and after when there was a short gathering for coffee and pastries. Everyone was politely distant. The words of the

Hymns we sang, however, touched me deeply. They were scripture verses, taken from the Bible; the word of God put to music. Tears welled up in my eyes during church services. No one around me seemed to be moved by the songs or the prayers we recited from the prayer books. The apparent lack of enthusiasm did not dampen my spirits. God had heard my prayers and healed me from sadness, from bitterness, from anger and so many of my personal woes. *"Then will I hear from heaven, and will forgive their sin and will heal their land"* Second Chronicles 7:14 (KJV): Said the Lord. A new feeling bubbled up from the now softening recesses of my heart. I looked at strangers with tenderness and felt joy at simply being alive.

My private talks at home with God became increasingly more meaningful. I had many questions I wanted to ask about God, Jesus, the Holy Ghost, and some of the things I was discovering during my periods of intense reading of the Bible. Luann, although pleased about my new experience did not invite me to the Baptist church she attended every Sunday. I suspected that it would be awkward for her if I showed up at her all White church so did not invite myself. People of all races seemed to be attending church together on the television programs I was watching, however. Blacks, Whites, Asians, Hispanics, and a variety of others of mixed ethnic backgrounds, men, women, young and old, talked, laughed, prayed, and sang together in church sanctuaries, in sitting rooms, openly in all sorts of places.

"I belong with them, the television people, we are all in the same family." I thought. One of the most inspiring comments, to me personally, that I treasured from civil rights leader Dr Martin Luther king Jr.'s speeches was that *"God never made anything inferior!"* Now that I was learning about God and his character through reading the Bible, I found confirmation of this over, and over. It saddened me that so much unnecessary heartache exists in the world when every creature is

treasured and loved by our Maker. The suffering I saw in Haiti, in particular, weighed on my mind when I realized how unnecessary it is. The situation in Haiti, as for the whole world has such a simple solution: *Stop serving the Devil, and turn to and serve God!* What a revolutionary idea! What would happen if Haiti land of revolutions were to embrace it, launch out on the Biblical promise? The answer is in Second Chronicles chapter seven verse fourteen: *"If my people, which are called by my name, shall humble themselves, and pray, and seek my face, and turn from their wicked ways; then will I hear from heaven, and will forgive their sin, and will heal their land." (KJV)*

Printed in the United States
93047LV00002B/1-96/A

9 781604 771275